Certification Study Companion Series

The Apress Certification Study Companion Series offers guidance and hands-on practice to support technical and business professionals who are studying for an exam in the pursuit of an industry certification. Professionals worldwide seek to achieve certifications in order to advance in a career role, reinforce knowledge in a specific discipline, or to apply for or change jobs. This series focuses on the most widely taken certification exams in a given field. It is designed to be user friendly, tracking to topics as they appear in a given exam and work alongside other certification material as professionals prepare for their exam.

More information about this series at `https://link.springer.com/bookseries/17100`

CompTIA CySA+ Certification Companion

Hands-on Preparation and Practice Guide

Kodi A. Cochran

Apress®

CompTIA CySA+ Certification Companion: Hands-on Preparation and Practice Guide

Kodi A. Cochran
Poca, OK, USA

ISBN-13 (pbk): 979-8-8688-1494-5   ISBN-13 (electronic): 979-8-8688-1495-2
https://doi.org/10.1007/979-8-8688-1495-2

Copyright © 2025 by Kodi A. Cochran

This work is subject to copyright. All rights are reserved by the Publisher, whether the whole or part of the material is concerned, specifically the rights of translation, reprinting, reuse of illustrations, recitation, broadcasting, reproduction on microfilms or in any other physical way, and transmission or information storage and retrieval, electronic adaptation, computer software, or by similar or dissimilar methodology now known or hereafter developed.

Trademarked names, logos, and images may appear in this book. Rather than use a trademark symbol with every occurrence of a trademarked name, logo, or image we use the names, logos, and images only in an editorial fashion and to the benefit of the trademark owner, with no intention of infringement of the trademark.

The use in this publication of trade names, trademarks, service marks, and similar terms, even if they are not identified as such, is not to be taken as an expression of opinion as to whether or not they are subject to proprietary rights.

While the advice and information in this book are believed to be true and accurate at the date of publication, neither the authors nor the editors nor the publisher can accept any legal responsibility for any errors or omissions that may be made. The publisher makes no warranty, express or implied, with respect to the material contained herein.

Managing Director, Apress Media LLC: Welmoed Spahr
Acquisitions Editor: Susan McDermott
Development Editor: Laura Berendson
Project Manager: Jessica Vakili

Distributed to the book trade worldwide by Springer Science+Business Media New York, 1 New York Plaza, New York, NY 10004. Phone 1-800-SPRINGER, fax (201) 348-4505, e-mail orders-ny@springer-sbm.com, or visit www.springeronline.com. Apress Media, LLC is a Delaware LLC and the sole member (owner) is Springer Science + Business Media Finance Inc (SSBM Finance Inc). SSBM Finance Inc is a **Delaware** corporation.

For information on translations, please e-mail booktranslations@springernature.com; for reprint, paperback, or audio rights, please e-mail bookpermissions@springernature.com.

Apress titles may be purchased in bulk for academic, corporate, or promotional use. eBook versions and licenses are also available for most titles. For more information, reference our Print and eBook Bulk Sales web page at http://www.apress.com/bulk-sales.

Any source code or other supplementary material referenced by the author in this book is available to readers on the Github repository: https://github.com/Apress/Cybersecurity-Essentials. For more detailed information, please visit https://www.apress.com/gp/services/source-code.

If disposing of this product, please recycle the paper

Table of Contents

About the Author xxix

About the Technical Reviewer xxxi

Chapter 1: Foundations of Cybersecurity Analysis 1

An Introduction to CompTIA 3

CompTIA CySA+ Certification Exam Domains 4

    Domain 1: Security Operations (33%) 4

    Domain 2: Vulnerability Management (30%) 5

    Domain 3: Incident Response and Management (20%) 5

    Domain 4: Reporting and Communication (17%) 6

Who This Certification Will Benefit 6

    IT Professionals Looking to Advance in Cybersecurity 7

    Organizations Needing Skilled Security Analysts 7

    Career Changers Entering the Cybersecurity Field 8

    Students and Early-Career Professionals 8

The Role of a Cybersecurity Analyst 8

    Key Responsibilities 9

The Bridge Between Technical Teams and Management 11

The CySA+ Exam Overview 12

Purpose of the CySA+ Certification 12

Exam Format and Structure 13

Building a Cybersecurity Mindset 14

    Critical Thinking in Cybersecurity 14

TABLE OF CONTENTS

- Adapting to Change 15
- Team Collaboration 15
- Core Principles of Cybersecurity 17
- The CIA Triad 17
  - Confidentiality 17
  - Integrity 18
  - Availability 18
- Defense-in-Depth Strategy 19
  - Core Components of Defense-in-Depth 20
  - Advantages of Defense-in-Depth 23
  - Implementing a Defense-in-Depth Strategy 24
- Understanding the Cybersecurity Landscape 25
- Measuring the Attack Surface 25
- Identifying Risk 26
- Common Threats 27
  - Malware 27
  - Phishing and Social Engineering 28
  - Insider Threats 29
  - Advanced Persistent Threats (APTs) 29
- Emerging Trends in Cybersecurity 30
  - Artificial Intelligence (AI) in Cyberattacks and Defenses 30
  - Securing Internet of Things (IoT) Devices 31
  - Cloud Security Concerns 31
- Cybersecurity Frameworks and Best Practices 32
  - NIST Cybersecurity Framework (CSF) 33
  - ISO/IEC 27001 35
  - MITRE ATT&CK Framework 36

Other Frameworks and Standards 37
    COBIT (Control Objectives for Information and Related Technologies) 37
    Center for Internet Security (CIS) Controls 37
Threat Intelligence Frameworks 37
Overview of Cybersecurity Tools 39
SIEM (Security Information and Event Management) 39
    Examples of SIEM Tools: 40
Endpoint Detection and Response (EDR) 40
    Examples of EDR Tools: 41
Vulnerability Scanners 42
    Examples of Vulnerability Scanners: 43
Threat Intelligence Platforms 43
    Examples of Threat Intelligence Platforms: 44
Chapter Summary 45

Chapter 2: Introduction to Threat Intelligence and Vulnerability Management Principles 47

Threat Intelligence and Analysis 48
Introduction to Threat Intelligence 49
The Role of Threat Intelligence in Cybersecurity 49
Types of Threat Intelligence 50
    Strategic Intelligence 50
    Operational Intelligence 50
    Tactical Intelligence 51
    Internal vs. External Threat Intelligence 51
Sources of Threat Intelligence 52
    Open-Source Intelligence (OSINT) 52
    Paid Intelligence Feeds 53
    Commercial Threat Intelligence Providers 53

TABLE OF CONTENTS

- Dark Web Monitoring 53
- Information-Sharing Platforms 54
- Information Sharing and Collaboration 54
- Threat Intelligence Life Cycle 55
  - Planning 55
  - Collection 55
  - Analysis 56
  - Dissemination 56
  - Feedback 56
- Types of Threat Actors 57
  - Hacktivists 57
  - Cybercriminals 57
  - Nation-States 58
  - Insider Threats 58
- Threat Intelligence Frameworks 58
  - MITRE ATT&CK Framework 59
  - Cyber Kill Chain 60
  - Diamond Model 61
- Threat Analysis and Evaluation 62
- Most Common Attack Vectors 62
- Phishing 62
- Forms of Phishing 63
  - Email Phishing 63
  - Spear Phishing 63
  - Whaling 64
  - Smishing (SMS Phishing) 64
  - Vishing (Voice Phishing) 65

TABLE OF CONTENTS

- Angler Phishing 65
- Clone Phishing 65
- Business Email Compromise (BEC) 66
- Best Practices to Prevent Phishing 66
- Malware 67
- Forms of Malware 68
  - Viruses 68
  - Worms 68
  - Trojans 69
  - Ransomware 69
  - Spyware 69
  - Adware 70
  - Rootkits 70
  - Keyloggers 71
  - Botnets 71
- Best Practices to Prevent Malware Attacks 71
- Exploits 73
- Types of Exploits 73
  - Zero-Day Exploits 73
  - Buffer Overflow Exploits 74
  - Privilege Escalation Exploits 74
  - Cross-Site Scripting (XSS) Exploits 75
  - SQL Injection Exploits 75
  - Man-in-the-Middle (MITM) Exploits 76
  - Denial of Service (DoS) Exploits 76
  - Command Injection Exploits 77
- Best Practices to Prevent Exploits 77
- Credential-Based Attacks 78

ix

TABLE OF CONTENTS

Common Methods of Credential-Based Attacks 79
    Brute-Force Attacks 79
    Credential Stuffing 80
    Phishing Attacks 81
    Keylogging and Malware-Based Attacks 81
    Password Spraying Attacks 82
    Man-in-the-Middle (MITM) Credential Interception 83
Impact of Credential-Based Attacks 84
Best Practices to Prevent Credential-Based Attacks 85
Emerging Attack Vectors 86
    Supply Chain Attacks 86
    Zero-Day Vulnerabilities 87
    Fileless Malware 88
Vulnerability Management 89
Scanning Tools and Techniques 90
    Network Scanners 90
    Web Application Scanners 92
    Host-Based Scanners 94
Common Vulnerabilities and Exposures (CVEs) 96
    Importance of Tracking CVEs 96
    Leveraging the National Vulnerability Database (NVD) 97
Risk Assessment in Vulnerability Management 97
Risk Scoring and Prioritization 98
    CVSS (Common Vulnerability Scoring System) 98
    Risk Matrix 98
    Contextualizing Risk 99
    Asset Criticality 99

TABLE OF CONTENTS

Exploitability 99

Attacker Motivation 100

Tailoring Risk Assessments to Organizational Goals and Regulatory Requirements 100

Remediation and Mitigation Strategies 101

Configuration Management 101

Compensating Controls 102

Incident Prevention Through Remediation 102

Threat Modeling 103

Key Methodologies 103

STRIDE 104

DREAD 106

Steps in Threat Modeling 108

Identify Assets 108

Define Threats 109

Assess Vulnerabilities 110

Implement Mitigations 110

Threat Hunting 112

Threat Hunting Methodologies 112

Hypothesis-Driven Hunting 112

Indicators of Attack (IOAs) 113

Behavioral Analytics 114

Tools for Threat Hunting 115

Endpoint Detection and Response (EDR) Solutions 116

Advanced SIEM Tools with Machine Learning Capabilities 117

Chapter Summary 119

xi

TABLE OF CONTENTS

Chapter 3: Comprehensive Vulnerability Management 123

Introduction to Vulnerability Management 125
Importance of Vulnerability Management 125
Key Components of Vulnerability Management 126
Vulnerability Scanning Tools and Techniques 129
Types of Vulnerability Scans 129
Popular Vulnerability Scanning Tools 131
Limitations of Vulnerability Scanners 133
The Vulnerability Management Life Cycle 134
Phase 1: Asset Discovery 135
    Inventorying Systems, Applications, and Devices 135
    Tools for Asset Discovery 135
    Nmap 135
    Asset Management Systems 136
    Network Discovery Tools 136
Phase 2: Vulnerability Identification 136
    Conducting Vulnerability Scans 136
    Leverage Threat Intelligence 137
    Regular Scanning 137
Phase 3: Risk Assessment 137
    Evaluating Impact and Likelihood 137
    Using CVSS Scores 138
    Considering Asset Criticality 138
    Threat Actor Capabilities 138
Phase 4: Prioritization 138
    Categorizing Vulnerabilities by Severity 139
    Risk Matrices and CVSS Scores 139
    Factors to Consider for Prioritization: 139

TABLE OF CONTENTS

Phase 5: Remediation and Mitigation 140
    Applying Patches and Updates 140
    Configuration Changes 140
    Compensating Controls 140
    Tracking Progress 141
Phase 6: Reporting and Review 141
    Documenting Findings 141
    Informed Stakeholders 141
    Continuous Improvement 141
Risk-Based Vulnerability Management 142
Why Risk-Based Approaches Matter 142
    Resource Constraint 142
    Focus on Critical Vulnerabilities 143
    Business Continuity 143
Steps in Risk-Based Vulnerability Management 143
    Identify High-Value Assets and Systems 143
    Assess Vulnerabilities That Impact High-Value Assets 144
    Prioritize Based on Likelihood of Exploitation and Potential Impact 144
Integration with Threat Intelligence 145
Patch Management 147
Role of Patch Management 147
    Patch Management Process 148
    Challenges in Patch Management 151
Vulnerability Management and Compliance 153
    Regulatory Requirements and Vulnerability Management 154
    Best Practices for Ensuring Compliance 159
Auditing Vulnerability Management Processes 160
Continuous Vulnerability Management 163

TABLE OF CONTENTS

    Why Continuous Management Is Necessary 163
    Strategies for Continuous Vulnerability Management 164
Integration with DevSecOps 166
Metrics and Reporting in Vulnerability Management 168
    Key Vulnerability Metrics 169
Creating Actionable Reports 171
Chapter Summary 174

Chapter 4: Cybersecurity Data Analysis 177

Data Collection and Sources 178
Understanding Data Sources 179
Types of Data Sources 179
    Logs 180
    Network Device Logs 180
    Server Logs 180
    Application Logs 181
    Telemetry Data 181
    Endpoint Data 182
    Cloud Activity Logs 182
    Threat Intelligence Feeds 183
    Real-Time Updates on Malicious Indicators 183
    Integration with SIEM Systems 183
Data Collection Best Practices 184
    Ensure Data Integrity 184
    Centralized Log Collection 185
    Adhere to Regulatory Requirements 185
    Why These Practices Matter 187
Data Normalization and Parsing 187

TABLE OF CONTENTS

Steps to Normalize Data 188
    Identify Key Data Fields 188
    Standardize Time Zones to UTC 189
    Eliminate Duplicate or Irrelevant Entries 190
    Why Data Normalization Matters 190
Data Parsing Tools 191
Log Analysis Tools 191
    Scripting Languages like Python 192
    Why Parsing Matters in Cybersecurity 194
Challenges in Data Normalization 194
    Handling Large Volumes of Data from Diverse Sources 194
Resolving Inconsistencies Caused by Proprietary Log Formats 195
    Why Addressing These Challenges Matters 196
Data Analysis Techniques: Understanding Cybersecurity Analytics 196
Types of Analysis in Cybersecurity 197
    Trend Analysis 197
    Anomaly Detection 198
    Correlation Analysis 199
Visualization Tools 200
Event Correlation 202
    Use Cases for Correlation Analysis 202
    Detecting Multistage Attacks 203
    Identifying Lateral Movement 204
The Importance of Correlation in Cybersecurity 204
    Correlation Rules 205
Benefits of Event Correlation 206
    Reduces Alert Fatigue 206
    Enhances Situational Awareness 207

TABLE OF CONTENTS

Strengthening the Security Posture 208
Data Enrichment 209
Enrichment Techniques in Cybersecurity 209
    Geo-IP Data 209
    Threat Intelligence Integration 210
    DNS Analysis 211
    Benefits of Data Enrichment 211
    Improved Threat Detection Accuracy 212
Machine Learning in Cybersecurity Analysis 213
    Common ML Applications in Cybersecurity 214
    Behavioral Analytics 214
    Predictive Models 214
Supervised vs. Unsupervised Learning in Cybersecurity 215
    Supervised Learning 215
    Unsupervised Learning 215
    Challenges in ML Adoption for Cybersecurity 216
    Need for High-Quality, Labeled Data 216
    Risk of False Positives or False Negatives 216
Using SIEM and Analytics Tools 217
    Popular SIEM Platforms 217
    Key SIEM Features 220
    Implementing SIEM Effectively 221
Metrics and Key Performance Indicators (KPIs) 223
    Examples of Key Metrics 223
    Using Metrics for Continuous Improvement 225
Chapter Summary 228

TABLE OF CONTENTS

Chapter 5: Security Operations and Monitoring 231
Logging and Log Management..232
What Are Logs?..233
Types of Logs..233
Log Collection and Aggregation 234
Importance of Log Correlation 235
Benefits of Effective Log Management...236
Challenges in Log Management 236
Monitoring and Detection Techniques..237
Continuous Monitoring..237
Key Monitoring Techniques..238
Anomaly-Based Detection vs. Signature-Based Detection.............................239
Anomaly-Based Detection 239
Signature-Based Detection 240
Key Differences and Practical Applications 241
Why Use Both? 241
Threat Hunting 241
Incident Detection and Alerts...242
Defining Incident Detection 243
Alerting Systems...243
Reducing False Positives 244
Strategies to Minimize False Positives...244
Incident Response Process 245
Defining Incident Response (IR) 245
Phases of Incident Response 246
Role of Incident Response Teams 248
Key Responsibilities of IRTs..248
SIEM and Security Tools...249

xvii

TABLE OF CONTENTS

What Is a SIEM System? 249
    Primary Objectives of a SIEM 249
    Key Features of SIEM Systems 250
Why Organizations Use SIEM Systems 250
Core Functions of SIEM Systems 250
Popular SIEM Tools 252
Advanced Monitoring Tools 252
    Endpoint Detection and Response (EDR) 253
    Network Detection and Response (NDR) 254
    Security Orchestration, Automation, and Response (SOAR) 254
Why Advanced Monitoring Tools Matter 255
    How SIEM and Advanced Tools Work Together 256
    Challenges in Implementing SIEM Systems 256
The Future of SIEM and Security Tools 257
Types of Threat Intelligence 258
    Tactical Threat Intelligence 258
    Operational Threat Intelligence 259
    Strategic Threat Intelligence 259
Integrating Threat Intelligence into Security Operations 260
    Benefits of Integration 261
Using Threat Feeds 262
Threat Intelligence Platforms (TIPs) 262
Automating Threat Intelligence Integration 263
Challenges in Threat Intelligence 264
Future Trends in Threat Intelligence 265
Chapter Summary 266

Chapter 6: Incident Response and Recovery 267
Introduction to Incident Response (IR) 268
Goals of Incident Response...268
The Importance of Preparedness 269
The Incident Response Life Cycle 270
    Preparation 270
Establishing Roles and Responsibilities..271
    Tools and Resources..273
    Identification..274
Common Indicators of Compromise 275
Initial Assessment and Triage 276
    Incident Documentation 277
    Containment 279
    Types of Containment Strategies...279
Minimizing Impact on Business Operations...................................281
Communication During Containment...282
    Eradication..284
Eliminating Threats 284
Patch Management and Security Updates....................................285
Collaborating with Forensics Teams 287
    Recovery...289
    System Restoration 289
Testing and Monitoring Post-recovery 291
Communication and Reporting..292
Post-incident Activities 294
    Lessons Learned 294
Improving Incident Response Plans..295
    Incident Response Policies and Procedures.........................297

TABLE OF CONTENTS

Establishing an Incident Response Policy 297
Developing Incident Response Playbooks 298
Incident Response Maturity Models 300
Maturity Levels 300
Frameworks for Maturity Assessment 302
    Key Takeaways 303
Testing an Incident Response Policy 304
Legal and Compliance Considerations 305
Roles and Responsibilities in Incident Response 307
Incident Response Team (IRT) 307
Third-Party Involvement 309
    Tools and Technologies for Incident Response 310
Essential Tools 310
    Security Information and Event Management (SIEM) 311
    Endpoint Detection and Response (EDR) 311
    Forensic Tools 311
Automation in Incident Response 312
SOAR (Security Orchestration, Automation, and Response) 312
Threat Intelligence Integration 312
Recovery Planning and Execution 314
    Key Objectives of Recovery 314
Developing a Recovery Plan 315
    Identify Critical Systems and Prioritize Restoration 315
Set Recovery Objectives: RPO and RTO 315
Validating Recovery 316
Business Continuity and Disaster Recovery (BC/DR) 317
Business Impact Analysis (BIA) 318

Disaster Recovery Plans (DRPs) 318
Continuity Plans 318
Testing and Updating Plans.. 319
    Incident Postmortem and Continuous Improvement 320
    Gather Stakeholders to Evaluate Response Effectiveness 320
    Document Findings and Recommendations 320
Updating Policies and Procedures 320
Adjust Response Strategies Based on New Threats or Gaps Identified 321
Strengthen Security Measures.. 321
    Best Practices for Policy Updates 322
Training and Awareness 323
Share Lessons Learned Across Teams to Build a Stronger Security Culture 323
Promote a Culture of Continuous Improvement 324
    Best Practices for Effective Training and Awareness 325
Metrics for Continuous Improvement.. 326
Chapter Summary 327

Chapter 7: Threat Intelligence, Indicators of Compromise, and Secure Operations 329

Types of Indicators of Compromise (IOCs) 329
    File-Based IOCs 329
    Network-Based IOCs 330
    Behavioral IOCs 332
Why Understanding IOCs Is Critical... 333
In Action: The Power of IOCs 333
Detecting and Using Indicators of Compromise (IOCs) 334
Collecting and Analyzing IOCs... 334
Integrating IOCs with Security Tools 336

TABLE OF CONTENTS

Sharing and Updating IOCs 337
Benefits of Proactive IOC Management 338
Threat Intelligence Platforms (TIPs): Enhancing Cybersecurity Operations 339
What Are Threat Intelligence Platforms? 339
    Key Functions of TIPs 339
    Why TIPs Are Critical 340
Core Features and Benefits of TIPs 340
Popular Threat Intelligence Platforms 342
How to Select the Right TIP 342
    Considerations for Small-to-Mid-Sized Organizations 343
    Considerations for Large Enterprises 343
Applying Threat Intelligence to Security Operations 344
Enhancing Detection and Prevention 344
    Improving Signature-Based Detection 344
    Enhancing Anomaly Detection 344
    Refining Security Policies 345
Threat Hunting: Proactive Threat Detection 345
    Role of Threat Intelligence in Threat Hunting 346
    Uncovering New and Unique Threats 346
    Operationalizing Threat Intelligence for Hunting 347
Incident Response and Threat Intelligence 347
    Speeding Up Detection and Remediation 347
    Guiding Incident Response Decisions 348
Threat Intelligence in the Context of Emerging Threats 349
Evolving Threat Landscape: Staying Ahead of Emerging Threats 349
    Case Study Examples: 351
AI and Machine Learning in Threat Intelligence 352

TABLE OF CONTENTS

Applications in Threat Intelligence 353
Threat Intelligence Sharing and Legal Considerations 354
Collaboration and Information Sharing: The Importance of Collaboration 354
The Benefits of Threat Intelligence Sharing 356
Legal and Compliance Issues 357
Privacy Concerns 358
Regulatory Compliance 358
Liability 360
Best Practices for Sharing Intelligence 360
The Importance of Proactive Threat Intelligence 362
Continuous Improvement and Adaptation 362
    Key Takeaways 363
Chapter Summary 364

Chapter 8: Security Operation Centers and Managing Security Incidents 365

Introduction to Security Operations 366
Defining Security Operations 366
    Goals of Security Operations 367
    Key Components of Security Operations 367
Introduction to Security Operation Centers 368
Role of Security Operations Centers (SOCs) 369
    Key Components of Security Operations 369
Types of Security Incidents 371
    1. Malware Incidents 371
    2. Phishing and Social Engineering 372
    3. Denial of Service (DoS) and Distributed Denial of Service (DDoS) 374

TABLE OF CONTENTS

    4. Data Breaches 375
    5. Insider Threats 376
Security Monitoring and Detection 377
    SIEM (Security Information and Event Management) 377
    Intrusion Detection and Prevention Systems (IDS/IPS) 379
    Endpoint Detection and Response (EDR) 380
    Network Traffic Analysis 381
Importance of Monitoring and Detection in Security Operations 382
Forms of Threat Hunting 383
    Proactive Threat Detection 383
    Hypothesis-Driven 383
    Manual Investigation 383
    Threat Hunting Methodologies 384
    Behavioral Analysis 384
    Data-Driven Hunting 385
Tools for Threat Hunting 385
    EDR (Endpoint Detection and Response) 385
    SIEM (Security Information and Event Management) 386
    YARA (Yet Another Recursive Acronym) 386
    Volatility 386
    Wireshark 387
Effective Communication During a Cybersecurity Incident 387
Internal Communication During Incidents 388
    Incident Reports 388
    Escalation Protocols 388
    Communication Plans 388
    Best Practices 389
External Communication 389

TABLE OF CONTENTS

    Law Enforcement 389
    Regulators and Compliance.. 389
    Third-Party Vendors 390
    Affected Customers 390
    Best Practices... 390
Public Relations and Crisis Management.................................. 391
    Managing Reputation 391
    Strategies for Media Communication 391
    Internal Coordination 391
    Crisis Management Plans 392
    Best Practices... 392
Role of Forensics in Incident Response 393
    Forensic Tools.. 394
    Chain of Custody... 395
    Post-Incident Analysis and Reporting................................. 395
    Creating Incident Reports 396
Continuous Improvement and Feedback Loop......................... 398
Incident Response and Legal/Compliance Considerations 399
    General Data Protection Regulation (GDPR)..................... 399
    Health Insurance Portability and Accountability Act (HIPAA) 400
    Payment Card Industry Data Security Standard (PCI DSS) 400
    Breach Notification Responsibilities.................................... 401
    Data Protection During an Incident...................................... 401
    Ethical Considerations in Incident Response...................... 401
    Protecting Privacy Rights 402
    Balancing Transparency and Confidentiality...................... 402
    Civil Liberties During Investigations 402
    Avoiding Conflicts of Interest.. 403

TABLE OF CONTENTS

Incident Transparency and Responsibility 403
Reporting and Accountability 403
Adapting to the Evolving Threat Landscape 404
Continuous Improvement 404
Chapter Takeaways 405
Chapter Summary 406

Chapter 9: Governance, Risk, and Compliance (GRC) 407
Introduction to Security Governance, Risk, and Compliance (GRC) 408
Cybersecurity Governance Frameworks 410
NIST Cybersecurity Framework (CSF) 410
COBIT (Control Objectives for Information and Related Technologies) 411
ISO/IEC 27001 and 27002 411
The Role of Senior Leadership in Cybersecurity Governance 412
Risk Management in Cybersecurity 412
Qualitative Risk Assessment 413
Quantitative Risk Assessment 413
Risk Treatment and Mitigation 414
Cybersecurity Risk Management Life Cycle 415
Regulatory Compliance Standards and Frameworks 416
General Data Protection Regulation (GDPR) 416
Health Insurance Portability and Accountability Act (HIPAA) 417
Payment Card Industry Data Security Standard (PCI DSS) 417
Federal Information Security Modernization Act (FISMA) 417
ISO/IEC 27001 and 27002 418
NIST SP 800-53 418
The Role of Audits and Assessments 418
Creating Effective Cybersecurity Policies 419

TABLE OF CONTENTS

Common Types of Cybersecurity Policies 420
    Acceptable Use Policy (AUP) 420
    Data Protection and Privacy Policy 420
    Incident Response Policy 421
    Access Control Policy 421
    Business Continuity and Disaster Recovery 421
    Disaster Recovery (DR) and its Relationship to Cybersecurity 422
The Role of Testing and Drills 423
Building a Strong Cybersecurity Culture 424
Continuous Improvement and Adaptation 424
The Future of GRC in Cybersecurity 425

Chapter 10: Final Review and Exam Preparation 427

Create a Study Plan 430
    1. Assess Your Starting Point 430
    2. Set Clear and Achievable Goals 430
    3. Stick to a Consistent Study Schedule 431
    4. Reinforce Learning with Practice Exams 431
    5. Adapt and Refine Your Plan 432
Use a Variety of Study Materials 432
    1. Official Study Guides and Books 432
    2. Video Tutorials and Online Courses 433
    3. Hands-on Labs and Simulations 433
    4. Practice Questions and Mock Exams 433
    5. Online Forums, Study Groups, and Discussion Boards 434
Focus on Hands-on Practice 434
    1. Set Up a Home Lab 435
    2. Use Simulation and Cloud-Based Labs 435

TABLE OF CONTENTS

    3. Engage in Open-Source Threat Intelligence and Incident Response 436

Take Practice Exams and Review Mistakes 437

    1. Understand the Exam Format 437

    2. Identify Weak Areas and Adjust Your Study Plan 437

    3. Improve Exam Stamina and Time Management 438

    4. Review Your Mistakes and Reinforce Key Concepts 439

Master Time Management 439

    1. Set a Realistic Pace 440

    2. Prioritize Easy Wins 440

    3. Use the Process of Elimination 440

    4. Manage PBQs Efficiently 441

    5. Leave Time for Review 441

Review Key Concepts the Day Before the Exam 441

    1. Focus on High-Yield Concepts 442

    2. Use Quick-Recall Tools 442

    3. Optimize Mental Readiness 443

Stay Calm and Confident on Exam Day 443

    1. Arrive Early and Be Prepared 443

    2. Stay Focused and Manage Stress 444

    3. Trust Your Preparation 444

Glossary of Key Terms 445

Wishing You the Best in Your Cybersecurity Journey 453

Index 455

About the Author

Kodi Cochran is highly invested in the field of cybersecurity, something he has followed as a hobbyist for the past decade and expanded to make it his field of study and work. He has both a bachelor's degree and a master's degree in Cybersecurity and Information Assurance, in addition to working as an Information Systems Manager for the Networking and Infrastructure team of the Department of Human and Health Resources under the agency of the Office of Management of Information Services at the state of West Virginia.

Kodi is responsible for networking administration, project management, system support, and site support for the state of West Virginia in all state-owned health care facilities, hospitals, and labs. In addition, he holds the following certifications: CompTIA A+, Network+, Security+, Project+, CySA+, and Pentest+. He's currently working on the CompTIA CASP+.

About the Technical Reviewer

David LeGrow is enrolled in the Cyber Forensics and Security program at Marshall University. His current project is performing as the Cyber Navigator through West Virginia Secretary of State and Marshall, where he and his team work with Cybersecurity and Infrastructure Security Agency (CISA) and West Virginia counties to ensure the election's security.

CHAPTER 1

Foundations of Cybersecurity Analysis

Welcome to the first chapter of your journey into the world of cybersecurity analysis. Before we get into the complexities and technicalities that make up the CySA+ certification, it's essential to build a strong foundation. In this chapter, we will lay the groundwork for understanding the core concepts, responsibilities, and frameworks that are pivotal to anyone working in cybersecurity analysis. Whether you're just starting out or looking to sharpen your skills, this chapter is designed to provide the clarity and context you need to move forward with confidence.

Cybersecurity is an ever-evolving field, and understanding its core components is crucial. We'll begin by exploring the overall cybersecurity landscape, including the key challenges organizations face when trying to protect their digital assets. This is where we will introduce essential concepts like **threats**, **vulnerabilities**, and **attacks**, explaining how they interact and why cybersecurity professionals must stay vigilant. You will also be introduced to the critical role that cybersecurity analysis plays within an organization—it's more than just monitoring systems; it's about understanding risk, identifying potential threats, and building strategies to mitigate those risks before they turn into full-blown incidents.

CHAPTER 1   FOUNDATIONS OF CYBERSECURITY ANALYSIS

We will also touch on the frameworks and standards that guide cybersecurity efforts across industries. You'll learn about popular frameworks like the **NIST Cybersecurity Framework** and **ISO/IEC 27001**, which offer structured approaches to managing cybersecurity risk. Understanding these frameworks is key for a cybersecurity analyst, as they provide both a strategic and operational approach to securing an organization's information systems. You will quickly see how these frameworks tie directly into the CySA+ exam, giving you the roadmap for tackling more complex cybersecurity challenges in future chapters.

Additionally, this chapter will introduce you to the tools that cybersecurity analysts use to keep systems secure. From vulnerability scanning tools to threat intelligence platforms and Security Information and Event Management (SIEM) systems, we'll discuss the core tools that make an analyst's job manageable and effective. While you won't become an expert in these tools overnight, having a working understanding of them is essential for mastering the material on the CySA+ exam.

As we progress, this chapter will guide you through the **best practices** every cybersecurity analyst should follow. These are the tried-and-tested strategies for defending against threats and minimizing risks, and they are an essential part of your cybersecurity toolkit. By the end of this chapter, you'll have a solid understanding of the foundational principles that will help you succeed not just on the CySA+ exam, but in the world of cybersecurity analysis.

In short, this chapter is not just about memorizing terms and definitions—it's about building the mental framework that will support your entire career in cybersecurity. By aligning the concepts in this chapter with the CySA+ domains, we ensure that what you're learning here will serve as a stepping stone for tackling the more advanced, specialized content in the chapters to follow. It's time to start your journey on the path to becoming a skilled and confident cybersecurity analyst.

CHAPTER 1   FOUNDATIONS OF CYBERSECURITY ANALYSIS

An Introduction to CompTIA

The Computing Technology Industry Association (CompTIA) is one of the world's leading providers of vendor-neutral IT certifications and training. Established in 1982, CompTIA has grown into a globally recognized authority in the IT industry, offering certifications that cover a wide range of skills, from foundational IT knowledge to specialized areas such as cybersecurity, cloud computing, and networking. CompTIA's mission is to empower professionals, businesses, and communities with the tools and certifications needed to excel in the ever-evolving technology landscape.

CompTIA certifications are structured to accommodate IT professionals at various stages of their careers, from beginners to advanced practitioners. For instance, the **CompTIA IT Fundamentals (ITF+)** certification introduces individuals to basic IT concepts, while certifications like **CompTIA Security+**, **Network+**, and **CySA+** focus on more specialized skills in cybersecurity and network management. These certifications are designed to align with industry standards and are frequently updated to ensure relevance in an ever-changing tech world.

What sets CompTIA apart is its emphasis on practical, hands-on skills. The certification exams are built around performance-based assessments, ensuring that candidates can apply their knowledge in real-world scenarios. This practical focus makes CompTIA credentials highly valued by employers and a critical benchmark for demonstrating competence in specific IT domains. By earning a CompTIA certification, professionals not only validate their technical skills but also gain a competitive edge in a rapidly growing and demanding job market.

CHAPTER 1   FOUNDATIONS OF CYBERSECURITY ANALYSIS

CompTIA CySA+ Certification Exam Domains

The CompTIA CySA+ certification exam, specifically the CS0-003 version, is organized into four main domains, each covering essential skills for cybersecurity analysts. Some of the chapters of the book may feel slightly redundant but due to the weighting of the domains, some items span across multiple categories. It is very likely that you will come across some legitimate redundancy, but please do your best to consider it with the context of that particular chapter's goals and objectives. Below is a breakdown of the CySA+ exam objectives and subobjectives:

Domain 1: Security Operations (33%)

This domain emphasizes understanding system and network architecture concepts critical to security operations, such as log ingestion, operating system concepts, and network architecture. Key objectives include

- **Analyze indicators of malicious activity** (network, host, application-related).

- **Use tools and techniques** to determine malicious activity, including common tools, programming languages, and techniques.

- **Understand threat-intelligence and threat-hunting concepts**, with a focus on threat actors, tactics, techniques, and procedures (TTPs).

- **Enhance efficiency in security operations** by standardizing processes, integrating technology, and improving tools.

Domain 2: Vulnerability Management (30%)

This domain focuses on the methods and processes involved in identifying and mitigating vulnerabilities:

- **Implement vulnerability scanning methods**, including asset discovery, scanning types (agent vs. agentless), and considerations like internal vs. external scanning.

- **Analyze vulnerability assessment output** using tools and understanding results.

- **Prioritize vulnerabilities** based on factors like the CVSS score, exploitability, and asset value.

- **Recommend and implement mitigation controls** for software vulnerabilities such as injection flaws, broken access control, and outdated components.

- **Vulnerability response management**, including patching, configuration management, and secure software development.

Domain 3: Incident Response and Management (20%)

This domain deals with the knowledge and skills required to effectively respond to and manage incidents:

- **Understand attack methodologies** like the Cyber Kill Chain and MITRE ATT&CK.

- **Perform incident response activities**, including detection, analysis, containment, eradication, and recovery.

- **Understand the phases of the incident management life cycle**, including preparation and post-incident activities.

Domain 4: Reporting and Communication (17%)

This domain focuses on the importance of clear reporting and communication during vulnerability management and incident response:

- **Vulnerability management reporting,** including compliance reports, action plans, and communicating with stakeholders.

- **Incident response communication** involving incident declaration, root cause analysis, and lessons learned.

Each of these domains is designed to ensure candidates can apply their knowledge to real-world cybersecurity scenarios, with an emphasis on proactive defense strategies, continuous monitoring, and effective communication. More details can be found in CompTIA's official resources and training guides

Who This Certification Will Benefit

The CompTIA Cybersecurity Analyst (CySA+) certification is a highly beneficial credential for individuals seeking to enhance their careers in cybersecurity and information technology. This certification is specifically designed for professionals who want to demonstrate their ability to proactively defend and continuously monitor an organization's network to protect against cybersecurity threats. It bridges the gap between foundational cybersecurity knowledge and advanced penetration testing or managerial roles, making it an ideal choice for intermediate-level IT professionals.

IT Professionals Looking to Advance in Cybersecurity

The CySA+ certification is perfect for IT professionals who already have experience in general IT or network administration and are ready to specialize in cybersecurity. Roles such as systems administrators, network administrators, or help desk analysts often involve exposure to security issues, making CySA+ a logical next step for deepening expertise. It validates essential skills such as threat detection, incident response, and vulnerability management, enabling professionals to take on more responsibility in protecting their organizations from cyber threats.

Organizations Needing Skilled Security Analysts

Organizations, especially those in sectors like finance, healthcare, and government, benefit significantly from employees who hold a CySA+ certification. Cybersecurity analysts certified in CySA+ bring practical skills to the table, such as analyzing and interpreting threat data, leveraging security tools effectively, and adhering to compliance regulations. These abilities are vital for businesses facing increasing cyberattacks and stringent regulatory requirements.

CHAPTER 1 FOUNDATIONS OF CYBERSECURITY ANALYSIS

Career Changers Entering the Cybersecurity Field

For individuals transitioning into cybersecurity from other fields, CySA+ offers a robust framework to build and validate their knowledge. This certification emphasizes hands-on, performance-based skills, which can help career changers demonstrate their readiness to handle real-world cybersecurity challenges. Paired with a foundational understanding of IT or networking, CySA+ provides a clear pathway into analyst and security-focused roles.

Students and Early-Career Professionals

Finally, students and entry-level IT professionals aiming to establish a career in cybersecurity will find CySA+ particularly valuable. While certifications like Security+ lay the groundwork, CySA+ builds on that knowledge by focusing on proactive defense and advanced analytical skills. This can help early-career professionals stand out in the job market and secure roles such as cybersecurity analysts, threat intelligence analysts, or SOC (Security Operations Center) analysts.

In summary, the CySA+ certification is an excellent investment for a wide audience, from seasoned IT professionals to newcomers entering the field. It equips individuals with the technical and analytical skills needed to address today's complex cybersecurity challenges, offering both personal career advancement and tangible value to their organizations.

The Role of a Cybersecurity Analyst

Cybersecurity analysts play a crucial role in defending organizations against an increasingly complex array of cyber threats. While they may not always be in the limelight, their work forms the backbone of an organization's defense against data breaches, malware attacks, and other cybercriminal activities. A cybersecurity analyst is responsible for proactively identifying threats, analyzing potential vulnerabilities, and responding to incidents in a way that minimizes damage and helps improve future security measures. The role requires a mix of technical knowledge, critical thinking, and communication skills, as analysts need to stay ahead of ever-evolving cyber threats while ensuring their organization's systems remain secure.

Key Responsibilities

Monitoring Security Systems: One of the primary duties of a cybersecurity analyst is to constantly monitor an organization's security systems for any signs of unusual activity or potential threats. Analysts utilize a variety of tools, such as Intrusion Detection Systems (IDS), Intrusion Prevention Systems (IPS), and Security Information and Event Management (SIEM) platforms to collect, aggregate, and analyze data from different sources. They review system logs, network traffic, and other critical data to detect anomalies or patterns that might indicate a security breach. These systems are designed to generate alerts, but it's the analyst's responsibility to sift through this data to identify the true threats, ensuring that security efforts are focused on actual risks rather than false positives.

Incident Identification and Response: When a cybersecurity incident occurs—whether it's a ransomware attack, phishing campaign, or a more sophisticated breach—an analyst's job is to quickly identify the problem, assess its scope, and respond appropriately. This includes everything from conducting a forensic investigation to understanding the nature of the attack to containing the incident to prevent further damage. Analysts may need to isolate affected systems, gather evidence, and communicate findings to key stakeholders. Their prompt and effective response can prevent attacks from escalating, saving the organization from significant financial, operational, and reputational harm. Additionally, once the incident is contained, analysts work to improve response protocols, ensuring that the organization is better prepared for future incidents.

Vulnerability Management: Cybersecurity analysts are also responsible for proactively identifying and managing vulnerabilities within the organization's infrastructure. This involves scanning systems and networks for known vulnerabilities, assessing their potential impact, and ensuring that they are remediated before attackers can exploit them. Regular patching and updates are crucial to keeping systems secure, and analysts must stay on top of the latest security patches from vendors, particularly for software or hardware with known weaknesses. Vulnerability management extends beyond just applying patches; it also includes risk assessments to determine which vulnerabilities are most critical and which can be mitigated through other means, such as network segmentation or access control.

Policy Development: Cybersecurity analysts assist in the creation and refinement of security policies and guidelines to ensure that security measures align with industry best practices and regulatory requirements. These policies often govern access control, data protection, incident response procedures, and user behavior. Analysts must ensure that security policies are not only effective but also practical, given the organization's specific operational needs and constraints. By staying up-to-date with evolving threats and compliance standards, analysts help shape policies that mitigate risks while supporting the business's goals.

Compliance Enforcement: In today's heavily regulated business environment, compliance is a key aspect of cybersecurity. Cybersecurity analysts ensure that their organization adheres to regulatory frameworks like GDPR, HIPAA, PCI-DSS, and others that impose strict requirements on data protection and security practices. Analysts track the organization's compliance with these regulations, help in preparing for audits, and implement necessary controls to meet security obligations. This includes ensuring that sensitive data is appropriately protected, encryption standards are met, and audit trails are maintained for accountability. Non-compliance can lead to hefty fines and reputational damage, which is why an analyst's role in enforcing compliance is vital.

The Bridge Between Technical Teams and Management

Cybersecurity analysts often serve as a bridge between the highly technical aspects of cybersecurity and the management or decision-making level of an organization. They are tasked with interpreting complex technical findings—such as data from security logs, threat reports, and vulnerability scans—and communicating those findings in a way that decision-makers can understand. This involves not only explaining the potential risks but also offering actionable insights that help leaders make informed decisions about where to allocate resources, how to prioritize initiatives, and what strategic steps to take next. Analysts must be able to translate the language of firewalls, malware, and encryption into a context that makes sense to business executives, often requiring the ability to distill technical jargon into clear, concise, and relevant information.

As organizations face an increasingly complex and dynamic threat landscape, the role of the cybersecurity analyst becomes ever more crucial. They are tasked with the responsibility of safeguarding the company's assets and ensuring that all security protocols are continually updated to meet emerging threats. By understanding and executing their duties in monitoring, incident response, vulnerability management, policy development, and compliance, cybersecurity analysts play a pivotal role in the overall security posture of the organization.

CHAPTER 1   FOUNDATIONS OF CYBERSECURITY ANALYSIS

The CySA+ Exam Overview

The **CySA+** (CompTIA Cybersecurity Analyst+) certification is designed to assess an analyst's ability to identify and respond to various cybersecurity threats, with a strong focus on practical, hands-on skills. Unlike other cybersecurity certifications, the CySA+ emphasizes not just theoretical knowledge but also the ability to apply cybersecurity principles to real-world scenarios. This makes it an invaluable certification for professionals looking to prove their expertise in defending against evolving cyber threats.

Purpose of the CySA+ Certification

The **CySA+** certification is geared toward individuals in cybersecurity roles who are tasked with actively defending and continuously monitoring the security posture of an organization. This includes identifying vulnerabilities, analyzing security incidents, and leveraging tools to detect, manage, and mitigate potential threats. The certification validates a candidate's ability to address and manage these threats through various techniques and processes, making it a crucial qualification for cybersecurity analysts.

The certification ensures that professionals are equipped with the skills to use critical security technologies and frameworks, perform risk assessments, and execute response plans. It's ideal for those who work in roles like security operations, vulnerability management, and threat detection, providing assurance that they have the skills to safeguard an organization from emerging cyber risks.

CHAPTER 1   FOUNDATIONS OF CYBERSECURITY ANALYSIS

Exam Format and Structure

The **CySA+** exam is a comprehensive test consisting of **85 questions**. These questions are presented in a mix of multiple-choice formats and performance-based questions, which require candidates to complete tasks or solve problems in a simulated environment. This format allows candidates to demonstrate their ability to perform key cybersecurity tasks rather than just answering theoretical questions.

- **Multiple-Choice Questions (MCQs):** These questions assess a candidate's theoretical understanding of cybersecurity concepts and their ability to apply that knowledge in different scenarios.

- **Performance-Based Questions (PBQs):** These require candidates to complete tasks that simulate real-world cybersecurity challenges. PBQs are designed to test practical, hands-on skills by having candidates demonstrate how they would approach specific security problems or tools in a controlled environment.

The **time limit** for completing the exam is **165 minutes**, which means candidates will need to manage their time effectively to complete both the multiple-choice and performance-based questions within the allotted time. The exam is designed to test the candidate's technical expertise as well as their ability to handle real-world security incidents under time pressure, providing a thorough measure of their readiness for cybersecurity analyst roles.

The CySA+ certification is widely recognized in the industry as an indicator of an individual's ability to safeguard organizations from a variety of cybersecurity threats. Successfully passing the exam demonstrates that a professional possesses a well-rounded skillset, making them a valuable asset to any cybersecurity team.

CHAPTER 1   FOUNDATIONS OF CYBERSECURITY ANALYSIS

Building a Cybersecurity Mindset

The journey to becoming a successful cybersecurity analyst involves more than just technical knowledge; it requires cultivating a strong cybersecurity mindset. This mindset is shaped by critical thinking, adaptability, and a collaborative approach to problem-solving. Cybersecurity analysts must be able to think strategically, remain flexible in the face of evolving threats, and work effectively with diverse teams to ensure the organization's security posture remains robust.

Critical Thinking in Cybersecurity

Critical thinking is an essential skill for cybersecurity analysts. It involves questioning assumptions, seeking evidence, and evaluating information logically and objectively. In the world of cybersecurity, analysts must constantly assess risks, evaluate threats, and determine the most effective ways to mitigate those risks. This requires more than just technical expertise; it requires the ability to think beyond the obvious, consider all possibilities, and use evidence to make informed decisions.

For example, when reviewing security logs or network traffic, an analyst might encounter suspicious activity. A critical thinker would not only recognize this activity as potentially malicious but would investigate the evidence, analyze patterns, and form hypotheses to determine whether the threat is real. They would also consider possible false positives and understand how different scenarios could affect the broader security landscape.

Critical thinking in cybersecurity also involves the ability to anticipate potential threats before they occur. Analysts must proactively identify weaknesses, anticipate attack methods, and implement measures to prevent security incidents. Being able to critically assess emerging technologies, new attack vectors, and changing organizational needs is a hallmark of a skilled cybersecurity professional.

Adapting to Change

Cybersecurity is a constantly evolving field, with new threats, technologies, and regulations emerging on a regular basis. As a result, cybersecurity analysts must be highly adaptable, continuously learning and updating their skills. They must stay informed about the latest trends in cyber threats, such as ransomware attacks, phishing tactics, and insider threats. Moreover, as technologies like cloud computing, the Internet of Things (IoT), and artificial intelligence (AI) change the landscape, analysts must remain flexible in adapting their strategies and tools to keep pace.

One of the biggest challenges in cybersecurity is staying ahead of attackers who are constantly evolving their tactics. To adapt, analysts must be committed to continuous learning, whether through formal certifications, training programs, or self-study. Regularly attending industry conferences, engaging with peer communities, and keeping up with the latest research are all critical for maintaining an up-to-date understanding of the ever-changing cybersecurity landscape.

Additionally, analysts must be able to apply their evolving knowledge to real-world scenarios. When new vulnerabilities or attack techniques are discovered, cybersecurity professionals must adapt their incident response protocols, update their defensive measures, and ensure that their systems remain secure. Being able to quickly pivot and adjust to new challenges is key to maintaining an organization's security in a fast-paced digital world.

Team Collaboration

While cybersecurity analysts are often seen as technical experts, their success depends on their ability to collaborate effectively with other departments. Cybersecurity is not an isolated function; it intersects with many areas of an organization, including IT, legal, compliance, and business operations. Analysts must be able to communicate effectively across teams to align technical efforts with broader organizational goals.

CHAPTER 1   FOUNDATIONS OF CYBERSECURITY ANALYSIS

For example, when a security incident occurs, the analyst's role is not limited to identifying the threat and mitigating its impact. They must also collaborate with IT teams to isolate affected systems, legal teams to understand regulatory implications, and compliance teams to ensure that the incident is documented and reported appropriately. Additionally, analysts may need to work with business leaders to assess the financial and reputational impact of a breach and communicate the importance of ongoing security initiatives.

Collaboration also extends to working with external partners, such as third-party vendors, security researchers, and law enforcement, especially when dealing with large-scale incidents or complex cyberattacks. Being able to build relationships, share insights, and work together toward common security goals is crucial for achieving the most effective outcomes.

Moreover, cybersecurity analysts must balance the need for technical expertise with the ability to communicate complex security concepts in a way that is understandable to non-technical stakeholders. This means translating technical jargon into actionable insights that can guide decision-making at the management level. Successful analysts do not only protect the organization's assets; they help shape security policies, raise awareness, and promote a culture of security across the entire organization.

Building a cybersecurity mindset requires more than just mastering technical tools and frameworks. It involves developing a critical thinking approach, staying adaptable in an ever-changing field, and fostering collaboration across teams. By cultivating these qualities, cybersecurity analysts can not only protect their organizations but also drive continuous improvement and strategic alignment in their security efforts. A strong cybersecurity mindset is the foundation upon which effective, proactive defense is built.

Core Principles of Cybersecurity

The following will be gone over in significantly more detail in upcoming chapters, but for the purpose of introductions, we are going to do a very brief analysis of the core principles. You do not have to know all of this information in order to understand the following chapters, at this moment this is solely to dip your feet in the water some and become acquainted with the terminology.

The CIA Triad

The **CIA Triad**—Confidentiality, Integrity, and Availability—forms the foundation of cybersecurity principles and practices. These three core pillars guide all security measures and serve as the standard for evaluating the security of systems and data. Understanding each component of the triad is essential for cybersecurity analysts, as these concepts will shape the strategies and decisions made to protect critical organizational assets.

Confidentiality

Confidentiality ensures that sensitive information is only accessible to individuals who are authorized to view or manage it. This prevents unauthorized users or entities from accessing confidential data, which could lead to data breaches or misuse. Confidentiality measures protect personal, financial, and proprietary data from external and internal threats. Common methods of ensuring confidentiality include encryption, secure authentication, and access controls.

- **Example:** Encrypting sensitive emails before sending them ensures that only the intended recipient can read the contents, protecting the email from being intercepted by unauthorized individuals.

Confidentiality extends beyond data and includes maintaining the confidentiality of communications, records, and operations. For cybersecurity analysts, it's essential to implement and regularly update encryption protocols, access control measures, and security policies to safeguard sensitive data.

Integrity

Integrity is the principle that ensures data remains accurate, reliable, and unaltered unless specifically authorized by the proper person or process. This concept is crucial to maintain trust in the data and systems used within the organization. Integrity focuses on ensuring that data cannot be tampered with, corrupted, or lost, either unintentionally (due to a system failure or human error) or intentionally (due to a malicious actor).

- **Example:** Hashing algorithms, like SHA-256, can be used to verify the integrity of files by creating a unique hash for the original data. If even a small change is made to the data, the hash will change, signaling that the file has been altered.

Integrity also applies to system configurations, logs, and operational processes. Cybersecurity analysts must deploy monitoring tools that can detect alterations in files, configurations, or data, ensuring that integrity is maintained and that any discrepancies are flagged for further investigation.

Availability

Availability ensures that systems, applications, and data are accessible when needed by authorized users. It focuses on minimizing downtime and ensuring that critical systems remain operational and accessible. Availability is not just about keeping services online but also ensuring they are accessible with sufficient performance and speed for users. Protecting availability involves both redundancy and robust disaster recovery plans to prevent disruptions.

- **Example:** Implementing redundant servers and systems, or using cloud services with multiple availability zones, ensures that services remain accessible in case of a hardware failure, natural disaster, or other unexpected events that could cause downtime.

For cybersecurity analysts, availability is a top priority because even short disruptions to key business systems can lead to financial losses, damage to reputation, and a decrease in user trust. Ensuring high availability often involves balancing security controls with system performance needs, making it a critical area of expertise.

Defense-in-Depth Strategy

A **Defense-in-Depth Strategy** refers to a security approach that uses multiple, overlapping layers of defense mechanisms to protect an organization's assets and operations. This multifaceted methodology acknowledges that no single security control is foolproof and ensures that if one layer fails, others are in place to detect, mitigate, or contain the threat. This layered defense philosophy applies to every aspect of an organization's infrastructure, from physical security measures to network segmentation and endpoint protection, making it a cornerstone of robust cybersecurity frameworks.

CHAPTER 1 FOUNDATIONS OF CYBERSECURITY ANALYSIS

Core Components of Defense-in-Depth

1. **Physical Security**

    Physical security serves as the first layer of defense, safeguarding access to facilities, servers, and other critical infrastructure. Measures include

    - **Controlled Access Points:** Security gates, ID badges, and biometric scanners restrict unauthorized entry.

    - **Surveillance Systems:** CCTV cameras monitor activity and provide forensic evidence if an incident occurs.

    - **Environmental Controls:** Fire suppression systems, temperature monitors, and uninterruptible power supplies (UPS) help protect hardware.

    - **Security Personnel:** Guards add an active deterrent against physical threats.

2. **Network Security**

    This layer protects data as it travels across internal and external networks. Techniques include

    - **Firewalls:** Monitor and control incoming and outgoing network traffic based on pre-defined security rules.

    - **Intrusion Detection and Prevention Systems (IDS/IPS):** Identify and stop malicious activity on the network.

CHAPTER 1 FOUNDATIONS OF CYBERSECURITY ANALYSIS

- **Network Segmentation:** Dividing the network into smaller, isolated segments limits the spread of attacks.

- **Virtual Private Networks (VPNs):** Secure connections for remote access, encrypting data to protect against interception.

3. **Endpoint Security**

    Endpoints such as laptops, mobile devices, and IoT devices are common entry points for attackers. Defense strategies include

    - **Antivirus and Anti-malware:** Regular scanning for malicious software.

    - **Endpoint Detection and Response (EDR):** Proactive identification and containment of suspicious activities.

    - **Patch Management:** Regular updates to close known vulnerabilities.

    - **Access Controls:** Limiting the privileges of endpoint users to reduce potential damage from compromised accounts.

4. **Application Security**

    Applications are often targeted by attackers seeking vulnerabilities in software. Safeguards include

    - **Code Reviews:** Rigorous testing and inspection of application code to identify and fix security flaws.

    - **Secure Development Practices:** Incorporating security measures during the software development life cycle (SDLC).

- **Application Firewalls:** Protecting web applications from common attacks like SQL injection and cross-site scripting (XSS).

5. **Data Security**

   Protecting sensitive data is a critical component of defense-in-depth. Methods include

   - **Encryption:** Encrypting data both at rest and in transit ensures it remains unreadable if intercepted.
   - **Data Loss Prevention (DLP):** Tools that monitor and restrict the transfer of sensitive data outside the organization.
   - **Backups:** Regular data backups enable recovery in the event of a ransomware attack or data corruption.

6. **Identity and Access Management (IAM)**

   Proper control of user identities is fundamental to preventing unauthorized access. Key measures include

   - **Multi-Factor Authentication (MFA):** Adds additional verification layers beyond a password.
   - **Role-Based Access Control (RBAC):** Ensures users only have access to the data and systems required for their roles.
   - **Privileged Access Management (PAM):** Limits and monitors access by privileged accounts.

7. **Monitoring and Logging**

   Continuous monitoring ensures that unusual activities are detected promptly.

   - **SIEM (Security Information and Event Management):** Centralizes and analyzes log data to identify threats.

   - **Behavioral Analytics:** Identifies deviations from normal patterns of user or system behavior.

   - **Alerts and Notifications:** Immediate alerts for critical security incidents.

Advantages of Defense-in-Depth

- **Comprehensive Protection:** Multiple layers of defense ensure that vulnerabilities in one layer are compensated by another.

- **Early Detection:** Defense mechanisms at different levels increase the likelihood of detecting threats before they cause harm.

- **Scalability:** The strategy is adaptable to organizations of varying sizes and industries.

- **Compliance:** Many regulatory frameworks, such as GDPR and HIPAA, require multilayered security approaches, which defense-in-depth inherently supports.

CHAPTER 1 FOUNDATIONS OF CYBERSECURITY ANALYSIS

Implementing a Defense-in-Depth Strategy

1. **Assessment and Planning**

   Conduct a thorough assessment of the organization's existing security measures and potential risks. Develop a plan that identifies critical assets and prioritizes layers of defense accordingly.

2. **Integration of Tools**

   Choose and integrate security tools that complement each other. Ensure seamless communication between systems, such as integrating EDR solutions with SIEM platforms.

3. **Employee Training**

   Equip employees with the knowledge to recognize phishing attempts, social engineering, and other tactics. A well-informed workforce is a crucial layer of defense.

4. **Regular Audits and Updates**

   Periodically review and update security protocols to address emerging threats and technological advancements.

5. **Incident Response Planning**

   Prepare for potential breaches by establishing a clear incident response plan. This ensures swift containment and minimizes damage in case of an attack.

A Defense-in-Depth Strategy is a robust and flexible approach to cybersecurity. By implementing multiple layers of defense, organizations can significantly reduce their vulnerability to attacks and increase their ability to detect, respond to, and recover from security incidents. The strategy requires careful planning, integration, and continuous improvement to remain effective in an ever-changing threat landscape.

Understanding the Cybersecurity Landscape

The **cybersecurity landscape** is dynamic, constantly evolving, and filled with diverse threats, challenges, and opportunities. Cybersecurity analysts must understand this landscape thoroughly to anticipate, identify, and mitigate risks effectively. This section will explore some of the most common cybersecurity threats and the emerging trends reshaping the field.

Measuring the Attack Surface

The attack surface refers to the total number of points in an organization's infrastructure where an unauthorized user could potentially access or manipulate systems, networks, or data. These points of entry include web applications, email systems, external devices, network ports, and even social engineering attack vectors. A larger attack surface increases the number of potential vulnerabilities and entry points that attackers could exploit. Therefore, understanding and reducing the attack surface is a critical component of cybersecurity strategy.

- **Example:** A company's website, email system, and employee mobile devices are all part of the organization's attack surface. Each point can potentially be exploited by attackers to gain unauthorized access.

CHAPTER 1   FOUNDATIONS OF CYBERSECURITY ANALYSIS

Cybersecurity analysts are responsible for continually assessing and reducing the attack surface by identifying vulnerable areas, removing unnecessary services, and applying appropriate security controls. The more a company can minimize its attack surface, the lower the risk of a successful attack.

Identifying Risk

Risk is the potential for loss, damage, or destruction resulting from a cybersecurity threat exploiting a vulnerability. Risk is a combination of three elements: threats, vulnerabilities, and the potential impact of a breach. Threats include anything from cyberattacks and natural disasters to insider threats, while vulnerabilities are weaknesses in systems, networks, or processes that could be exploited. The potential impact refers to the consequences of a successful attack, which could range from financial loss to reputational damage or legal repercussions.

Cybersecurity analysts must continuously evaluate the risk to the organization by conducting risk assessments and prioritizing risks based on their likelihood and potential impact. By understanding the risk profile of the organization, analysts can guide the implementation of appropriate countermeasures, such as firewalls, encryption, access controls, and user awareness training, to reduce risk exposure.

- **Example:** If a company stores sensitive customer data without proper encryption, the risk of a data breach is high, as the sensitive data could be accessed by unauthorized parties. The analyst would recommend encryption, among other security measures, to mitigate this risk.

Common Threats

Cybersecurity analysts are at the front line of defending against various threats. These threats can come from external attackers, internal employees, or even automated systems designed to exploit vulnerabilities. Understanding these threats is crucial for analysts to develop robust defenses and stay prepared for new attack vectors.

Malware

Malware is a broad category of software that is intentionally designed to cause harm to systems, steal data, or disrupt operations. Types of malware include:

- **Viruses:** Programs that attach themselves to files and spread to other systems. They can cause significant damage, corrupt data, or slow down systems.

- **Worms:** Similar to viruses, worms can replicate themselves and spread across networks without requiring user interaction. They often exploit vulnerabilities in systems and can bring down entire networks.

- **Ransomware:** A form of malware that locks a user's system or encrypts their files and demands a ransom for their release. This is one of the most lucrative forms of attack for cybercriminals, as it often targets both individuals and businesses.

- **Spyware:** Software that secretly monitors user activity and collects sensitive information without the user's consent. It can track browsing habits, record keystrokes, or steal credentials.

CHAPTER 1   FOUNDATIONS OF CYBERSECURITY ANALYSIS

Phishing and Social Engineering

Phishing attacks are designed to deceive users into revealing sensitive information, such as passwords, credit card details, or access to organizational systems. Social engineering, which phishing is a part of, manipulates individuals into trusting malicious actors. These attacks often leverage psychological manipulation and can take many forms:

- **Email Phishing:** Cybercriminals send fraudulent emails that appear to come from legitimate sources, like banks, government organizations, or even internal departments, prompting users to click malicious links or open attachments.

- **Spear Phishing:** A more targeted form of phishing, spear phishing is aimed at specific individuals or organizations, often involving in-depth research about the victim to craft more convincing messages.

- **Vishing (Voice Phishing):** Attackers use phone calls or voicemail messages to deceive individuals into disclosing sensitive information.

- **Pretexting:** The attacker creates a fabricated scenario to persuade a person into divulging confidential information.

Cybersecurity analysts need to train users to recognize phishing attempts and other forms of social engineering to reduce the risk of these attacks.

Insider Threats

An insider threat refers to a security risk posed by individuals within the organization, such as employees, contractors, or business partners, who have access to internal systems. These threats can be intentional or unintentional:

- **Malicious Insiders:** Employees or contractors who deliberately steal or damage company data or systems. These threats are often difficult to detect, as insiders already have authorized access to sensitive information.

- **Negligent Insiders:** Employees who inadvertently expose data through careless actions, such as falling for phishing emails, misconfiguring security settings, or sharing passwords with unauthorized individuals.

To combat insider threats, cybersecurity analysts should implement strong access controls, user monitoring, and employee training on security best practices.

Advanced Persistent Threats (APTs)

APTs are highly sophisticated, long-term attacks that often target specific organizations or industries. These threats are usually state-sponsored or carried out by well-funded and skilled cybercriminal groups. APTs typically involve multiple stages of attack, including initial entry, persistence, lateral movement within networks, and exfiltration of data over an extended period.

- **Example:** AAPT targeting a government agency might begin with spear-phishing emails to gain access to an employee's credentials. Once inside, the attackers establish footholds in the system, steal sensitive information, and attempt to avoid detection.

CHAPTER 1   FOUNDATIONS OF CYBERSECURITY ANALYSIS

Cybersecurity analysts need advanced detection systems, threat intelligence, and incident response plans to counter APTs effectively.

Emerging Trends in Cybersecurity

As technology evolves, so do the threats and opportunities within the cybersecurity landscape. Cybersecurity analysts must stay informed of emerging trends to anticipate future threats, refine their defenses, and remain effective in an ever-changing environment.

Artificial Intelligence (AI) in Cyberattacks and Defenses

Artificial Intelligence (AI) is playing an increasingly prominent role in both cyberattacks and cybersecurity defenses. Attackers use AI to enhance the effectiveness and sophistication of their attacks, while defenders use it to automate threat detection, response, and analysis.

- **In Cyberattacks:** AI can be used to power more advanced malware that adapts to evade detection. For example, AI-driven malware can change its code or behavior to bypass signature-based antivirus software.

- **In Defenses:** AI is also used in cybersecurity tools like intrusion detection systems (IDS) that analyze traffic patterns and learn to recognize anomalies, allowing them to identify potential threats faster and more accurately than traditional methods.

As AI becomes more integrated into both offensive and defensive tactics, cybersecurity analysts will need to keep pace with these technologies to understand and mitigate the associated risks.

CHAPTER 1   FOUNDATIONS OF CYBERSECURITY ANALYSIS

Securing Internet of Things (IoT) Devices

The rise of **Internet of Things (IoT)** devices—ranging from smart thermostats and security cameras to industrial sensors and medical devices—has introduced a new wave of security challenges. While these devices offer tremendous benefits, they also create significant vulnerabilities. Many IoT devices are not designed with robust security measures, making them prime targets for cybercriminals.

- **Example:** A smart refrigerator with poor security could be exploited to access a home network, or a vulnerable industrial IoT device could be hijacked to launch a botnet attack.

Cybersecurity analysts must understand the unique risks IoT devices pose and implement proper security measures, such as network segmentation, strong authentication protocols, and regular vulnerability assessments, to mitigate these risks.

Cloud Security Concerns

As more organizations migrate their infrastructure and services to the cloud, securing cloud environments has become a major priority. The shared responsibility model between cloud service providers and customers means that while cloud providers handle the physical security of the cloud infrastructure, the responsibility for securing data and applications remains with the organization. The following are some of the most common talking points in regard to cloud infrastructure concerns:

- **Data Security:** Cloud environments may store sensitive data off-site, which can be vulnerable to breaches if not properly secured.

- **Misconfiguration:** Many cloud security incidents are the result of poor configuration practices, such as improper access controls or public-facing storage buckets.

- **Compliance:** Ensuring that cloud services comply with industry regulations (such as GDPR or HIPAA) is a critical concern for organizations that store sensitive or regulated data in the cloud.

Cybersecurity analysts must stay knowledgeable about cloud security best practices and implement tools that monitor and secure cloud environments, including encryption, identity and access management (IAM), and continuous configuration monitoring.

Understanding the common threats and emerging trends in cybersecurity is critical for analysts to effectively defend their organizations. The ever-evolving nature of cybersecurity requires continuous learning, adaptation, and vigilance to stay one step ahead of cyber adversaries. By gaining a deep understanding of these threats and trends, analysts can better prepare to mitigate risks, respond to incidents, and protect their organization's data and assets.

Cybersecurity Frameworks and Best Practices

In the ever-changing world of cybersecurity, frameworks and best practices provide a structured approach to managing security risks, detecting threats, and responding effectively to incidents. These frameworks help organizations of all sizes establish a comprehensive security posture and streamline their defense efforts. This section dives deep into some of the most widely recognized cybersecurity frameworks and standards, explaining their components, benefits, and practical applications.

CHAPTER 1   FOUNDATIONS OF CYBERSECURITY ANALYSIS

NIST Cybersecurity Framework (CSF)

The **NIST Cybersecurity Framework (CSF)**, developed by the National Institute of Standards and Technology (NIST), is one of the most widely used frameworks designed to help organizations manage and reduce cybersecurity risk. It was created in response to the increasing frequency and complexity of cyberattacks and is widely used by both private and public sector organizations across the globe.

The NIST CSF is organized into five core functions, which together provide a comprehensive approach to cybersecurity:

- **Identify:** This function involves understanding and managing cybersecurity risks to systems, assets, data, and capabilities. It emphasizes the importance of asset management, risk assessments, and the identification of vulnerabilities within the organization's environment. For example, identifying critical assets such as intellectual property or customer data and assessing the risks that they face is crucial to building a solid cybersecurity strategy.

- **Protect:** Protecting systems and data from cybersecurity threats involves implementing appropriate safeguards. This includes technical measures such as firewalls, encryption, and access controls, as well as organizational measures like employee training and the development of strong security policies. This function ensures that an organization's critical assets are secure from unauthorized access or disclosure.

- **Detect:** Early detection of cybersecurity incidents is key to minimizing damage. This involves continuously monitoring systems for signs of abnormal activity and deploying tools such as Intrusion Detection Systems (IDS), Security Information and Event Management (SIEM) tools, and behavior analytics to detect potential threats. Timely detection enables organizations to respond quickly and mitigate potential threats before they escalate.

- **Respond:** Once a cybersecurity incident is detected, it is critical to have a clear response plan in place. This function involves developing procedures for incident management, including containment, communication, and investigation. Response activities can include analyzing the attack, notifying relevant stakeholders, and initiating mitigation steps to stop the threat from spreading.

- **Recover:** After an incident, the recovery process focuses on restoring normal operations and minimizing the impact of the attack. This involves data recovery strategies, disaster recovery planning, and updating security protocols to ensure future incidents are prevented. Recovery is an ongoing process that includes analyzing the incident to improve overall security posture and avoid similar threats in the future.

The NIST CSF is valuable for organizations because it provides a flexible, risk-based approach to cybersecurity, which can be tailored to the organization's specific needs. By using the NIST CSF, cybersecurity analysts can establish a proactive cybersecurity strategy, focusing on continuous improvement.

ISO/IEC 27001

ISO/IEC 27001 is an international standard for information security management. It provides a comprehensive set of requirements for establishing, implementing, operating, monitoring, reviewing, maintaining, and improving an organization's information security management system (ISMS). This framework helps organizations protect sensitive data through risk management, ensuring business continuity, and safeguarding stakeholder interests.

Key aspects of **ISO/IEC 27001** include

- **Risk Management:** ISO/IEC 27001 emphasizes the importance of identifying risks to information security and implementing controls to mitigate them. This involves a systematic risk assessment and treatment process.

- **Continuous Improvement:** One of the core principles of ISO/IEC 27001 is continuous improvement. Organizations are required to regularly assess their security posture, identify weaknesses, and implement improvements over time.

- **Documentation:** The standard also places significant importance on documentation, requiring organizations to maintain records of security measures, audits, and incidents to demonstrate their commitment to security best practices.

ISO/IEC 27001 aligns with various industry regulations, making it a valuable framework for global organizations that need to meet compliance requirements such as the EU General Data Protection Regulation (GDPR), Health Insurance Portability and Accountability Act (HIPAA), and others.

CHAPTER 1   FOUNDATIONS OF CYBERSECURITY ANALYSIS

MITRE ATT&CK Framework

The **MITRE ATT&CK Framework** (Adversarial Tactics, Techniques, and Common Knowledge) is a knowledge base that catalogs adversary tactics, techniques, and procedures (TTPs) based on real-world observations. It provides cybersecurity professionals with insights into the ways cybercriminals and threat actors conduct their operations. This framework helps analysts understand attack methodologies and design more effective defense strategies.

Key elements of the **MITRE ATT&CK Framework**:

- **Tactics:** These represent the goals or objectives of an attacker during a cybersecurity attack. For example, an attacker's tactic might be "Initial Access," meaning their goal is to gain access to a target network.

- **Techniques:** These are the specific methods or tools attackers use to achieve their goals. For instance, phishing or exploiting a vulnerability to gain access to a network falls under the "Initial Access" tactic.

- **Procedures:** These describe how an adversary performs a technique in practice. For example, a specific phishing email designed to exploit a vulnerability in an email client.

By mapping real-world attacks to the MITRE ATT&CK matrix, cybersecurity analysts can improve threat detection and response strategies. It also assists in threat-hunting activities and incident response by providing insights into common attack patterns.

Other Frameworks and Standards

In addition to the frameworks mentioned above, several other frameworks and standards are widely used in cybersecurity analysis. These frameworks help organizations ensure security governance, compliance, and effective protection from cyber threats.

COBIT (Control Objectives for Information and Related Technologies)

COBIT is a framework for the governance and management of enterprise IT. It focuses on aligning IT with business goals and ensuring IT risks are properly managed. It helps cybersecurity professionals understand the controls necessary to meet business objectives and mitigate cybersecurity risks.

Center for Internet Security (CIS) Controls

The CIS Controls consist of a prioritized set of best practices and actions designed to protect organizations from known attack vectors. The framework covers essential cybersecurity controls such as inventorying hardware and software, implementing strong access controls, and maintaining an incident response plan. The CIS Controls are a practical, actionable guide for organizations to improve their cybersecurity posture.

Threat Intelligence Frameworks

In addition to these established frameworks, threat intelligence plays a crucial role in identifying and mitigating emerging threats. Threat intelligence frameworks, such as the **MITRE ATT&CK** and **The Diamond Model of Intrusion Analysis**, provide a structured approach to analyzing and sharing information about threats.

CHAPTER 1   FOUNDATIONS OF CYBERSECURITY ANALYSIS

Threat intelligence involves the collection, analysis, and sharing of data on threats, attackers, and attack techniques. Key aspects of threat intelligence frameworks include

- **Tactics, Techniques, and Procedures (TTPs):** As previously mentioned, understanding the TTPs used by attackers is key to anticipating and defending against future attacks. Cybersecurity analysts use frameworks like MITRE ATT&CK to map out the behavior of threat actors and develop proactive defense measures.

- **Threat Actors:** Threat intelligence frameworks also help organizations identify the threat actors behind cyberattacks. These can include nation-state actors, cybercriminal groups, hacktivists, or insiders.

- **Indicators of Compromise (IOCs):** Threat intelligence frameworks provide valuable data on IOCs, which include artifacts left behind by attackers, such as IP addresses, file hashes, and domain names. This information helps analysts identify ongoing attacks and stop them before they escalate.

In summary, cybersecurity frameworks and best practices are vital for organizing and enhancing an organization's security posture. By using frameworks like the **NIST CSF**, **ISO/IEC 27001**, and **MITRE ATT&CK**, organizations can proactively identify and mitigate risks, detect incidents early, and ensure effective incident response and recovery. Additionally, staying updated on emerging trends and leveraging threat intelligence frameworks will help cybersecurity analysts stay ahead of potential attacks. Understanding and implementing these frameworks is crucial for any cybersecurity professional looking to protect systems and data from increasingly sophisticated threats.

CHAPTER 1   FOUNDATIONS OF CYBERSECURITY ANALYSIS

Overview of Cybersecurity Tools

As cybersecurity threats continue to evolve, the tools that analysts use to detect, respond, and mitigate these threats are constantly improving. A broad range of tools exists, each designed to address specific aspects of security, from monitoring to threat detection and vulnerability management. This section will provide an overview of some of the most essential cybersecurity tools used by analysts, breaking down their functions, examples, and how they contribute to overall security efforts.

SIEM (Security Information and Event Management)

SIEM tools are essential in modern cybersecurity, serving as centralized platforms for collecting, analyzing, and correlating security event data from various sources. They aggregate logs from different systems, devices, and applications, allowing analysts to monitor and respond to security incidents effectively. By centralizing event data, SIEM tools provide real-time visibility into the network and can generate alerts when suspicious activities or anomalies are detected.

Key functions of **SIEM** tools include

- **Log Aggregation:** SIEM systems collect logs from diverse data sources such as firewalls, routers, intrusion detection/prevention systems (IDS/IPS), and servers.

- **Correlation:** SIEM tools correlate data from different logs to identify potential security incidents or attacks that might go unnoticed if viewed in isolation.

- **Incident Detection:** SIEM platforms provide automated detection of abnormal behavior and can alert analysts to potential threats or security breaches.
- **Compliance Reporting:** Many SIEM tools include built-in compliance templates, which make it easier for organizations to meet regulatory requirements by automatically generating reports.

Examples of SIEM Tools:

- **Splunk:** One of the most widely used SIEM solutions, Splunk offers a comprehensive platform for searching, monitoring, and analyzing machine data. It excels in scalability and flexibility, making it suitable for large enterprises.
- **QRadar:** Developed by IBM, QRadar is a robust SIEM tool known for its ability to analyze vast amounts of data, correlate events, and offer actionable insights for threat response.
- **LogRhythm:** LogRhythm provides a unified security intelligence platform that combines SIEM, log management, and network monitoring to deliver comprehensive security solutions.

Endpoint Detection and Response (EDR)

EDR tools are designed to focus on detecting and responding to threats targeting endpoint devices like laptops, servers, and mobile devices. With more organizations adopting bring-your-own-device (BYOD) policies

CHAPTER 1 FOUNDATIONS OF CYBERSECURITY ANALYSIS

and remote work environments, endpoints have become prime targets for cybercriminals. EDR tools provide continuous monitoring of endpoint activities and respond to any suspicious behavior, often providing automated remediation.

Key functions of **EDR** tools include

- **Continuous Monitoring:** EDR tools constantly monitor endpoints for unusual activities that might indicate a security breach, such as unauthorized file access or malicious processes running in the background.

- **Threat Detection:** They leverage advanced behavioral analysis, signature-based detection, and machine learning to identify and flag suspicious activity in real time.

- **Incident Response:** Once a potential threat is detected, EDR tools enable quick remediation by isolating affected devices, terminating malicious processes, or rolling back to a secure state.

- **Data Collection and Analysis:** EDR systems collect rich data from endpoints to assist in forensic investigations, helping analysts understand how the threat infiltrated the system.

Examples of EDR Tools:

- **CrowdStrike Falcon:** Known for its cloud-native platform, CrowdStrike Falcon provides real-time endpoint protection and threat intelligence. It offers advanced AI-driven detection and prevention, ensuring minimal impact on system performance.

- **SentinelOne:** SentinelOne uses autonomous AI to detect and respond to endpoint threats. Its platform is designed for real-time protection and incident response, with a strong focus on automated remediation.

Vulnerability Scanners

Vulnerability scanners are tools designed to identify weaknesses in systems, networks, and applications that could be exploited by attackers. These tools are essential for cybersecurity analysts to conduct regular assessments of their organization's infrastructure and ensure that systems are secure. Vulnerability scanning helps identify security gaps, misconfigurations, outdated software, and other potential entry points for cybercriminals.

Key functions of **vulnerability scanners** include

- **Automated Scanning:** Vulnerability scanners automatically scan systems and networks for known vulnerabilities, misconfigurations, and missing patches.

- **Reporting:** They generate detailed reports on discovered vulnerabilities, often prioritizing them based on risk severity and potential impact.

- **Remediation Recommendations:** Many scanners provide suggestions for fixing vulnerabilities, such as applying patches or reconfiguring settings.

- **Compliance:** Vulnerability scanning tools are useful for ensuring compliance with security standards and regulations such as PCI DSS, HIPAA, and NIST guidelines.

Examples of Vulnerability Scanners:

- **Nessus:** One of the most popular vulnerability scanners, Nessus is used by security professionals to identify and fix vulnerabilities in systems. It provides a comprehensive list of potential vulnerabilities, along with detailed risk assessments.

- **Qualys:** A cloud-based vulnerability management platform, Qualys provides continuous monitoring and scanning for vulnerabilities across an organization's IT environment. It supports a wide range of devices, from on-premises servers to cloud resources.

- **OpenVAS:** An open-source vulnerability scanner that is widely used in the cybersecurity community. OpenVAS provides thorough vulnerability scanning with a focus on network and host-based vulnerabilities.

Threat Intelligence Platforms

Threat Intelligence Platforms (TIPs) are designed to aggregate and analyze data about potential threats from a variety of sources. These platforms provide actionable insights into emerging threats, adversary tactics, and indicators of compromise (IOCs). By collecting intelligence from external and internal sources, TIPs help organizations proactively defend against evolving cyber threats, allowing cybersecurity teams to anticipate attacks and strengthen defenses.

Key functions of **Threat Intelligence Platforms** include

- **Data Aggregation:** TIPs collect data from various sources, such as open-source intelligence (OSINT), commercial threat feeds, and internal logs. This allows analysts to have a comprehensive view of the threat landscape.

- **Threat Analysis:** These platforms analyze collected data, identifying patterns and providing insights on emerging threats. They often use machine learning and AI to predict and prioritize potential risks.

- **Sharing Intelligence:** TIPs facilitate the sharing of threat intelligence across organizations, industries, and sectors, enhancing the collective defense against cyber threats.

- **Integration with Other Tools:** Threat intelligence platforms integrate with SIEM, EDR, and other security tools to enrich threat detection and response efforts by providing up-to-date intelligence on adversary tactics and known IOCs.

Examples of Threat Intelligence Platforms:

- **Recorded Future:** A leading threat intelligence platform that uses machine learning to analyze vast amounts of data from various sources. It helps organizations understand the threat landscape and make informed decisions about risk management.

- **Anomali:** Anomali provides threat intelligence solutions that aggregate, analyze, and operationalize threat data. Their platform is designed to help security teams identify, detect, and respond to emerging threats efficiently.

In summary, cybersecurity tools such as **SIEM**, **EDR**, **vulnerability scanners**, and **threat intelligence platforms** play crucial roles in the detection, prevention, and mitigation of cyber threats. These tools enable cybersecurity analysts to monitor networks, protect endpoints, identify vulnerabilities, and stay informed about evolving threats. Understanding and effectively leveraging these tools is essential for creating a comprehensive and proactive security posture that can defend against today's complex cyber risks.

Chapter Summary

In this chapter, we have laid the groundwork for understanding the crucial role of a cybersecurity analyst. By defining the core responsibilities of the profession and introducing key cybersecurity concepts, tools, and frameworks, we've provided readers with the necessary foundation to succeed in the field. From exploring the critical elements of the CIA Triad to understanding defense-in-depth strategies, the concepts discussed in this chapter are essential for any aspiring analyst.

The chapter also emphasizes the importance of cultivating a proactive cybersecurity mindset. We explored how critical thinking, adaptability, and teamwork are integral to navigating the dynamic and ever-evolving world of cybersecurity. These qualities not only enhance an analyst's ability to protect an organization's systems but also contribute to creating a culture of security within the company.

CHAPTER 1   FOUNDATIONS OF CYBERSECURITY ANALYSIS

Additionally, readers have been introduced to the NIST Cybersecurity Framework and other vital standards, which will serve as key references throughout the rest of the book. With a solid grasp of these foundational elements, readers are now prepared to dive deeper into the specific domains of the CySA+ certification, which will be addressed in the following chapters. By the end of this chapter, readers should feel confident in their ability to approach cybersecurity analysis with a clear understanding of its importance and the tools needed for success.

CHAPTER 2

Introduction to Threat Intelligence and Vulnerability Management Principles

In this chapter, we explore the essential components of Threat and Vulnerability Management, which is central to the role of a cybersecurity analyst. The chapter focuses on the core responsibilities of identifying, assessing, and mitigating risks related to threats and vulnerabilities within an organization's infrastructure. With an emphasis on both proactive defense and continuous monitoring, we will cover the key concepts and methodologies that cybersecurity analysts employ to detect and manage potential risks effectively.

We will begin by defining threats and vulnerabilities, highlighting the different types that analysts need to recognize. From there, we'll dive into the process of vulnerability management, including identification, prioritization, and remediation. Risk assessment models will also be

CHAPTER 2   INTRODUCTION TO THREAT INTELLIGENCE AND VULNERABILITY
             MANAGEMENT PRINCIPLES

examined to help analysts understand how to assess and manage potential risks. Finally, we'll look at strategies for mitigating threats and vulnerabilities, with an eye toward real-world applications that organizations can implement to minimize their exposure.

By the end of this chapter, readers will have the knowledge and tools necessary to approach threat and vulnerability management in a structured, informed manner—ensuring they are prepared to defend against evolving cybersecurity risks.

Threat Intelligence and Analysis

Threat intelligence is the cornerstone of proactive cybersecurity. In an age where threats evolve faster than ever, having actionable insights into the tactics, techniques, and procedures (TTPs) of attackers can make the difference between a thwarted attempt and a full-scale breach. This chapter delves into the world of threat intelligence, exploring how organizations gather, analyze, and apply data to enhance their security posture and protect critical assets. The value of threat intelligence lies in its ability to provide context. It transforms raw data—such as IP addresses, malware signatures, or attack patterns—into meaningful insights that can inform decisions. By understanding the motivations and methodologies of adversaries, organizations can take proactive measures to mitigate risks before they escalate into incidents. Threat intelligence also serves as a powerful tool for aligning cybersecurity efforts with broader business objectives, ensuring resources are focused on the most relevant threats.

In this chapter, we'll explore the various categories of threat intelligence—strategic, tactical, operational, and technical—and their unique roles in a comprehensive security strategy. We'll examine how intelligence is sourced, from internal logs and external feeds to collaborative sharing initiatives. Additionally, we'll discuss the importance of analyzing this information to separate valuable insights from noise and how to apply those insights to improve threat detection, incident response, and overall resilience. By the end of this chapter, readers will have a deep understanding of how threat intelligence functions as a dynamic, essential component of cybersecurity. You'll gain practical knowledge on integrating intelligence into your organization's defenses and learn how to stay ahead in an ever-changing threat landscape.

Introduction to Threat Intelligence

In today's digital landscape, cyber threats are evolving at an unprecedented pace, making it critical for organizations to stay ahead of attackers. **Threat intelligence** serves as a cornerstone of modern cybersecurity strategies, providing actionable insights into potential risks and adversarial behaviors. At its core, threat intelligence involves collecting, analyzing, and sharing information about cyber threats—ranging from malware and phishing campaigns to nation-state activities. By leveraging these insights, organizations can anticipate attacks, improve their defensive postures, and react swiftly when incidents occur.

The Role of Threat Intelligence in Cybersecurity

Threat intelligence transforms the reactive nature of traditional cybersecurity into a proactive approach. Instead of waiting for an attack to occur, organizations can leverage intelligence to identify vulnerabilities, monitor adversarial tactics, and deploy defenses before incidents arise. It also empowers security teams to detect threats earlier, mitigate risks more effectively, and reduce the time required for recovery. This proactive posture significantly strengthens an organization's resilience to cyberattacks.

CHAPTER 2 INTRODUCTION TO THREAT INTELLIGENCE AND VULNERABILITY MANAGEMENT PRINCIPLES

Types of Threat Intelligence

Threat intelligence is not a one-size-fits-all approach, and it can be categorized into several types, each providing a different perspective on the threat landscape. These different types of intelligence help organizations to stay ahead of attackers and strengthen their security defenses.

Strategic Intelligence

Strategic intelligence is high-level information that provides insight into long-term trends and emerging threats in the cybersecurity landscape. Often used by executives and senior decision-makers, this type of intelligence helps shape the organization's overall security strategy and risk management. It provides valuable insights into industry-wide trends, geopolitical risks, and the evolving nature of cyber threats. For example, understanding how nation-state actors are targeting critical infrastructure can help an organization better prepare for potential risks in the future.

Operational Intelligence

Operational intelligence is more focused and timelier, offering insights into specific attacks or campaigns currently underway. This intelligence helps organizations understand the tactics and techniques used by attackers in a given campaign. It provides crucial information on the "who, what, when, and how" of a specific attack, enabling organizations to take swift action and counteract these threats. Operational intelligence often includes details like attack vectors, targeted systems, and the profile of the threat actor, all of which can be used to prevent or mitigate similar incidents in the future.

Tactical Intelligence

Tactical intelligence dives deep into the technical aspects of attacks, specifically focusing on the tools, techniques, and procedures (TTPs) used by cybercriminals. This intelligence provides actionable insights into the specific ways attackers infiltrate systems, conduct reconnaissance, or move laterally through a network. By understanding the TTPs of threat actors, organizations can implement defenses tailored to block specific attack methods. This type of intelligence also includes indicators of compromise (IOCs) such as file hashes, malicious IP addresses, and other artifacts that can be used to detect active intrusions.

Internal vs. External Threat Intelligence

- **Internal Intelligence**: This is generated from within the organization and reflects its unique environment. Sources include system logs, network traffic analysis, endpoint detections, and incidents identified by security tools such as SIEMs or EDR platforms. Internal intelligence helps identify vulnerabilities specific to the organization and provides actionable insights for tailored defense strategies.

- **External Intelligence**: External intelligence is sourced from entities outside the organization. This includes feeds from threat intelligence providers, security vendors, and industry collaborations. External intelligence provides broader context, offering details about global threat campaigns, attack vectors, and actor profiles that may target similar organizations or industries.

CHAPTER 2   INTRODUCTION TO THREAT INTELLIGENCE AND VULNERABILITY MANAGEMENT PRINCIPLES

Sources of Threat Intelligence

Threat intelligence is derived from multiple sources, each contributing a unique set of data points that help organizations get a clearer picture of the threat landscape. By combining information from various sources, analysts can obtain a more comprehensive and nuanced understanding of emerging risks.

Open-Source Intelligence (OSINT)

Open-source intelligence (OSINT) refers to publicly available data that can be used to gather information about threats. This can include information from news articles, social media posts, public databases, blogs, or even forums where cybercriminals discuss tactics. OSINT provides valuable early warnings about potential threats and allows organizations to monitor current events, vulnerabilities, and suspicious activities that might pose a threat. Because OSINT is freely available, it is a cost-effective way for organizations to stay informed about the latest cybersecurity trends.

- **Common OSINT Tools:**
    - **Shodan**: A search engine for discovering Internet-connected devices, revealing potential misconfigurations or vulnerabilities.
    - **VirusTotal**: Analyzes suspicious files and URLs to detect malware and threat indicators.
    - **Maltego**: A powerful tool for data visualization and correlation across multiple sources.

Paid Intelligence Feeds

Paid intelligence feeds offer high-quality, curated threat data from commercial vendors. These providers offer detailed threat reports that include up-to-date information about emerging threats, malware analysis, and cyberattack tactics. Unlike OSINT, which can sometimes be fragmented or delayed, paid feeds provide real-time data that is essential for organizations looking to defend against the latest threats. These feeds often come with in-depth analysis and the ability to track specific threat actor groups, making them an invaluable resource for any security team.

Commercial Threat Intelligence Providers

Many organizations subscribe to commercial threat intelligence services to access curated, actionable data tailored to their specific needs.

- **Leading Vendors**: Companies like **FireEye**, **CrowdStrike**, and **Anomali** offer robust platforms that integrate threat feeds, analytics, and automated defenses.

- **Benefits**: These services provide in-depth analysis of threats, historical data for context, and actionable indicators that can be directly integrated into security tools. They save time and resources by delivering intelligence in a readily usable format.

Dark Web Monitoring

The dark web is an encrypted part of the Internet where illicit activities, including the sale of stolen data and hacking tools, take place. Monitoring the dark web is a critical aspect of threat intelligence as it helps organizations detect early signs of a breach or attack. For example, if an organization's customer data is being sold on the dark web, it can take immediate action to notify impacted parties and remediate vulnerabilities. Dark web monitoring can also help track the activities of cybercriminals, providing a heads-up before attacks unfold.

Information-Sharing Platforms

Information Sharing and Analysis Centers (ISACs) are collaborative platforms where organizations can share threat intelligence with each other. These platforms allow members to exchange information about new threats, vulnerabilities, and emerging attack methods in real time. ISACs are often industry-specific, allowing members to discuss and address threats that are particularly relevant to their sector. Sharing intelligence in this manner strengthens the collective defense of the industry, ensuring that all organizations are aware of the same risks and can take coordinated actions to prevent them.

Information Sharing and Collaboration

Threat intelligence is most effective when shared within trusted networks, allowing organizations to learn from each other and strengthen collective defenses.

- **Information Sharing and Analysis Centers (ISACs)**: Industry-specific groups where members collaborate to exchange threat data and best practices. For example, the Financial Services ISAC (FS-ISAC) serves banks and financial institutions.

- **Computer Emergency Response Teams (CERTs)**: These teams coordinate national or regional incident responses, share intelligence, and provide guidance to organizations.

Collaboration fosters a stronger community defense by enabling faster detection and response to widespread threats. Sharing insights also enhances collective knowledge, benefiting all participants in the intelligence ecosystem. By leveraging internal and external sources, organizations can build a robust threat intelligence framework that strengthens their ability to predict, detect, and mitigate cyber threats effectively.

Threat Intelligence Life Cycle

Threat intelligence is a dynamic process that involves multiple phases, from collection to feedback. The goal is not just to collect data but to ensure that intelligence is actionable and effective in strengthening security defenses. Here's how the life cycle typically unfolds:

Planning

The first phase in the intelligence life cycle involves setting objectives and determining what type of threat intelligence is needed. During planning, organizations define the specific threats they are concerned about, the resources they have available, and the stakeholders involved. Clear planning ensures that the threat intelligence gathered is aligned with the organization's overall security strategy.

Collection

In this phase, data is collected from various sources. Analysts gather information from open-source platforms, threat intelligence feeds, dark web monitoring tools, and other sources. The collection process is focused on acquiring as much relevant data as possible, ensuring that the team has the necessary context to analyze the data effectively.

Analysis

Once data is collected, it must be analyzed to identify patterns and extract actionable insights. This is often the most critical step in the process, as it turns raw data into valuable intelligence. Analysts examine trends, correlate information, and identify potential threats that could impact the organization. The analysis may also involve understanding the motivations and behaviors of threat actors to help predict their next move.

Dissemination

After analysis, the threat intelligence is shared with relevant stakeholders, such as security teams, executives, and other departments within the organization. The goal is to ensure that decision-makers have the information they need to act. This could involve updating firewalls, applying patches, or altering security policies based on the intelligence.

Feedback

The feedback phase is essential for continuous improvement. Organizations assess how effectively the intelligence was used to mitigate threats and what impact it had on their security posture. Feedback is gathered from stakeholders and integrated into future intelligence cycles to refine processes and make them more efficient.

Through the process of collecting, analyzing, and disseminating threat intelligence, cybersecurity professionals can stay ahead of evolving risks and implement proactive defense strategies. The key to effective threat intelligence is not just in understanding the data but in turning it into actionable insights that lead to informed decision-making and stronger organizational security.

Types of Threat Actors

Understanding who the threat actors are is crucial in developing effective cybersecurity strategies. These actors can vary widely in their motivations, methods, and targets. By identifying the types of threat actors, organizations can better anticipate the tactics and techniques they might employ.

Hacktivists

Hacktivists are individuals or groups who are driven by ideological or political motives rather than financial gain. They often target organizations or governments they see as promoting policies or actions that conflict with their beliefs. Their primary goal is to create disruption or draw attention to a cause, sometimes through cyberattacks like website defacements, DDoS attacks, or data leaks. Hacktivism can also extend to campaigns of misinformation or social media manipulation, aimed at swaying public opinion.

Cybercriminals

Cybercriminals are financially motivated individuals or groups that engage in illegal activities, ranging from fraud and identity theft to large-scale data breaches and ransomware attacks. Their goal is to extract money from individuals, businesses, or organizations, often through methods such as phishing, the deployment of malicious software, or extorting victims for ransom payments. Cybercriminals typically exploit weaknesses in systems to gain unauthorized access, steal sensitive data, or cripple an organization's operations for financial gain.

Nation-States

Nation-state actors are state-sponsored attackers who are generally well-funded, highly skilled, and focused on achieving political, economic, or military objectives. These attackers typically target critical infrastructure, sensitive government data, intellectual property, or national security interests. Nation-state attacks can be sophisticated and long-term, often employing a variety of techniques, including cyber espionage, data theft, and even cyber warfare, to gain strategic advantages over other countries. The impact of nation-state attacks can extend far beyond a single organization, affecting entire industries or even geopolitical stability.

Insider Threats

Insider threats involve individuals within an organization—such as employees, contractors, or business partners—who pose a risk to security. These threats can be intentional, such as a disgruntled employee stealing sensitive data, or unintentional, such as an employee falling for phishing scams or mishandling confidential information. Regardless of intent, insider threats can be particularly damaging because the attackers have authorized access to the organization's systems, making it harder to detect malicious activity. Preventing and mitigating insider threats requires strong security policies, user access management, and monitoring tools to detect suspicious behavior.

Threat Intelligence Frameworks

Frameworks in threat intelligence provide structured approaches to analyzing, understanding, and responding to cyber threats. They help security teams identify patterns in attacker behavior, determine vulnerabilities, and develop targeted defense strategies. Among the most widely used frameworks are the **MITRE ATT&CK Framework**, the **Cyber Kill Chain**, and the **Diamond Model**.

MITRE ATT&CK Framework

The **MITRE ATT&CK Framework** is a globally recognized resource for categorizing and understanding adversary behaviors. It provides a detailed knowledge base of tactics, techniques, and procedures (TTPs) used by threat actors, making it an essential tool for cybersecurity professionals.

- **Categories**: The framework organizes adversary behaviors into tactical categories such as **Initial Access**, **Execution**, **Persistence**, **Privilege Escalation**, **Defense Evasion**, and others. Each category outlines specific techniques attackers use during an operation.

- **Use Cases:**

  - **Incident Mapping**: Analysts can map detected activities to specific ATT&CK techniques, providing a comprehensive understanding of an incident.

  - **Detection Strategies**: The framework suggests potential detection methods and mitigations for each technique, helping teams refine their defenses.

The ATT&CK Framework fosters a shared language across organizations, enabling consistent threat analysis and collaboration.

CHAPTER 2   INTRODUCTION TO THREAT INTELLIGENCE AND VULNERABILITY MANAGEMENT PRINCIPLES

Cyber Kill Chain

Developed by Lockheed Martin, the **Cyber Kill Chain** is a model that breaks down the life cycle of a cyberattack into distinct phases. This approach helps defenders understand how attackers operate and where defenses can be implemented to disrupt their activities.

- **Phases of the Kill Chain:**
    1. **Reconnaissance**: Gathering information about the target
    2. **Weaponization**: Creating malicious payloads
    3. **Delivery**: Transmitting the payload to the target (e.g., via email or USB)
    4. **Exploitation**: Exploiting vulnerabilities to execute the payload
    5. **Installation**: Installing malware or backdoors on the target system
    6. **Command and Control (C2)**: Establishing communication with compromised systems
    7. **Actions on Objectives**: Achieving the attacker's ultimate goal, such as data theft or system disruption
- **Defensive Applications**: Security teams can apply countermeasures at each phase, such as using email filters during **Delivery** or monitoring outbound traffic during **C2**.

The Cyber Kill Chain emphasizes understanding the life cycle of attacks, allowing defenders to proactively disrupt them.

Diamond Model

The **Diamond Model** focuses on analyzing cyber incidents by examining four key components:

1. **Adversary**: The threat actor behind the attack

2. **Capability**: The tools and techniques used by the adversary

3. **Infrastructure**: The systems and networks leveraged to carry out the attack

4. **Victim**: The target of the attack

    - **Usefulness:**

        - The Diamond Model helps security teams identify relationships between the components of an incident, such as how an adversary uses specific capabilities against a victim.

        - It is particularly effective for modeling attacker behavior and uncovering patterns across multiple incidents.

By providing a structured way to analyze incidents, the Diamond Model enables deeper insights into attacker strategies and their underlying motivations.

Using frameworks like MITRE ATT&CK, the Cyber Kill Chain, and the Diamond Model allows organizations to systematically analyze threats and develop effective defensive measures. These models not only improve threat intelligence processes but also enhance collaboration across teams, ensuring a well-coordinated security posture.

CHAPTER 2   INTRODUCTION TO THREAT INTELLIGENCE AND VULNERABILITY
            MANAGEMENT PRINCIPLES

Threat Analysis and Evaluation

Effective threat analysis and evaluation are cornerstones of robust cybersecurity practices. By understanding the motives and behaviors of threat actors, analyzing intelligence data, and employing a systematic approach through the intelligence cycle, organizations can make informed decisions to protect their assets.

Most Common Attack Vectors

Attack vectors are the methods or pathways through which attackers infiltrate systems, steal data, or cause damage. Understanding common attack vectors helps organizations strengthen their defenses and reduce the likelihood of successful breaches.

Phishing

Phishing is one of the most common and effective attack vectors in the cybersecurity landscape. It involves sending deceptive emails or messages, often disguised as legitimate communications, to trick individuals into revealing sensitive information, such as usernames, passwords, credit card details, or other personal data. These attacks typically aim to exploit human trust, manipulating victims into taking actions they would not normally do, such as clicking a malicious link or downloading an infected attachment. Phishing campaigns can vary in complexity, from simple emails that look suspiciously similar to legitimate ones, to highly sophisticated social engineering schemes designed to impersonate trusted sources like colleagues, financial institutions, or popular businesses.

Once an attacker acquires sensitive information, they can gain unauthorized access to networks, systems, or financial accounts, leading to potentially severe consequences like data breaches, identity theft, and financial loss. It is crucial for organizations to educate employees and users on how to recognize phishing attempts and implement technical controls to prevent successful attacks.

Forms of Phishing

Phishing attacks can come in many forms, each tailored to exploit different vulnerabilities. Understanding these types can help individuals and organizations better defend themselves against them.

Email Phishing

Email phishing is the most common and well-known form of phishing. Attackers send fraudulent emails that appear to come from a trusted source, such as a bank, a well-known company, or a colleague. These emails often contain links that lead to fake websites designed to harvest personal information, or attachments that contain malware.

Example: An email that looks like it comes from a well-known online retailer like Amazon, informing the recipient that their account has been compromised, with a link to "verify" or "reset" their password. Clicking the link leads to a counterfeit website that looks identical to the retailer's official site, designed to steal login credentials.

Spear Phishing

Unlike general email phishing, spear phishing targets specific individuals or organizations. The attacker customizes the message to appear more legitimate by gathering personal information about the target. This can involve using public social media profiles or other publicly available data to craft highly convincing messages.

Example: A spear phishing email might come from a supposed colleague, with details about a current project or conversation, making the request for sensitive data or actions seem legitimate. For instance, an email might ask for access to a shared drive or login credentials for a company system, seemingly from the target's manager or IT department.

Whaling

Whaling is a specific type of spear phishing aimed at high-profile targets, such as executives or other senior personnel in an organization. The goal is often to steal sensitive corporate information or execute fraudulent transactions.

Example: A whaling email might appear to come from the CEO of a company, directing a lower-level employee to transfer funds or share sensitive business information. The email might look like a routine communication but is actually a fraudulent request designed to exploit the employee's trust in their superior.

Smishing (SMS Phishing)

Smishing is phishing that occurs via SMS (text messages). Attackers send fraudulent text messages that often contain a link or phone number for the target to call. Like email phishing, the text usually requests sensitive information or prompts the victim to perform an action that compromises their security.

Example: A text message claiming to be from a bank or credit card company warns the recipient that their account has been compromised and instructs them to call a phone number or click on a link to resolve the issue. The phone number leads to an attacker-controlled line, and the website may steal credit card numbers or other personal data.

Vishing (Voice Phishing)

Vishing involves phishing over the phone. Attackers use social engineering tactics to impersonate legitimate entities, such as banks, government agencies, or customer service departments, in order to gather sensitive information.

Example: A phone call that appears to come from the recipient's bank, asking them to confirm their account number or PIN to prevent fraud. The attacker might claim to be a fraud investigator and instruct the target to provide personal information over the phone.

Angler Phishing

Angler phishing is a type of social media-based phishing where attackers impersonate legitimate customer service accounts to deceive users into sharing personal information or clicking malicious links.

Example: An attacker creates a fake social media account that closely resembles the official customer service page of a well-known company, like Netflix or Twitter. The attacker then responds to real user complaints or queries with fake links to support websites, where victims are prompted to enter login credentials or download malicious files.

Clone Phishing

In clone phishing, attackers duplicate a legitimate email that was previously sent to the victim, replacing an attachment or link with a malicious one. The victim believes the email is legitimate because it appears to be a re-send of a message they've received before.

Example: A person receives a cloned email that looks exactly like an important document they received previously. The attacker replaces the attachment with a malicious one that contains malware, leading the victim to open it and infect their system.

Business Email Compromise (BEC)

Business Email Compromise (BEC) is a sophisticated phishing attack where attackers target employees of a company to commit fraud. Often, attackers impersonate an executive or a trusted business partner to request a wire transfer or the sharing of sensitive data.

Example: An email appears to come from the CEO requesting the finance department to make an urgent transfer to a foreign bank account. The email is crafted to appear as if it is from a trusted internal source, leading the employee to comply with the request, resulting in the loss of substantial funds.

Best Practices to Prevent Phishing

1. **User Awareness Training**: Educate users on the different types of phishing attacks and how to recognize suspicious messages. Regular training should be conducted to stay updated on new tactics.

2. **Multi-Factor Authentication (MFA)**: Implement MFA for all accounts to provide an additional layer of protection. Even if login credentials are compromised, MFA can prevent unauthorized access.

3. **Email Filtering**: Use advanced email filtering technologies to automatically detect and block phishing emails before they reach users' inboxes.

4. **Verify Requests**: Always verify any sensitive or unusual requests, especially those related to financial transactions, directly through a trusted communication method (e.g., phone call).

5. **Regular Updates and Patching**: Ensure that all software, including email systems and web browsers, are regularly updated to protect against known vulnerabilities.

6. **Incident Reporting**: Encourage users to report any suspected phishing attempts immediately so that appropriate action can be taken to mitigate further risks.

Malware

Malware is a broad term used to describe malicious software that is specifically designed to harm, disrupt, or gain unauthorized access to a computer system or network. Malware can take many forms, each with its own method of attack and consequences. Whether it's damaging files, stealing sensitive information, or holding systems hostage for ransom, malware is a persistent and serious threat to both individuals and organizations. Attackers often use malware to achieve various goals, such as financial gain, espionage, or sabotage. The impact of a successful malware attack can be devastating, ranging from data corruption and system failure to severe financial losses and reputation damage.

Malware can be spread through various methods, including email attachments, malicious websites, infected software downloads, and vulnerabilities in outdated software. Once installed on a system, malware can remain hidden for extended periods, sometimes going unnoticed until significant damage has occurred. It's crucial for individuals and organizations to implement robust defenses, including antivirus software, firewalls, regular updates, and employee training, to prevent malware infections.

Forms of Malware

Malware exists in many different forms; each designed to exploit specific vulnerabilities or achieve particular malicious objectives. Below are some of the most common types of malware:

Viruses

A virus is a type of malware that attaches itself to legitimate files or programs and spreads when the infected file is executed. A virus typically replicates and spreads to other files on the same system or network. Once executed, viruses can cause a range of damages, including corrupting files, stealing data, or compromising system functionality.

Example: A file downloaded from an untrusted website appears to be a legitimate program, but it contains a virus. When the user opens the file, the virus begins replicating, spreading to other files on the system, and damaging important data.

Worms

Unlike viruses, worms are stand-alone programs that do not require a host file to spread. Worms typically exploit vulnerabilities in a system or network to replicate and distribute themselves across devices without user interaction. They can spread rapidly across networks and often carry payloads that cause significant harm, such as deleting files or installing other malicious software.

Example: A worm that exploits a security vulnerability in a network router might spread to every device connected to that network. As the worm infects more systems, it may launch a denial-of-service attack or install ransomware on all infected devices.

Trojans

A Trojan, or Trojan horse, is malware that disguises itself as a legitimate program or file. Trojans are typically spread through social engineering, where users are tricked into downloading and executing the malicious software, often thinking it is harmless. Once installed, Trojans can create backdoors, giving attackers remote access to the infected system.

Example: A Trojan disguised as a software update appears on a user's screen. When downloaded and executed, it secretly installs malicious code that opens a backdoor, allowing the attacker to access the system and steal sensitive data.

Ransomware

Ransomware is one of the most dangerous types of malware. It encrypts the victim's files and demands a ransom payment (usually in cryptocurrency) in exchange for the decryption key. Ransomware attacks can cripple organizations by locking access to critical data, leading to severe operational and financial disruptions. In some cases, attackers may also threaten to release sensitive data unless the ransom is paid.

Example: A business receives an email with an attachment that appears to be a legitimate invoice. When the attachment is opened, the ransomware encrypts all the files on the company's network. The attacker demands payment to restore access, threatening to leak sensitive client information if the ransom is not paid within a specified time.

Spyware

Spyware is a type of malware designed to secretly monitor and collect information about the user's activities without their knowledge. This can include tracking keystrokes, capturing passwords, taking screenshots, or even recording webcam footage. Spyware is often bundled with other software or installed via vulnerabilities, and its purpose is typically to steal sensitive personal or financial data.

Example: A user unknowingly installs a program that appears to be a legitimate free tool. Once installed, the software silently records the user's keystrokes, sending the information to cybercriminals who then use the stolen data to access bank accounts or steal personal information.

Adware

Adware is software that automatically displays or downloads unwanted advertisements on a user's computer. While not always directly harmful, adware can slow down system performance, cause browser hijacking, and display intrusive ads that might lead to additional malware infections. In some cases, adware is bundled with free software, and users unknowingly install it.

Example: A user downloads a free video player from an untrusted website, and upon installation, the software also installs adware. The user starts seeing a barrage of pop-up ads that slow down their computer, and in some cases, the ads may link to malicious websites.

Rootkits

A rootkit is a type of malware designed to gain unauthorized access to a system and maintain that access without being detected. Rootkits can be installed through other types of malware and are often used to hide the presence of other malicious programs, such as Trojans or keyloggers, by modifying system files and processes.

Example: An attacker installs a rootkit on a compromised server, allowing them to hide their activities from administrators. The rootkit ensures that the attacker can continue accessing the system without detection, even if other security measures are in place.

Keyloggers

Keyloggers are a type of surveillance software that records the keystrokes made by the user on a device. These tools are commonly used by cybercriminals to steal login credentials, credit card numbers, or other sensitive information by monitoring what the victim types.

Example: A keylogger is installed on a user's computer through a phishing email attachment. It silently tracks every keystroke made by the user, including passwords and credit card information, and sends this data to the attacker, allowing them to use the stolen credentials for fraud or identity theft.

Botnets

A botnet is a network of compromised devices that are controlled remotely by an attacker. Botnets are typically created by infecting a large number of devices with malware, which then communicate with the attacker's command and control servers. Once a botnet is established, the attacker can use it for various malicious purposes, including launching distributed denial-of-service (DDoS) attacks, sending spam emails, or executing ransomware campaigns.

Example: A botnet of thousands of infected devices is used to launch a DDoS attack against a major website. The botnet floods the target's servers with traffic, causing the website to become slow or completely unavailable.

Best Practices to Prevent Malware Attacks

1. **Regular Software Updates**: Ensure all operating systems, applications, and antivirus software are regularly updated to patch vulnerabilities and defend against known threats.

2. **Antivirus and Anti-malware Software**: Use reputable antivirus and anti-malware programs to detect and block known malware. Keep these tools updated to provide protection against the latest threats.

3. **Network Segmentation**: Implement network segmentation to isolate critical systems and minimize the spread of malware if an infection occurs.

4. **Employee Training**: Regularly train employees to recognize phishing attempts and malware threats. Encourage them to avoid downloading files from untrusted sources and clicking on suspicious links.

5. **Backup Data Regularly**: Regularly back up important data to prevent data loss in the event of a ransomware attack or system failure. Store backups offline or in a secure cloud environment.

6. **Implement Strong Access Controls**: Use strong passwords and multi-factor authentication (MFA) to reduce the likelihood of unauthorized access to systems. Limit administrative privileges to minimize the damage that malware can cause.

7. **Use Firewalls**: Implement both network and host-based firewalls to monitor and block malicious traffic that could be used to deliver malware to systems.

8. **Isolate Infected Systems**: If malware is suspected or detected on a system, disconnect it from the network immediately to prevent the spread of the infection.

Exploits

Exploits are a critical class of cyber threats where attackers take advantage of vulnerabilities in software, hardware, or network systems to gain unauthorized access or perform malicious actions. These vulnerabilities can exist in a variety of places, including operating systems, applications, hardware devices, or network protocols. Once an exploit is successfully executed, attackers can manipulate or control the affected system, potentially causing significant harm, such as stealing sensitive data, installing malware, or disrupting normal operations. Exploits are particularly dangerous because they can grant attackers privileged access to systems, bypass security mechanisms, and lead to severe security breaches.

Exploits typically target weaknesses or flaws that exist in the design or implementation of software or hardware. These vulnerabilities might arise from coding errors, incorrect configurations, or insufficient access controls. Since attackers can take advantage of these weaknesses to bypass defenses, exploits are often used as the first step in a larger attack chain.

Types of Exploits

Exploits can be classified based on the nature of the vulnerability they target and the tactics used by the attacker. Below are some common types of exploits:

Zero-Day Exploits

A **zero-day exploit** occurs when attackers exploit a vulnerability that is unknown to the software vendor or security community. Since the vulnerability has not yet been discovered or patched, there is no available fix at the time of the attack, leaving systems vulnerable until the vulnerability is addressed. Zero-day exploits are particularly dangerous because they give attackers a window of opportunity to carry out attacks before any countermeasures can be implemented.

Example: A cybercriminal discovers a flaw in a popular operating system that allows them to execute arbitrary code when a user opens a specially crafted email attachment. Since this flaw is unknown to the vendor, the attacker can exploit it until a patch is created and deployed, potentially compromising thousands of systems.

Buffer Overflow Exploits

Buffer overflow exploits take advantage of weaknesses in software that improperly handle memory allocation. When an attacker sends more data to a buffer (temporary memory storage) than it can hold, the extra data can overflow into adjacent memory, potentially allowing the attacker to overwrite important control structures, such as return addresses. This allows them to execute arbitrary code, often giving the attacker the ability to take control of the system.

Example: An attacker sends a specially crafted input to a vulnerable application with a buffer overflow, causing the program to crash. However, instead of crashing normally, the overflow allows the attacker to run malicious code, such as installing malware or gaining unauthorized access to the system.

Privilege Escalation Exploits

Privilege escalation exploits occur when an attacker gains higher-level permissions than they are authorized to have. These exploits take advantage of flaws in operating systems or applications that improperly assign user permissions. There are two types of privilege escalation:

- **Vertical Privilege Escalation**: Involves gaining higher levels of access or privileges, such as moving from a regular user account to an administrator or root account.

- **Horizontal Privilege Escalation**: Involves accessing resources or data belonging to other users at the same privilege level.

Example: An attacker exploiting a vulnerability in an operating system's access control system may gain administrative privileges, allowing them to perform unauthorized actions such as installing malware or modifying critical system files.

Cross-Site Scripting (XSS) Exploits

Cross-Site Scripting (XSS) is a type of exploit that targets web applications. It occurs when an attacker injects malicious scripts into webpages that are then executed by unsuspecting users who visit those pages. These scripts can steal sensitive data, such as session cookies or login credentials, or perform malicious actions on behalf of the user.

Example: An attacker injects a script into a comment section of a website. When a legitimate user views the comment, the script is executed in the user's browser and sends their session cookies to the attacker, allowing them to impersonate the user and access their account.

SQL Injection Exploits

SQL injection occurs when an attacker exploits vulnerabilities in a web application's database interaction. By injecting malicious SQL queries into input fields, the attacker can manipulate the database, retrieve sensitive information, delete data, or even execute administrative commands.

Example: A login page that does not properly sanitize user input may allow an attacker to input a malicious SQL statement, such as OR '1'='1'. This query can bypass authentication mechanisms, allowing the attacker to gain unauthorized access to the application or database.

Man-in-the-Middle (MITM) Exploits

A **Man-in-the-Middle (MITM) exploit** occurs when an attacker intercepts and potentially alters communications between two parties, often without their knowledge. MITM attacks can target various types of communication, such as email, web traffic, or even encrypted data. Attackers can use this technique to steal sensitive information, inject malicious code, or manipulate the data exchanged between the victim and the intended recipient.

Example: An attacker sets up a rogue Wi-Fi access point at a coffee shop. When users connect to the Wi-Fi, the attacker can intercept and modify any data sent between the user and the websites they visit, potentially capturing login credentials, credit card details, or sensitive business data.

Denial of Service (DoS) Exploits

Denial of Service (DoS) exploits aim to disrupt the normal functioning of a system or network by overwhelming it with excessive requests. The goal is to make a system or service unavailable to its legitimate users, often by flooding it with more traffic than it can handle. DoS exploits can lead to significant downtime and loss of service.

Example: An attacker exploits a vulnerability in a web server's ability to handle simultaneous connections, causing the server to crash when an overwhelming number of requests are made. This can make the website or service unavailable to users until the issue is resolved.

Command Injection Exploits

Command injection exploits occur when an attacker is able to insert malicious commands into a system's execution process. These commands are typically executed with the same privileges as the application or server running the system, giving the attacker the ability to execute arbitrary system commands that can compromise security.

Example: A vulnerable web application allows users to input data that is later passed to the operating system for execution. If the input is not properly sanitized, the attacker can input a command like ; rm -rf / to delete all files on the server.

Best Practices to Prevent Exploits

1. **Patch Management**: Regularly apply patches and updates to all software, operating systems, and hardware devices to close known vulnerabilities. This is crucial for preventing exploits that target already discovered weaknesses.

2. **Input Validation and Sanitization:** Ensure that all user inputs are properly validated and sanitized before they are processed by applications or systems. This helps prevent injection-based exploits, such as SQL injection or command injection.

3. **Use of Firewalls and Intrusion Detection Systems (IDS):** Implement firewalls and IDS to monitor for suspicious activity and block known attack vectors. These tools can help detect and prevent exploits before they cause damage.

4. **Least Privilege Principle**: Limit the privileges granted to users and applications to only what is necessary for their function. This helps mitigate the impact of privilege escalation exploits and prevents attackers from gaining full system control.

5. **Security Audits and Penetration Testing**: Regularly conduct security audits and penetration testing to identify vulnerabilities in your systems before attackers do. This proactive approach helps to uncover and mitigate potential exploits.

6. **Employee Training and Awareness**: Train employees on recognizing phishing attempts, handling sensitive data securely, and adhering to security best practices. Educating users is key to preventing social engineering attacks that could lead to system compromises.

Credential-Based Attacks

Credential-based attacks are a category of cyberattacks in which malicious actors use stolen, guessed, or compromised credentials to gain unauthorized access to systems, networks, or services. Credentials are typically usernames and passwords, but can also include other forms of authentication, such as tokens or biometric data. Attackers employ various techniques to acquire or bypass these credentials, enabling them to access systems and potentially cause significant damage. Once attackers have gained access through compromised credentials, they can steal sensitive information, escalate privileges, pivot to other systems, or execute additional malicious actions.

The goal of credential-based attacks is often to exploit the trust and access that legitimate users have to systems. Attackers rely on methods such as brute-force attacks, credential stuffing, and phishing to gain entry. The impact of these attacks can range from the theft of personal or financial data to the compromise of entire networks, resulting in serious consequences for both individuals and organizations.

Common Methods of Credential-Based Attacks

Credential-based attacks can take various forms, each leveraging different techniques to gain access to a system or network. Below are the most common methods used in these types of attacks:

Brute-Force Attacks

A **brute-force attack** is a method where an attacker systematically attempts every possible password combination until the correct one is found. This type of attack relies on computational power to test a vast number of possible combinations quickly. Brute-force attacks are particularly effective against weak passwords, such as short or easily guessable ones. These attacks can be automated using tools that can try millions of combinations per second, making them a significant threat to poorly secured systems.

Example: An attacker uses a brute-force tool to guess the password for a user account by entering every possible combination of letters, numbers, and special characters. If the password is weak (e.g., "123456" or "password123"), the attacker will likely succeed in gaining access.

Mitigation:

- Implement strong password policies, requiring a mix of characters, numbers, and symbols.

- Use account lockout mechanisms after a certain number of failed login attempts.

- Enable multi-factor authentication (MFA) to add an extra layer of security.

Credential Stuffing

Credential stuffing is an attack technique where attackers use large sets of previously leaked usernames and passwords (often from data breaches) to attempt to gain access to multiple accounts on different services. Since many users reuse the same credentials across multiple websites and platforms, attackers can exploit this behavior by taking advantage of data breaches to launch credential stuffing attacks. This attack is automated, using bots to test millions of credential pairs rapidly.

Example: After a breach of a popular social media platform exposes millions of usernames and passwords, an attacker uses these credentials to try logging into other services (e.g., email accounts, online banking, shopping platforms). If users have reused the same passwords, the attacker can easily gain access to other accounts.

Mitigation:

- Encourage users to use unique passwords for each service and enable password managers to help manage them.

- Use CAPTCHA or bot detection to block automated login attempts.

- Enable MFA to ensure that stolen credentials alone are not enough to gain access.

Phishing Attacks

Phishing is a social engineering attack where attackers trick individuals into revealing their credentials by masquerading as legitimate entities, such as trusted companies or colleagues. This is typically done through deceptive emails, fake websites, or phone calls. Phishing attacks often use urgency or fear (e.g., a claim that an account has been compromised or needs to be verified) to pressure the victim into entering their login credentials on a malicious website or providing them directly to the attacker.

Example: An attacker sends an email that appears to be from a bank, asking the recipient to verify their account by clicking on a link. The link directs the user to a fake login page that looks identical to the bank's real website. When the victim enters their credentials, the attacker steals them.

Mitigation:

- Train users to recognize phishing attempts, such as suspicious email addresses, misspelled words, and generic greetings.

- Use email filtering systems to block known phishing sources.

- Implement MFA, so that even if credentials are compromised, attackers cannot easily gain access to the account.

Keylogging and Malware-Based Attacks

In a **keylogging** attack, malware is installed on a victim's device to record keystrokes, capturing login credentials and other sensitive data as the victim types. This malware may be delivered via phishing emails, malicious websites, or software downloads. Keyloggers can be configured to operate stealthily, transmitting stolen credentials to the attacker without the victim's knowledge.

Example: An attacker sends a victim a malicious email with an attachment. When the victim opens the attachment, it installs a keylogger on their device. The keylogger records all keystrokes, including passwords, credit card numbers, and other private information, which is then sent back to the attacker.

Mitigation:

- Use anti-malware software to detect and block keyloggers.

- Implement endpoint security measures and restrict administrative privileges to minimize the risk of malware installation.

- Regularly update operating systems and applications to patch vulnerabilities that malware could exploit.

Password Spraying Attacks

Password spraying is a variation of brute-force attacks where an attacker attempts a small number of common passwords across many user accounts, rather than targeting a single account with numerous guesses. This method reduces the likelihood of triggering account lockout mechanisms, making it a more stealthy and scalable approach.

Example: An attacker attempts to log in to hundreds of employee accounts at a company using a common password, such as "Summer2024" or "Welcome123". Since only one or two accounts might use that password, the attacker avoids triggering lockout policies and successfully gains access to one or more accounts.

Mitigation:

- Require employees to create complex and unique passwords.

- Implement account lockout policies to limit the number of login attempts from a single IP address or account.

- Use MFA, especially for access to critical systems, to protect against credential-based attacks.

Man-in-the-Middle (MITM) Credential Interception

Man-in-the-Middle (MITM) attacks occur when an attacker intercepts communication between two parties. In the context of credential-based attacks, the attacker can intercept login credentials transmitted over insecure channels, such as unencrypted Wi-Fi or HTTP connections. Once the attacker has captured the credentials, they can use them to log in to the target system or network.

Example: An attacker sets up a fake Wi-Fi hotspot in a public place, such as a coffee shop. When users connect to the hotspot, the attacker intercepts their unencrypted login credentials as they access online accounts.

Mitigation:

- Use encryption (e.g., HTTPS, VPNs) to protect data in transit and ensure login credentials are transmitted securely.

- Educate users on the dangers of public Wi-Fi and encourage the use of VPNs for secure connections.

- Implement MFA to ensure that stolen credentials alone cannot be used to access accounts.

Impact of Credential-Based Attacks

Credential-based attacks can have a devastating impact on both individuals and organizations. Once an attacker gains access using stolen credentials, they can

1. **Steal Sensitive Information**: Attackers can access personal data, financial records, intellectual property, or confidential business documents, leading to financial loss, reputational damage, and legal ramifications.

2. **Escalate Privileges**: Once inside the system, attackers may escalate their privileges, gaining access to more sensitive or critical systems, which could lead to further compromises or data destruction.

3. **Widen the Attack Surface**: Compromised credentials can be used to move laterally across networks, accessing additional systems, servers, or applications, often escalating the scope and severity of the attack.

4. **Launch Further Attacks**: With access to valid credentials, attackers may deploy additional malware, initiate ransomware attacks, or exfiltrate large amounts of data, causing significant disruption to business operations.

Best Practices to Prevent Credential-Based Attacks

1. **Enforce Strong Password Policies**: Require users to create complex, unique passwords for each account. Passwords should be at least 12-16 characters and include a mix of upper and lowercase letters, numbers, and special characters.

2. **Implement Multi-Factor Authentication (MFA)**: Require multiple forms of verification, such as a password combined with a phone number or biometric data. This makes it more difficult for attackers to gain access using only stolen credentials.

3. **Monitor for Suspicious Activity**: Implement security tools that monitor login attempts and detect unusual behavior, such as repeated login failures or access from unfamiliar locations.

4. **Educate Users**: Regularly train employees on the risks of credential-based attacks, such as phishing, and teach them to recognize signs of compromise. Encourage them to use password managers to generate and store strong passwords.

5. **Conduct Regular Audits**: Regularly audit access logs and conduct penetration testing to identify weak spots in authentication systems and ensure credentials are being managed securely.

CHAPTER 2 INTRODUCTION TO THREAT INTELLIGENCE AND VULNERABILITY
MANAGEMENT PRINCIPLES

Emerging Attack Vectors

As technology advances, cybercriminals and other malicious actors continuously adapt and refine their methods of attack. Emerging attack vectors are becoming more sophisticated and harder to detect, requiring organizations to evolve their cybersecurity strategies accordingly. This section covers some of the most notable new and evolving attack vectors that pose significant risks to organizations in today's digital landscape.

Supply Chain Attacks

A **supply chain attack** targets third-party vendors, service providers, or partners that have access to an organization's systems or data. These attacks exploit weaknesses in the cybersecurity practices of these external parties, often bypassing the security measures of the primary target. Attackers leverage the trust that exists between organizations and their suppliers or partners to infiltrate the system. Once access is gained through a vulnerable third party, attackers can move laterally through the network and compromise the target organization.

Example:

One of the most infamous examples of a supply chain attack is the **SolarWinds attack**. In this case, cybercriminals inserted malware into a legitimate software update from SolarWinds, an IT management company trusted by thousands of organizations, including government agencies, tech firms, and critical infrastructure. The malware was distributed as part of the company's Orion software update, allowing the attackers to gain access to thousands of networks before the breach was discovered.

Mitigation:

- **Vendor Risk Management**: Organizations should evaluate and continuously monitor the cybersecurity posture of third-party vendors and partners.

- **Zero Trust Models**: Implement a Zero Trust security framework, where access is never implicitly trusted, even if the connection originates from a known vendor or trusted partner.

- **Multi-Factor Authentication (MFA)**: Use MFA and strong authentication protocols to secure access between organizations and their suppliers or service providers.

- **Continuous Monitoring**: Implement robust network monitoring to detect abnormal activities and anomalous behaviors from third-party systems.

Zero-Day Vulnerabilities

A **zero-day vulnerability** refers to a flaw or weakness in software or hardware that is not known to the vendor or the broader security community. These vulnerabilities are particularly dangerous because there is no patch or fix available when they are discovered, leaving systems exposed to exploitation. Zero-day vulnerabilities are often discovered and exploited by attackers before they are detected and patched, giving attackers a window of opportunity to access systems or data.

Example:

In 2020, a zero-day vulnerability in Microsoft's Windows operating system (CVE-2020-0601) was exploited by hackers. The flaw, which affected the Windows CryptoAPI, could allow attackers to spoof digital signatures and impersonate trusted applications, leading to unauthorized access. The attack was particularly troubling because the vulnerability was unknown to the public or Microsoft at the time it was exploited.

Mitigation:

- **Patch Management**: While zero-day vulnerabilities are hard to defend against, organizations should implement a robust patch management strategy to apply updates and patches as soon as they are released.

- **Intrusion Detection and Prevention Systems (IDPS)**: Use advanced network monitoring and intrusion detection systems to identify unusual or malicious activities that may indicate the exploitation of a zero-day vulnerability.

- **Redundant Security Layers**: Implement a multilayered defense strategy, such as using firewalls, endpoint protection, and behavior-based anomaly detection to minimize the impact of zero-day exploits.

- **Threat Intelligence Sharing**: Participate in threat intelligence networks to stay informed about emerging zero-day threats and vulnerabilities.

Fileless Malware

Fileless malware is a type of attack that does not rely on traditional malicious files or executables. Instead, this malware operates directly in the memory of a system, leveraging legitimate system processes or applications to execute its payload. Because fileless malware does not leave traditional traces on a system's hard drive, it is much harder to detect using conventional antivirus or endpoint protection software, which typically focuses on file-based threats.

Fileless attacks typically exploit system vulnerabilities or misconfigurations to run scripts in memory, such as PowerShell scripts, without writing malicious files to disk. These attacks are particularly difficult to detect because they do not create the typical artifacts associated with traditional malware infections, such as executables or registry modifications.

Example:

An attacker might exploit a vulnerability in a web browser or operating system to run a PowerShell script in memory. This script can download and execute additional malicious code without leaving any trace on the file system, making it harder for traditional security tools to detect the attack.

Mitigation:

- **Advanced Endpoint Detection and Response (EDR)**: Deploy EDR solutions that monitor system memory and behavior to detect malicious activities, even if no files are involved.

- **Application Whitelisting**: Use application whitelisting to ensure that only trusted and authorized software can run on systems.

- **System Hardening**: Disable unnecessary system tools, such as PowerShell, or restrict their execution to minimize the attack surface.

- **Behavior-Based Detection**: Focus on detecting abnormal behavior or system anomalies rather than relying solely on signature-based detection methods.

Vulnerability Management

Vulnerabilities refer to weaknesses or flaws in software, hardware, or processes that attackers can exploit to gain unauthorized access or perform malicious activities. These vulnerabilities can exist in operating systems, applications, network protocols, or even in organizational procedures. Attackers often look for these weaknesses to bypass security controls and infiltrate systems, steal data, or disrupt operations. It's essential to identify, assess, and address vulnerabilities in a timely manner to reduce the likelihood of exploitation. Vulnerability management plays a key role in maintaining the overall security posture of an organization by proactively identifying and mitigating these risks.

This will be covered in significantly greater detail in Chapter Four.

Scanning Tools and Techniques

Effective vulnerability management is crucial for identifying and mitigating weaknesses within an organization's infrastructure, ensuring that security risks are proactively addressed before attackers can exploit them. Scanning tools and techniques are essential in this process, as they help identify vulnerabilities in various areas, such as network security, web application security, and host-level security. Below, we explore some of the key scanning tools and techniques used to identify vulnerabilities and protect organizations against cyber threats.

Network Scanners

Network scanners are tools designed to analyze the security of an organization's network infrastructure. They scan networks to detect vulnerabilities such as open ports, misconfigured firewalls, weak encryption protocols, outdated software, and improperly secured devices. By identifying these weaknesses, network scanners help organizations understand potential attack vectors that could allow unauthorized access or compromise of their network.

Common Vulnerabilities Detected:

- **Open Ports**: Unnecessarily open ports that expose systems to external attacks.

- **Misconfigured Devices**: Routers, switches, or other networked devices configured incorrectly.

- **Outdated Software**: Networked systems running outdated or unpatched software versions that may contain exploitable vulnerabilities.

- **Weak Encryption**: Use of weak encryption protocols (e.g., SSL instead of TLS), which could be susceptible to attacks like man-in-the-middle (MITM).

Example Tools:

- **Nessus**: One of the most widely used vulnerability scanning tools, Nessus scans for a wide range of vulnerabilities and misconfigurations across network devices and systems. It can also be customized with plugins to identify specific vulnerabilities.

- **OpenVAS**: An open-source network scanner that provides comprehensive vulnerability scanning features. OpenVAS allows for deep network scanning and includes a large database of known vulnerabilities.

- **Nmap**: Primarily known as a network discovery tool, Nmap also offers vulnerability scanning capabilities. It can be used to identify open ports and detect various network services, operating systems, and potential security issues.

Best Practices for Network Scanning:

- Perform regular scans to keep your network security configurations up-to-date.

- Use network segmentation to minimize the impact of vulnerabilities by limiting access between different areas of the network.

- Automate vulnerability scanning and reporting to quickly address any identified issues.

Web Application Scanners

Web application scanners are specialized tools that identify vulnerabilities specific to web applications, which are often targeted by attackers due to their accessibility over the Internet. These scanners help detect common vulnerabilities in web applications, such as SQL injection, cross-site scripting (XSS), insecure session management, and authentication issues. Securing web applications is critical, as they often handle sensitive user data and interact with back-end databases.

Common Vulnerabilities Detected:

- **SQL Injection**: A technique where attackers inject malicious SQL queries into input fields, potentially gaining unauthorized access to databases.

- **Cross-Site Scripting (XSS)**: A vulnerability where malicious scripts are injected into web pages viewed by other users, allowing attackers to steal sensitive information or hijack user sessions.

- **Insecure Session Management**: Flaws in the way sessions are managed, such as weak session cookies or poor session expiration mechanisms, can be exploited to hijack user sessions.

- **Cross-Site Request Forgery (CSRF)**: An attack where a malicious request is sent from an authenticated user's browser without their consent, potentially performing unauthorized actions on a web application.

Example Tools:

- **Acunetix**: A widely used web application scanner that automates the detection of web-based vulnerabilities, including SQL injection, XSS, and others. It provides detailed reports and remediation steps.

- **Burp Suite**: A powerful suite of tools for web application security testing. Burp Suite includes features like vulnerability scanning, proxying traffic, and fuzz testing to identify common web application flaws.

- **OWASP ZAP (Zed Attack Proxy)**: An open-source web application scanner that automates the detection of vulnerabilities such as XSS, SQL injection, and others. It also includes an active scanner for real-time testing and a passive scanner for inspecting traffic.

Best Practices for Web Application Scanning:

- Conduct regular scans of web applications, particularly after updates or changes to the codebase.

- Use a combination of both static and dynamic analysis tools to detect vulnerabilities in source code and during runtime.

- Implement a Web Application Firewall (WAF) in conjunction with regular scanning to filter and monitor HTTP requests that may contain malicious input.

Host-Based Scanners

Host-based scanners focus on individual systems—such as servers, workstations, and endpoints—and evaluate their security configurations. These scanners check for vulnerabilities like outdated software, missing patches, insecure system configurations, and potential weaknesses in the operating system or installed applications. Since these scanners work directly on the host machine, they are often more detailed and comprehensive in identifying vulnerabilities specific to each device.

Common Vulnerabilities Detected:

- **Outdated Software:** Systems running outdated versions of software or operating systems that are known to have vulnerabilities.

- **Missing Patches:** Systems missing critical security patches that could be exploited by attackers.

- **Insecure Configurations**: Weak or misconfigured security settings, such as improper file permissions or unencrypted sensitive files.

- **File Integrity Issues**: Unauthorized changes to files or system binaries, which could indicate malware infections or unauthorized tampering.

CHAPTER 2   INTRODUCTION TO THREAT INTELLIGENCE AND VULNERABILITY MANAGEMENT PRINCIPLES

Example Tools:

- **Qualys**: A cloud-based vulnerability scanner that offers host-based scanning capabilities. Qualys can scan individual systems for vulnerabilities, missing patches, and configuration issues, and provides detailed reports for remediation.

- **Tripwire**: A host-based security tool that provides file integrity monitoring, vulnerability management, and configuration auditing. It scans systems for vulnerabilities and tracks changes to critical files and configurations.

- **Nessus** (also used for network scanning): Nessus can also perform host-based vulnerability assessments, checking the configurations and patches of individual systems, making it a versatile tool for both network and host scanning.

Best Practices for Host-Based Scanning:

- Ensure that host-based scans are part of your routine vulnerability management process, especially for high-value systems like servers and endpoints.

- Regularly apply patches and updates to all systems to reduce the attack surface.

- Use file integrity monitoring to detect any unauthorized changes to critical files or configurations.

- Leverage host-based scanning tools in conjunction with network scanning and web application testing to provide a comprehensive security assessment.

Scanning tools and techniques are vital components of an organization's vulnerability management strategy. By using network scanners, web application scanners, and host-based scanners, organizations can identify and remediate potential security weaknesses before they can be exploited by attackers. These tools enable proactive risk management by assessing security configurations, detecting vulnerabilities, and providing actionable insights for remediation.

To effectively manage vulnerabilities, it is crucial to perform regular scans across all levels of an organization's infrastructure. By doing so, organizations can ensure their systems remain secure, up-to-date, and resilient against the ever-evolving landscape of cyber threats.

Common Vulnerabilities and Exposures (CVEs)

Tracking and managing vulnerabilities is crucial for any organization's cybersecurity strategy. The Common Vulnerabilities and Exposures (CVE) system provides a standardized way to identify and categorize known vulnerabilities. Each CVE entry contains detailed information about a specific vulnerability, including its description, severity, and any available patches or mitigation strategies.

Importance of Tracking CVEs

Staying up-to-date with the latest CVEs is essential for organizations to manage their exposure to known vulnerabilities. Cybercriminals often exploit publicly known CVEs to launch attacks, so organizations that do not track CVEs and apply patches in a timely manner are at a higher risk of compromise. The CVE system helps prioritize which vulnerabilities to address based on the threat landscape and the criticality of affected systems.

Leveraging the National Vulnerability Database (NVD)

The National Vulnerability Database (NVD) is a public resource that provides detailed information about vulnerabilities, including CVE entries, risk ratings, and mitigation recommendations. By regularly consulting the NVD, organizations can keep track of new vulnerabilities, access remediation guidance, and ensure that their systems remain secure. Security professionals often use the NVD to monitor trends in vulnerabilities, helping them stay proactive in identifying and addressing emerging threats.

Vulnerability management is an ongoing process that requires continuous effort, regular scanning, and a comprehensive approach to address weaknesses in systems and applications. By following the vulnerability management life cycle and utilizing the appropriate tools, organizations can effectively reduce their exposure to cyberattacks and maintain a strong security posture.

Risk Assessment in Vulnerability Management

In the context of cybersecurity, **risk** is the potential for a threat to exploit a vulnerability within an organization's systems, processes, or infrastructure, resulting in a negative impact. Risk is typically evaluated by two primary factors: the likelihood of the threat exploiting the vulnerability and the potential consequences or impact that such an exploitation would have on the organization. This definition highlights that risk is not solely about the presence of vulnerabilities but also the probability and severity of their exploitation. Understanding risk allows organizations to make informed decisions about where to allocate resources for mitigation and which vulnerabilities require immediate attention.

CHAPTER 2 INTRODUCTION TO THREAT INTELLIGENCE AND VULNERABILITY
         MANAGEMENT PRINCIPLES

Risk Scoring and Prioritization

Once risks are defined, organizations need a structured approach to assess and prioritize them effectively. Risk scoring systems and prioritization methods allow security teams to focus on vulnerabilities that pose the greatest potential harm.

CVSS (Common Vulnerability Scoring System)

The **Common Vulnerability Scoring System (CVSS)** is a standardized method used to assess the severity of vulnerabilities based on several metrics, such as exploitability, impact, and the existence of mitigating controls. CVSS scores range from 0 to 10, with higher scores indicating more severe vulnerabilities. A score of **10** represents a critical vulnerability that requires immediate action, such as patching or isolating the affected system. CVSS helps security teams compare the relative severity of vulnerabilities across different systems and prioritize remediation efforts.

Risk Matrix

A **risk matrix** is a visual tool used to categorize and prioritize risks based on their likelihood and impact. Typically, a risk matrix plots these two factors on an X-Y axis, where one axis represents the likelihood of a threat exploiting a vulnerability, and the other represents the potential impact of that exploitation. Based on the position within the matrix, risks are categorized into levels such as **low**, **medium**, **high**, or **critical**. This method provides a clear, visual representation of risks, helping decision-makers prioritize their resources and actions accordingly.

CHAPTER 2   INTRODUCTION TO THREAT INTELLIGENCE AND VULNERABILITY
            MANAGEMENT PRINCIPLES

Contextualizing Risk

While tools like CVSS and the risk matrix offer a standardized method for evaluating vulnerabilities, **contextualizing risk** is equally important for accurate prioritization. Several factors should be considered to tailor the risk assessment to the specific environment, goals, and regulatory needs of the organization.

Asset Criticality

The value of an asset to the organization plays a significant role in determining its risk level. Critical assets, such as financial systems, customer databases, or intellectual property, should be given higher priority in risk assessments. A vulnerability in a highly valuable asset could have severe consequences, making it more urgent to address, even if the likelihood of exploitation is low. Conversely, vulnerabilities in non-critical systems may pose less immediate concern.

Exploitability

The likelihood of an attacker successfully exploiting a vulnerability should also be considered. Some vulnerabilities are easily exploitable with readily available tools, while others may require sophisticated techniques or insider knowledge. The easier it is for an attacker to exploit a vulnerability, the higher the associated risk. For example, a vulnerability with a well-known exploit and no available patch is a far higher risk than one that requires custom development or internal access.

Attacker Motivation

The **motivation** behind an attack is also a key factor. Threat actors with financial or political goals may focus on high-value targets, while hacktivists may target organizations for ideological reasons. Understanding the potential motivations behind attacks helps in predicting which vulnerabilities are more likely to be exploited and allows organizations to prioritize defenses accordingly.

Tailoring Risk Assessments to Organizational Goals and Regulatory Requirements

Each organization operates within its own unique context, so risk assessments should align with both its strategic objectives and any **regulatory** requirements it must comply with. For instance, a financial institution may prioritize vulnerabilities that affect data integrity and privacy due to strict regulations like GDPR or PCI-DSS, while a healthcare organization may focus on vulnerabilities that could expose patient data. Tailoring risk assessments to these specific factors ensures that the organization's efforts are aligned with its risk tolerance and compliance obligations.

Risk assessment is an essential component of vulnerability management. By accurately defining, scoring, and contextualizing risks, organizations can prioritize vulnerabilities in a way that minimizes exposure and aligns with their security goals. Implementing a structured, risk-based approach allows security teams to focus on addressing the most critical vulnerabilities first and to implement security measures that effectively safeguard the organization's assets and reputation.

Remediation and Mitigation Strategies

One of the most fundamental strategies for remediating vulnerabilities is **patch management**. This process involves regularly updating software and systems to fix known vulnerabilities that could be exploited by attackers. A key element of effective patch management is creating a consistent **patching schedule**. By ensuring that patches are applied promptly, organizations can reduce the window of opportunity for attackers to exploit weaknesses. However, patching is not without its risks; updates can sometimes introduce new issues, so it is critical to **test patches** in a **controlled environment** before full deployment. This testing ensures that the patch resolves the vulnerability without negatively impacting system functionality or performance. A well-organized patch management process minimizes the risk of successful exploitation while maintaining system integrity.

Configuration Management

Configuration management focuses on ensuring that systems and applications are configured securely from the start and are consistently maintained in a secure state. The **CIS Controls** (Center for Internet Security) provide a widely respected set of benchmarks for secure system configurations. These benchmarks offer guidelines on securing everything from network devices to operating systems, reducing the potential attack surface. To improve efficiency, many organizations choose to **automate configuration checks**. Automation tools can continuously monitor system configurations to ensure compliance with security policies, alerting administrators when deviations from best practices occur. This proactive approach ensures that systems remain secure and aligned with organizational security standards, minimizing the likelihood of misconfigurations that can create vulnerabilities.

Compensating Controls

In some cases, remediation strategies such as applying patches or reconfiguring systems may not be feasible, particularly in situations where critical systems cannot be disrupted or where no patch exists for a specific vulnerability. In these scenarios, **compensating controls** offer an alternative way to reduce risk. These controls are designed to mitigate the impact of a vulnerability when the primary control (such as a patch) cannot be applied. For example, if a vulnerable system cannot be patched immediately, **segmenting** the system on the network can help limit its exposure to other parts of the network, reducing the likelihood that an attacker will be able to exploit the vulnerability. Compensating controls are temporary solutions but can be highly effective in maintaining security while waiting for a more permanent fix.

Incident Prevention Through Remediation

While remediation focuses on resolving vulnerabilities, **incident prevention** aims to stop attacks from succeeding in the first place. Several proactive measures can be taken to strengthen defenses and prevent incidents from occurring. For instance, regularly updating **antivirus definitions** ensures that security software can detect and block newly discovered malware. Likewise, refining and **updating firewall rules** can prevent unauthorized traffic from reaching vulnerable systems or services. These preventative actions, when combined with other strategies like intrusion detection and behavior analysis, help ensure that even if a vulnerability exists, the chances of exploitation are minimized. Incident prevention requires ongoing attention and a comprehensive security strategy, as attackers are constantly evolving their tactics.

Together, these remediation and mitigation strategies form a holistic approach to vulnerability management. By applying a combination of patching, configuration management, compensating controls, and proactive incident prevention, organizations can significantly reduce their risk of exploitation and improve their overall cybersecurity posture. The key to success lies in consistent, ongoing efforts to adapt to emerging threats and maintain secure systems.

Threat Modeling

Threat modeling is a structured approach to identifying, quantifying, and mitigating potential threats during the design phase of systems. Rather than waiting until a system is live or until an attack occurs, threat modeling proactively examines the architecture and components of a system to anticipate possible vulnerabilities and threats. This allows organizations to build defenses into their systems from the outset, reducing the potential for security breaches. By systematically analyzing the threats and weaknesses before deployment, organizations can make informed decisions on how to address risks, whether through design adjustments or the implementation of specific security controls.

Key Methodologies

Threat modeling is a crucial process for identifying, assessing, and mitigating potential security risks in a system. Several well-established methodologies provide structured approaches to help security teams analyze threats and devise appropriate strategies to address them. Two of the most widely used frameworks for conducting effective threat modeling are **STRIDE** and **DREAD**.

CHAPTER 2   INTRODUCTION TO THREAT INTELLIGENCE AND VULNERABILITY
            MANAGEMENT PRINCIPLES

STRIDE

STRIDE is a threat modeling methodology developed by Microsoft that categorizes threats into six distinct areas. It helps security teams systematically assess a system's vulnerabilities by focusing on each of these categories. By breaking down potential threats into recognizable components, STRIDE aids in identifying weaknesses and developing specific countermeasures for each type of threat.

STRIDE Categories:

- **Spoofing**: This involves impersonating a legitimate user or system to gain unauthorized access or perform malicious actions. For example, an attacker might use stolen credentials to masquerade as a trusted user.

- **Tampering**: Tampering refers to the unauthorized modification of data or system functionality. An attacker might alter sensitive data in transit or manipulate the configuration of a system to disrupt operations.

- **Repudiation**: In repudiation attacks, users or systems deny actions or events, making them difficult to trace or verify. For example, an attacker might delete logs or modify timestamps to cover their tracks after an attack.

- **Information Disclosure**: This threat involves the unauthorized exposure of sensitive data, such as credit card numbers or personal information. This could occur due to poor encryption practices or vulnerabilities in the application.

- **Denial of Service (DoS)**: A DoS attack aims to disrupt or disable access to a system or service, rendering it unavailable to legitimate users. This could be achieved through methods like overwhelming the system with traffic (Distributed Denial of Service—DDoS).

- **Elevation of Privilege**: This occurs when an attacker gains unauthorized access to restricted system functions, allowing them to perform actions that should be limited to higher-privileged users, such as administrators.

How STRIDE Helps

By systematically analyzing each of these categories within the context of a given system, security teams can identify potential risks that might not be immediately obvious. STRIDE encourages comprehensive analysis of every aspect of a system, helping teams think through various attack scenarios and vulnerabilities that could affect the system.

Best Practices:

- Use STRIDE at the design phase of system development to ensure that security is integrated from the beginning.

- Regularly revisit threat modeling with STRIDE as the system evolves to account for new risks.

- Conduct workshops or team sessions to brainstorm potential threats under each STRIDE category, ensuring a thorough and collaborative approach.

DREAD

DREAD is a scoring model used to assess and prioritize risks based on five criteria. Unlike STRIDE, which focuses on identifying types of threats, DREAD helps quantify the severity of those threats to determine which require immediate attention and resources. The DREAD model assigns a numerical score to each risk, providing a clear method for prioritization.

DREAD Criteria:

- **Damage**: This measures the potential harm or impact a threat could cause if it were to occur. The more severe the consequences, the higher the damage score. For example, a data breach exposing sensitive customer data would score higher in damage than a minor service disruption.

- **Reproducibility**: This assesses how easily an attacker can replicate the attack. If the attack can be easily reproduced with minimal effort, it is considered a higher risk. For instance, a vulnerability in a web application that can be exploited with a single script would score higher than a complex attack requiring specific conditions.

- **Exploitability**: This looks at how easy it is for an attacker to exploit the vulnerability. A vulnerability that can be easily exploited with common tools or techniques will score high in exploitability. For example, a flaw in user authentication that can be exploited via a brute-force attack would be highly exploitable.

- **Affected Users**: This criterion considers the number of users or systems that would be impacted by the threat. A vulnerability affecting a critical component or a large number of users would receive a higher score. For example, a vulnerability in a widely used web application that exposes all users' data would impact many users, thus increasing the score.

- **Discoverability**: This assesses how easily an attacker can discover the vulnerability. A vulnerability that is easy to find, perhaps because of poor security practices or publicly known weaknesses, will score higher for discoverability. For example, a misconfigured database that is accessible to anyone on the Internet would be easily discovered.

How DREAD Helps

DREAD provides a structured, quantitative approach to risk assessment. By scoring each threat across these five factors, security teams can calculate an overall risk score, which helps prioritize which threats should be mitigated first. This methodology is particularly useful when dealing with multiple vulnerabilities and need to determine which ones pose the greatest risk to the organization.

Best Practices:

- Use DREAD in combination with STRIDE to both identify threats and assess their relative importance.

- Regularly reassess risks as the environment changes, particularly after updates or new deployments.

- Use the scores derived from DREAD to allocate resources effectively, focusing on high-priority risks.

Combining STRIDE and DREAD

While STRIDE and DREAD each serve different purposes, they complement each other well. STRIDE helps teams identify potential threats, while DREAD quantifies the risks associated with each threat. By using both methodologies together, organizations can effectively model and prioritize their security risks, ensuring that critical vulnerabilities are addressed promptly.

In threat modeling, both **STRIDE** and **DREAD** provide invaluable frameworks for identifying, categorizing, and prioritizing security risks. STRIDE is particularly useful for systematically breaking down potential threats into key areas, ensuring comprehensive coverage of all possible attack vectors. Meanwhile, DREAD helps security teams assess the severity of these threats and prioritize them based on impact, exploitability, and discoverability. Together, these methodologies help organizations understand and address security risks effectively, making threat modeling a powerful tool for proactive cybersecurity defense.

Steps in Threat Modeling

Effective threat modeling is a structured process that helps organizations identify, assess, and mitigate security risks in their systems. By following a clear sequence of steps, security teams can proactively safeguard their infrastructure and respond to emerging threats. Below are the key stages involved in threat modeling.

Identify Assets

The first step in threat modeling is to pinpoint the critical assets that require protection. These are the systems, data, and components essential to the organization's operations or those containing sensitive information. Assets can include customer data, intellectual property, proprietary code, infrastructure, or even key personnel.

Identifying and valuing these assets is crucial for understanding which areas require the highest level of protection. Once assets are prioritized, the next steps can focus on evaluating the risks they face.

Best Practices:

- Classify assets based on their value and the potential consequences if they were compromised.

- Include both digital and physical assets, considering infrastructure, software, personnel, and organizational reputation.

- Engage with business stakeholders to ensure that all critical assets, including those not immediately obvious, are considered.

Define Threats

After recognizing the assets, the next step is to define the potential threats that could target those assets. Threats can take many forms—ranging from malicious attacks to natural disasters—and understanding how adversaries might exploit system weaknesses is essential for creating a robust defense strategy.

Leveraging frameworks such as **MITRE ATT&CK** provides insight into adversary tactics, techniques, and procedures (TTPs), offering a structured way to predict and prepare for various attack scenarios. Threats may be internal or external and should be considered in light of the organization's unique environment and threat landscape.

Best Practices:

- Use established threat intelligence sources to identify common attack vectors (e.g., MITRE ATT&CK, OWASP Top Ten).

- Continuously monitor emerging threats and adapt your threat model accordingly.

- Consider the range of potential attackers, including cybercriminals, nation-states, insiders, and hacktivists.

Assess Vulnerabilities

Once threats are defined, the next step is to identify vulnerabilities in the system that could be exploited. Vulnerabilities are weaknesses that may allow an attacker to compromise an asset, bypass security measures, or escalate their privileges. This step involves reviewing the system architecture, applications, and configurations for potential security gaps.

For example, if an application lacks proper encryption, it may be vulnerable to data breaches. Identifying vulnerabilities before an attack occurs gives organizations the opportunity to address weaknesses and prioritize mitigation efforts based on severity.

Best Practices:

- Conduct regular vulnerability scans using automated tools and manual penetration testing.

- Cross-reference vulnerabilities with defined threats to evaluate which are most likely to be exploited.

- Prioritize vulnerabilities based on their potential impact on assets and the likelihood of exploitation.

Implement Mitigations

The final step in the threat modeling process is implementing mitigations to reduce or eliminate identified risks. Mitigations are countermeasures designed to safeguard systems against the identified threats. They can range from technical solutions, such as deploying encryption or implementing multi-factor authentication, to procedural changes like access control policies or employee training.

It's important to not only address the most critical threats but also to ensure the cost-effectiveness and practicality of the mitigations. A robust mitigation strategy should aim for defense in depth, ensuring multiple layers of protection that can prevent or minimize the impact of attacks.

Best Practices:

- Adopt a layered security approach (defense in depth), utilizing firewalls, intrusion detection/prevention systems, encryption, and other tools.

- Assess the feasibility of implementing mitigations, considering both the technical and operational aspects.

- Continuously monitor and test mitigations to ensure they remain effective in the face of evolving threats.

Threat modeling is an ongoing, iterative process that helps organizations stay ahead of potential cyber threats. By systematically identifying assets, defining threats, assessing vulnerabilities, and implementing mitigations, organizations can proactively strengthen their security posture. This process not only protects valuable assets but also ensures that security measures evolve with changing threats.

Incorporating threat modeling into the design, deployment, and maintenance of systems provides a comprehensive approach to cybersecurity, enabling teams to reduce risks, prevent attacks, and ultimately secure critical infrastructure.

CHAPTER 2 INTRODUCTION TO THREAT INTELLIGENCE AND VULNERABILITY
MANAGEMENT PRINCIPLES

Threat Hunting

Threat hunting is a proactive cybersecurity practice focused on actively searching for hidden threats within an organization's network, rather than waiting for alerts triggered by automated defenses. The goal of threat hunting is to identify malicious activity that may have evaded detection by traditional security measures. This approach assumes that threats are already present within the system, so it is up to the analyst to detect and neutralize them before they can cause harm. Threat hunting is often an ongoing and iterative process, relying on the expertise of skilled analysts to track down sophisticated attackers who may be operating in the shadows of the network.

Threat Hunting Methodologies

Threat hunting involves proactive searches for signs of potential threats within an organization's systems, aiming to uncover threats that might evade traditional security measures. By using different methodologies, security teams can improve their chances of detecting sophisticated attacks, such as advanced persistent threats (APTs) or insider threats. Below are some common and effective threat hunting methodologies.

Hypothesis-Driven Hunting

In hypothesis-driven threat hunting, analysts begin by formulating educated guesses or hypotheses based on knowledge of adversary tactics, techniques, and procedures (TTPs). These hypotheses are informed by the analyst's understanding of how attackers typically operate and which methods they might use to breach a system.

The goal is to search for specific attack behaviors that could suggest an intruder is present, such as the presence of certain types of malware or unusual communication patterns. Analysts may hypothesize that an attacker has already infiltrated the network and is trying to escalate privileges or move laterally.

To validate these hypotheses, analysts actively search through various data sources, including logs, network traffic, endpoint behavior, and even threat intelligence reports. This approach is particularly useful for detecting more advanced attacks like APTs, where adversaries often use custom or less well-known attack vectors to evade detection.

Best Practices:

- Base hypotheses on past attack data, threat intelligence, and attacker behavior patterns.

- Use data from multiple sources (e.g., endpoints, network traffic, and logs) to test hypotheses.

- Focus on detecting complex attack chains or tactics that may be missed by signature-based detection.

Indicators of Attack (IOAs)

The Indicators of Attack (IOAs) methodology involves hunting for signs of active attacks that are occurring or have just started. Unlike Indicators of Compromise (IOCs), which are retrospective markers used to identify past breaches (e.g., malicious IP addresses, file hashes), IOAs look for signals that suggest an attack is in progress, often before any damage has been done.

IOAs can include suspicious activities such as:

- Unusual network traffic patterns (e.g., large volumes of data being sent to unknown external addresses)

- Abnormal command-line arguments or system calls indicative of exploit attempts

- Sudden spikes in failed login attempts or unexpected user behaviors, such as accessing files outside of a typical workflow

By focusing on IOAs, threat hunters can detect intruders early in the attack life cycle, giving them the chance to mitigate or stop attacks before they escalate. This methodology is often used in combination with other techniques like network traffic analysis and endpoint monitoring.

Best Practices:

- Monitor for anomalies or behaviors that could indicate the early stages of an attack.

- Leverage tools that support real-time detection of potential IOAs.

- Correlate IOAs with other data sources to gain a full picture of an ongoing attack.

Behavioral Analytics

Behavioral analytics focuses on identifying deviations from normal system or user behavior patterns. Instead of relying solely on predefined indicators, this methodology looks for unusual activities that may signal malicious behavior, even if they do not directly match known attack signatures or IOAs.

For example, a user who typically accesses a limited set of files might suddenly begin accessing large volumes of data, or a device that usually communicates with a set range of IP addresses might start connecting to external, unrecognized locations. These changes in behavior are often indicative of an attacker trying to move laterally within the network or exfiltrate data.

Behavioral analytics helps uncover sophisticated threats that attempt to blend in with normal activity, such as insider threats or attacks involving compromised credentials. By analyzing behavior patterns over time, analysts can establish baselines and detect anomalies that could indicate a security breach.

Best Practices:

- Continuously monitor system and user behaviors to establish baselines.

- Use machine learning and AI to identify subtle behavioral changes that may indicate attacks.

- Look for signs of lateral movement, data exfiltration, or privilege escalation based on deviations from typical activity.

These methodologies provide powerful frameworks for proactive threat hunting and enable security teams to uncover attacks before they cause significant damage. Whether through hypothesis-driven searches based on known attack patterns, focusing on Indicators of Attack for early detection, or leveraging behavioral analytics to spot deviations from normal activity, these techniques empower analysts to identify emerging threats more effectively.

By combining these methodologies, organizations can implement a comprehensive threat-hunting strategy that improves their ability to detect and respond to threats in real time.

Tools for Threat Hunting

Effective threat hunting relies on a variety of specialized tools that assist analysts in collecting and analyzing data across the organization's systems and networks. These tools are crucial for identifying potential threats before they can cause significant damage. Below are some of the most commonly used tools in threat hunting, each tailored for specific aspects of monitoring and detection.

Endpoint Detection and Response (EDR) Solutions

Endpoint Detection and Response (EDR) solutions are essential for monitoring the activity on individual endpoints within an organization's network. Endpoints include computers, servers, mobile devices, and other connected devices. EDR tools provide detailed insights into what's happening on each endpoint, capturing data such as file changes, network connections, processes, and user activities.

By continuously monitoring endpoints, EDR tools enable security teams to detect and investigate suspicious behavior in real time. They also offer powerful capabilities for forensic analysis, helping analysts trace back the steps of an attacker and understand how a breach unfolded.

Key features of EDR solutions include

- Real-time monitoring and alerting for abnormal activities

- Detailed data collection on endpoint activities such as file execution, system processes, and network communication

- Advanced forensic capabilities to investigate potential incidents

- Incident response capabilities for isolating compromised systems and containing threats

Popular EDR tools include

- **CrowdStrike Falcon**: Known for its cloud-native approach, Falcon offers powerful real-time monitoring, advanced threat detection, and AI-driven incident response.

- **SentinelOne**: This platform uses AI and machine learning to automatically detect and respond to attacks, offering autonomous threat prevention and remediation across endpoints.

Best Practices:

- Regularly update and configure EDR solutions to ensure comprehensive coverage across all endpoints.

- Leverage EDR data to investigate incidents, perform root cause analysis, and improve future defense strategies.

- Integrate EDR with other security tools for a unified view of the organization's threat landscape.

Advanced SIEM Tools with Machine Learning Capabilities

Security Information and Event Management (SIEM) systems aggregate and analyze data from various sources within an organization's infrastructure, such as firewalls, intrusion detection/prevention systems, servers, and network traffic logs. SIEM tools play a critical role in threat hunting by providing a centralized location for monitoring, detecting, and responding to security events.

CHAPTER 2 INTRODUCTION TO THREAT INTELLIGENCE AND VULNERABILITY MANAGEMENT PRINCIPLES

Recent advancements in SIEM platforms include the integration of machine learning and artificial intelligence (AI). These technologies enable the tools to process vast amounts of data, identify patterns, and detect anomalous behavior that could indicate a potential threat.

Key features of advanced SIEM tools include

- Aggregation and normalization of security logs from multiple sources

- Real-time event correlation to detect potential threats across different systems

- Machine learning-based anomaly detection to flag unusual patterns that may be signs of a breach

- Threat intelligence integration to provide additional context for detected events

Some popular SIEM platforms with machine learning capabilities include

- **Splunk**: A highly customizable SIEM platform that offers real-time monitoring, powerful data search capabilities, and advanced analytics. Splunk's machine learning tools help detect new threats by analyzing trends and deviations in system behavior.

- **QRadar**: Known for its ease of use and strong correlation capabilities, QRadar uses machine learning to analyze large datasets and identify previously unseen threats. It offers powerful visualizations and insights that make it easier to manage and respond to incidents.

- **LogRhythm**: This platform integrates machine learning, behavioral analytics, and threat intelligence to provide comprehensive threat detection, response, and management. It is designed to help security teams identify emerging threats quickly.

Best Practices:

- Use SIEM tools to centralize security data and perform in-depth analysis across the entire network.

- Regularly fine-tune machine learning algorithms to improve detection accuracy and reduce false positives.

- Leverage threat intelligence feeds within SIEM systems to stay informed about emerging threats and attack techniques.

Threat hunting is a crucial component of proactive cybersecurity, allowing organizations to identify and mitigate potential threats before they cause damage. By using sophisticated tools like EDR solutions and advanced SIEM platforms, security teams can enhance their threat detection capabilities and uncover signs of sophisticated attacks that may otherwise go undetected.

Incorporating machine learning and AI into these tools has made it easier for analysts to sift through vast amounts of data and identify emerging threats. This proactive and data-driven approach helps organizations stay ahead of attackers, improving overall security posture and reducing the risk of a breach.

Chapter Summary

In this chapter, readers are introduced to the critical domain of threat and vulnerability management, which is central to the role of cybersecurity analysts. The chapter covers the entire life cycle of managing threats and vulnerabilities, beginning with the identification and classification of various types of threats, including cybercriminals, nation-states, hacktivists, and insider threats. It provides a deep dive into threat intelligence, explaining how to gather and analyze data to proactively address emerging threats. The concept of intelligence is broken down

CHAPTER 2 INTRODUCTION TO THREAT INTELLIGENCE AND VULNERABILITY MANAGEMENT PRINCIPLES

into various categories—strategic, operational, and tactical—each serving different purposes and audiences, from executives to analysts. The chapter also explores key sources of threat intelligence, such as open-source intelligence (OSINT), paid feeds, dark web monitoring, and information-sharing platforms like ISACs.

A significant portion of the chapter is devoted to understanding the vulnerability management life cycle, which includes discovering vulnerabilities, prioritizing them based on risk, remediating issues, and verifying the effectiveness of the remediation. It highlights the importance of using tools like vulnerability scanners, patch management systems, and host-based scanners to identify weaknesses within systems and networks. Additionally, readers are introduced to the Common Vulnerabilities and Exposures (CVEs) system and how tracking these vulnerabilities through resources like the National Vulnerability Database (NVD) aids in staying ahead of threats.

Risk assessment is explored as a critical part of vulnerability management, with a focus on risk scoring systems such as the Common Vulnerability Scoring System (CVSS) and visual tools like risk matrices to prioritize vulnerabilities. The chapter emphasizes how risk assessment must consider factors like asset criticality, exploitability, and potential attacker motivations to tailor remediation efforts that align with the organization's objectives and regulatory requirements.

Beyond identifying and remediating vulnerabilities, the chapter delves into threat modeling as a structured approach to anticipating and mitigating threats in the design phase of systems. Readers learn methodologies like STRIDE and DREAD, which help in evaluating and mitigating various types of risks. The chapter also covers the proactive practice of threat hunting, guiding readers through hypothesis-driven hunting, the use of Indicators of Attack (IOAs), and behavioral analytics to identify potential threats before they cause damage.

CHAPTER 2   INTRODUCTION TO THREAT INTELLIGENCE AND VULNERABILITY
             MANAGEMENT PRINCIPLES

The final section discusses mitigation strategies, including patch management, configuration management, and the use of compensating controls when direct remediation is not feasible. The chapter underscores the importance of applying these strategies to not only prevent security incidents but also to minimize their impact if they do occur.

By the end of the chapter, readers have a well-rounded understanding of how to proactively manage and mitigate threats and vulnerabilities. With a combination of threat intelligence analysis, risk assessment, vulnerability scanning, and advanced practices like threat hunting and modeling, cybersecurity analysts are equipped to safeguard their organizations against a wide range of potential attacks. This chapter sets the stage for the hands-on skills and strategies necessary to build a resilient, future-proof cybersecurity posture.

CHAPTER 3

Comprehensive Vulnerability Management

In the ever-evolving landscape of cybersecurity, vulnerabilities present a constant threat to organizations, making vulnerability management a cornerstone of any comprehensive security strategy. Vulnerabilities—whether in operating systems, software applications, or network configurations—are often the gateways through which cyberattacks occur. In many cases, attackers exploit these weaknesses to gain unauthorized access, escalate privileges, exfiltrate sensitive data, or disrupt business operations. Effective vulnerability management helps organizations identify, assess, prioritize, and remediate these weaknesses before they can be exploited.

However, with the growing complexity of modern IT environments, the sheer volume and variety of vulnerabilities make this task increasingly challenging. An organization may have thousands of systems, each with its own set of vulnerabilities that could be targeted by attackers. Additionally, vulnerabilities are constantly being discovered—sometimes even in previously secure systems—requiring ongoing vigilance and adaptation to new threats. As a result, vulnerability management is not a one-time task but a continuous process that requires both proactive and reactive measures.

CHAPTER 3　COMPREHENSIVE VULNERABILITY MANAGEMENT

This chapter looks into the entire vulnerability management life cycle, breaking down each phase from discovery to remediation. It explores how organizations can systematically identify vulnerabilities using automated tools, how to assess the potential risks associated with these vulnerabilities, and how to prioritize them based on their potential impact. Given the breadth of potential vulnerabilities, it's crucial for cybersecurity teams to not only know how to scan for weaknesses but also how to interpret the data effectively and make informed decisions on where to focus their resources.

We will also look at how frameworks and industry standards, such as the Common Vulnerability Scoring System (CVSS) and the National Institute of Standards and Technology (NIST) Cybersecurity Framework, can be leveraged to create a structured and consistent approach to vulnerability management. Furthermore, we'll explore the various tools available to cybersecurity teams—from vulnerability scanners to configuration management systems—and examine how these tools can help streamline the process of discovering, categorizing, and addressing vulnerabilities. One of the most crucial aspects of vulnerability management is the ability to assess and prioritize vulnerabilities effectively. Given the limited resources and the constant flow of vulnerabilities being discovered, it is essential to understand which vulnerabilities pose the greatest threat to the organization. This chapter discusses different risk assessment strategies, including the use of risk matrices and the role of asset classification in determining priority.

Lastly, we will address the importance of ongoing vulnerability management in a broader cybersecurity strategy. Vulnerability management is not isolated from other security practices, such as incident response, threat hunting, and risk management. By integrating vulnerability management into an organization's overall security posture, cybersecurity teams can ensure they are not only responding to threats but proactively defending against them.

CHAPTER 3   COMPREHENSIVE VULNERABILITY MANAGEMENT

By the end of this chapter, readers will have a comprehensive understanding of the vulnerability management life cycle, the tools and frameworks that support it, and best practices for ensuring that vulnerabilities are consistently and effectively mitigated. The goal is to equip cybersecurity analysts with the knowledge and skills needed to implement a robust vulnerability management program, minimize risk exposure, and improve the overall security posture of the organization.

Introduction to Vulnerability Management

Vulnerability management is a systematic approach to identifying, evaluating, and addressing weaknesses within an organization's IT infrastructure. It aims to reduce the attack surface by ensuring that known vulnerabilities are mitigated or remediated before they can be exploited by malicious actors. Vulnerabilities can be present in various forms, including software bugs, configuration errors, weak security policies, or outdated hardware. The vulnerability management process is ongoing and ensures that an organization's systems remain secure, compliant, and resilient against evolving cyber threats.

Importance of Vulnerability Management

The significance of vulnerability management cannot be overstated. In an age of rapidly evolving cyber threats, organizations are under constant pressure to secure their systems from attackers seeking to exploit weaknesses. By proactively identifying and addressing vulnerabilities, organizations can significantly reduce the risk of data breaches, financial loss, and reputational damage. Here are a few key reasons why vulnerability management is critical:

- **Reduces Attack Surface**: By addressing vulnerabilities, organizations can minimize the entry points that attackers may exploit, reducing the likelihood of a successful attack.

- **Ensures Compliance**: Many regulatory standards, such as the **Payment Card Industry Data Security Standard (PCI DSS)** and **Health Insurance Portability and Accountability Act (HIPAA)**, require organizations to maintain a process for managing vulnerabilities to ensure the protection of sensitive data. Non-compliance can result in fines, legal actions, or loss of customer trust.

- **Protects Sensitive Data and Critical Infrastructure**: Vulnerability management protects valuable and sensitive assets, including personal customer data, financial information, and proprietary intellectual property. Additionally, it ensures the integrity of critical infrastructure, such as servers, networks, and cloud environments, all of which play an essential role in an organization's operations.

Key Components of Vulnerability Management

Effective vulnerability management encompasses several key components, each of which contributes to a comprehensive strategy for identifying and addressing vulnerabilities in a timely manner. These components work together to provide a robust framework for managing vulnerabilities across the enterprise.

1. **Discovery**: The discovery phase is the first step in identifying vulnerabilities within an organization's systems. This involves mapping out all IT assets, including hardware, software, networks, and applications, to ensure nothing is overlooked. Vulnerability scanners and automated tools are often used to detect known vulnerabilities and configuration issues within these assets. Discovery also involves continuously monitoring systems to catch newly introduced vulnerabilities or emerging threats.

2. **Assessment**: Once vulnerabilities are discovered, the next step is assessing their risk levels. This process involves evaluating the potential impact of each vulnerability in terms of its exploitability, severity, and potential damage to the organization. Tools like the **Common Vulnerability Scoring System (CVSS)** can help assign a score to vulnerabilities based on factors such as the ease of exploitation, the affected assets, and the potential consequences of an attack. The assessment phase also considers external threats, such as hacker tactics and known exploits.

3. **Prioritization**: Given that not all vulnerabilities pose an equal risk, prioritization is critical. Vulnerabilities must be addressed in order of their potential impact, exploitability, and the criticality of the affected systems. This is where risk-based models come into play. Asset criticality, business impact, and regulatory requirements all factor into prioritizing vulnerabilities for remediation.

For instance, vulnerabilities in systems housing sensitive customer data or critical business operations should be addressed before less impactful issues.

4. **Remediation**: Remediation involves implementing fixes or mitigation strategies to address identified vulnerabilities. This can include applying patches, reconfiguring systems, or updating software. In some cases, if immediate remediation is not feasible, compensating controls, such as network segmentation or the application of firewalls, may be used to reduce the potential exposure of the vulnerability. Remediation requires coordination across multiple teams within the organization to ensure that the appropriate fixes are applied in a timely manner.

5. **Reporting**: After vulnerabilities have been identified, assessed, prioritized, and remediated, reporting is the final key component in the vulnerability management process. This involves documenting the findings, actions taken, and the status of each vulnerability to ensure transparency and accountability. Reporting also helps management and security teams track progress, identify trends, and ensure compliance with internal policies and regulatory standards. Detailed reporting can provide valuable insights into the organization's overall security posture and areas that require ongoing attention.

By following these components, organizations can establish an effective vulnerability management program that reduces risk and strengthens overall security resilience. Vulnerability management is not just about fixing vulnerabilities but also about embedding a culture of continuous monitoring and improvement. In today's threat landscape, proactive vulnerability management is essential for protecting critical assets, maintaining compliance, and safeguarding an organization's reputation.

Vulnerability Scanning Tools and Techniques

Vulnerability scanners are automated tools designed to identify weaknesses and security flaws within an organization's IT infrastructure, including networks, applications, systems, and databases. These tools are essential in proactively managing vulnerabilities by providing regular assessments and detecting potential entry points for attackers. Vulnerability scanners work by comparing the current state of systems against known vulnerabilities and security best practices, often using databases of common vulnerabilities such as the **Common Vulnerabilities and Exposures (CVE)** list. The scanners help security teams efficiently identify issues that need remediation, thereby reducing the attack surface and improving overall security posture.

Types of Vulnerability Scans

Vulnerability scanning can be categorized into different types, each focusing on specific aspects of an organization's infrastructure. The type of scan selected depends on the scope, purpose, and assets being assessed.

- **Network Scans**: Network scans focus on identifying vulnerabilities within the organization's network infrastructure. These scans assess both **external** and **internal** networks, checking for issues like open ports, weak encryption protocols, misconfigured network devices, and improper access control configurations. External scans typically simulate attacks from outside the network, while internal scans look at vulnerabilities that could be exploited by insiders or attackers who have already gained network access.

- **Application Scans**: Application scans are designed to identify vulnerabilities within software applications, including web applications, APIs, and server-side applications. These scans are critical in detecting **SQL injection, cross-site scripting (XSS), broken authentication mechanisms**, and other vulnerabilities specific to application code and logic. Web application scanners, such as **Burp Suite**, are specialized tools that focus on finding vulnerabilities unique to web environments.

- **Host-Based Scans**: Host-based scans target individual devices, such as servers, workstations, and endpoints. These scans look for unpatched software, missing security configurations, outdated antivirus definitions, and unauthorized changes to system settings. Host-based scans are typically run on a scheduled basis or as part of a larger endpoint security strategy. They are particularly useful for detecting vulnerabilities specific to the operating system and installed software on individual machines.

CHAPTER 3   COMPREHENSIVE VULNERABILITY MANAGEMENT

- **Database Scans**: Database scans focus on vulnerabilities within the organization's databases. This includes assessing the configuration of database management systems (DBMS), identifying improper access control settings, weak user authentication, insecure connections, and other security misconfigurations. Vulnerabilities like **SQL injection**, improper user privileges, or unencrypted data storage are frequently identified during these scans.

Popular Vulnerability Scanning Tools

There are several well-established vulnerability scanning tools that organizations can use to assess their infrastructure. Each tool offers unique features and focuses on different aspects of vulnerability management:

- **Nessus**: Nessus is one of the most widely used vulnerability scanners, known for its comprehensive vulnerability database and ability to scan both network and host-based vulnerabilities. Nessus is particularly effective at detecting known vulnerabilities in a variety of systems, including operating systems, network devices, and databases. It also offers advanced features like credentialed scanning, which allows for more thorough scanning of systems that require privileged access.

- **OpenVAS**: OpenVAS is an open-source vulnerability scanner that offers similar functionality to Nessus. It provides a wide range of scanning capabilities, including network and host-based scanning, and has a large repository of vulnerability checks. While it is free to use, it may require more configuration and maintenance compared to commercial solutions.

- **Qualys**: Qualys is a cloud-based vulnerability management platform that provides scalable scanning solutions for businesses of all sizes. It offers automated vulnerability scanning for assets across global networks, with real-time vulnerability assessment capabilities. Qualys is often praised for its flexibility, ease of integration with other security tools, and comprehensive coverage of both IT and cloud environments.

- **Rapid7 Nexpose**: Nexpose, developed by Rapid7, is another popular vulnerability management tool known for its robust scanning features and intuitive user interface. It allows users to perform network, web application, and database vulnerability scans and provides detailed reports with actionable remediation steps. Nexpose integrates well with other security tools, including **Metasploit**, for automated exploitation testing.

- **Burp Suite (for Web Applications)**: Burp Suite is a specialized vulnerability scanning tool that focuses on web applications. It is widely used by penetration testers and security teams to identify vulnerabilities like **SQL injection**, **XSS**, and other web-based threats. Burp Suite allows for comprehensive scanning of both static and dynamic content, along with tools for manual testing and vulnerability exploitation.

CHAPTER 3   COMPREHENSIVE VULNERABILITY MANAGEMENT

Limitations of Vulnerability Scanners

While vulnerability scanners are invaluable tools in the vulnerability management process, they do have limitations. Understanding these limitations is essential to ensure that the results of a vulnerability scan are used effectively.

- **False Positives and False Negatives**: One of the most significant challenges of vulnerability scanners is the possibility of false positives and false negatives. False positives occur when a scanner incorrectly flags a benign issue as a vulnerability, which can lead to wasted time and resources during remediation efforts. False negatives, on the other hand, occur when the scanner misses an actual vulnerability, which may allow attackers to exploit an unaddressed weakness. To mitigate these risks, manual validation is often required to confirm critical findings.

- **Limited Scope for Zero-Day Vulnerabilities**: Vulnerability scanners rely on known vulnerability databases, such as CVE lists, to detect weaknesses. However, they cannot identify **zero-day vulnerabilities**—security flaws that are unknown to the vendor or security community and are often exploited by attackers before patches are available. While scanners can identify a wide range of known vulnerabilities, zero-day threats often require more advanced detection methods, including behavior analysis or machine learning.

- **Lack of Context:** Vulnerability scanners provide technical data regarding vulnerabilities but often lack the contextual information needed to assess the true risk of a vulnerability in a given environment. For instance, a vulnerability may be flagged in a system that is not exposed to the Internet or in a low-risk environment. Thus, additional factors, such as asset criticality and network segmentation, need to be considered in the risk assessment.

- **Resource Intensive:** Running regular vulnerability scans can be resource-intensive, especially in large organizations with a vast number of systems to scan. Scanning large environments, particularly network-based scans or credentialed host scans, can result in system slowdowns or performance issues. It is important to schedule scans during off-peak hours or to use scanning tools that are optimized for large environments.

Despite these limitations, vulnerability scanners are a critical component of any organization's security strategy. By using a combination of scanning tools and manual validation, organizations can effectively identify and address vulnerabilities before they can be exploited by attackers.

The Vulnerability Management Life Cycle

The **Vulnerability Management Life Cycle** is a structured approach to identifying, assessing, prioritizing, and remediating vulnerabilities within an organization's systems and infrastructure. By following a repeatable process, security teams can ensure that vulnerabilities are addressed in a timely and effective manner, reducing the risk of exploitation by threat actors. Below are the key phases in the vulnerability management life cycle, each of which plays a crucial role in maintaining a strong security posture.

Phase 1: Asset Discovery

Asset discovery is the first step in the vulnerability management life cycle. Without a comprehensive understanding of what assets are present within the network, it becomes impossible to effectively secure them. This phase involves creating an inventory of all systems, applications, and devices in the organization.

Inventorying Systems, Applications, and Devices

Security teams need to know what systems are in use, including hardware, software, virtualized systems, and cloud-based resources. This process helps in identifying which systems need to be monitored for vulnerabilities.

Tools for Asset Discovery
Nmap

A widely used network scanning tool that can detect live hosts, open ports, and services running on a network. It helps in identifying unknown or rogue devices.

Asset Management Systems

Automated tools that track and manage IT assets across the organization. These systems can feed into the vulnerability management process by providing real-time visibility of assets.

Network Discovery Tools

Tools like **SolarWinds Network Discovery** or **Advanced IP Scanner** allow security teams to automatically identify devices connected to the network and monitor them for vulnerabilities.

By completing a thorough asset discovery process, organizations gain the foundational knowledge necessary to evaluate vulnerabilities accurately and ensure all assets are covered in the subsequent scanning and remediation processes.

Phase 2: Vulnerability Identification

The next phase in the life cycle is **vulnerability identification**, where security teams actively search for weaknesses within their systems. This step involves conducting regular scans and staying up to date with newly disclosed vulnerabilities.

Conducting Vulnerability Scans

Vulnerability scanning tools, such as **Nessus**, **Qualys**, and **Rapid7 Nexpose**, are employed to scan assets for known vulnerabilities. These tools help identify common security flaws like unpatched software, weak passwords, misconfigurations, and unsecure protocols.

Leverage Threat Intelligence

Threat intelligence feeds are a valuable resource for identifying new vulnerabilities as they are disclosed. Organizations often integrate threat intelligence sources such as **US-CERT** or commercial threat intelligence providers to stay informed about emerging threats and zero-day vulnerabilities.

Regular Scanning

Scans should be conducted regularly to ensure newly introduced vulnerabilities, as well as those introduced by software updates or configuration changes, are quickly detected and mitigated.

Phase 3: Risk Assessment

Once vulnerabilities are identified, the next step is to assess their potential impact and the likelihood of their exploitation. This is where the **risk assessment** phase comes into play. It's important to understand the risk that a vulnerability poses to the organization before deciding on remediation efforts.

Evaluating Impact and Likelihood

The impact of a vulnerability is determined by how severe the consequences would be if it were exploited. For example, a vulnerability in a critical database may have far-reaching consequences compared to a flaw in a non-critical system.

The likelihood of exploitation is based on factors like the complexity of the exploit, the availability of exploit code, and whether the vulnerability is being actively targeted by threat actors.

Using CVSS Scores

The **Common Vulnerability Scoring System (CVSS)** is a standardized method for assessing the severity of vulnerabilities. CVSS scores range from 0 to 10, with higher scores indicating more severe vulnerabilities. CVSS considers factors such as exploitability, impact, and the availability of attack vectors.

Considering Asset Criticality

Not all vulnerabilities are equal in terms of risk. For example, vulnerabilities in mission-critical systems or databases may pose a higher risk than vulnerabilities in less critical systems. Asset criticality and exposure must be factored into the assessment process to determine which vulnerabilities require the most immediate attention.

Threat Actor Capabilities

Understanding the capabilities of potential threat actors is also crucial. Some vulnerabilities may be more attractive to advanced threat actors, such as nation-state actors, whereas others may be primarily exploited by opportunistic hackers.

Phase 4: Prioritization

After assessing the risk of identified vulnerabilities, the next step is **prioritization**. This phase involves determining the order in which vulnerabilities should be addressed based on their severity and the risk they pose to the organization.

Categorizing Vulnerabilities by Severity

Vulnerabilities are typically categorized into severity levels such as **critical**, **high**, **medium**, and **low**. Critical vulnerabilities should be prioritized for immediate remediation, while low-severity vulnerabilities may be addressed later or included in routine maintenance.

Risk Matrices and CVSS Scores

Risk matrices are often used to prioritize vulnerabilities based on their CVSS score, criticality, and potential impact. A risk matrix can help visualize which vulnerabilities are the highest priority and should be tackled first.

CVSS scores are a valuable tool in the prioritization process, providing an objective measure of vulnerability severity that helps security teams make data-driven decisions.

Factors to Consider for Prioritization:

- Exposure level: Is the vulnerability accessible from the public Internet or behind a firewall?

- Business impact: How does the vulnerability impact the organization's ability to function or the safety of its data?

- Remediation complexity: Some vulnerabilities may require simple patches, while others may need more complex fixes.

Phase 5: Remediation and Mitigation

The **remediation and mitigation** phase involves taking action to address the identified vulnerabilities. This phase includes applying patches, making configuration changes, or implementing compensating controls when immediate fixes are not feasible.

Applying Patches and Updates

The most common method of addressing vulnerabilities is by applying patches released by software vendors or operating system providers. Security teams must ensure that patches are tested and deployed promptly to avoid leaving systems exposed.

Configuration Changes

In some cases, vulnerabilities may be mitigated by adjusting configurations. For example, changing default credentials, disabling unnecessary services, or enabling multi-factor authentication (MFA) can reduce the risk of exploitation.

Compensating Controls

If remediation isn't possible due to technical or business constraints, **compensating controls** can be implemented. These are alternative measures that reduce the risk of exploitation, such as enhanced monitoring, additional network segmentation, or the use of firewalls.

Tracking Progress

Remediation efforts should be tracked to ensure all identified vulnerabilities are addressed. This may involve verifying patch deployment or confirming that systems are re-scanned after remediation.

Phase 6: Reporting and Review

The final phase of the vulnerability management life cycle is **reporting and review**, which focuses on documenting vulnerabilities, remediation actions taken, and any residual risks that remain.

Documenting Findings

Comprehensive reports should be generated after each vulnerability scan and remediation cycle. These reports should detail the vulnerabilities found, the severity of each, the actions taken to address them, and any outstanding risks.

Informed Stakeholders

Reports should be shared with key stakeholders, including senior management, IT teams, and compliance officers, to ensure that decision-makers are aware of the current security posture and the efforts being made to address vulnerabilities.

Continuous Improvement

Vulnerability management is an ongoing process, and organizations should regularly review their practices to ensure they are effective. The insights gained from vulnerability assessments can be used to improve future detection, assessment, and remediation efforts.

By following the **vulnerability management life cycle**, organizations can ensure that vulnerabilities are continuously identified, assessed, and addressed, thereby minimizing the risk of exploitation and strengthening overall cybersecurity defenses.

Risk-Based Vulnerability Management

In modern cybersecurity, managing vulnerabilities is not a one-size-fits-all approach. Given the vast number of vulnerabilities that can exist within an organization's systems, it is not always feasible or practical to address each one immediately. This is where **Risk-Based Vulnerability Management (RBVM)** becomes crucial. Rather than applying resources indiscriminately to every identified vulnerability, a risk-based approach focuses on addressing the vulnerabilities that present the most significant risk to the organization's critical assets and operations.

Why Risk-Based Approaches Matter

The core idea behind risk-based vulnerability management is that not all vulnerabilities pose the same level of threat. The importance of prioritizing vulnerabilities based on their potential impact and the likelihood of exploitation cannot be overstated. Here's why a risk-based approach is critical:

Resource Constraint

Security teams are often limited by time, personnel, and tools. With thousands of vulnerabilities discovered annually, it's unrealistic to expect teams to remediate them all at once. Focusing on the most impactful vulnerabilities helps ensure that resources are used efficiently.

Focus on Critical Vulnerabilities

Vulnerabilities in systems or applications that are critical to the business need to be prioritized. Exploiting these vulnerabilities can cause substantial financial damage, operational disruption, or reputational harm. Addressing the most critical vulnerabilities first helps to protect the most valuable assets.

Business Continuity

A risk-based approach aligns the remediation efforts with the business's risk tolerance, ensuring that the focus remains on protecting assets that are crucial to the organization's continued operation and success.

Steps in Risk-Based Vulnerability Management

A risk-based vulnerability management process consists of several key steps. These steps help identify, assess, and prioritize vulnerabilities based on their potential to cause harm to the organization.

Identify High-Value Assets and Systems

- **Asset Inventory**: Understanding which systems, applications, and data are most important to the organization's operations is the first step in risk-based vulnerability management. These assets may include critical servers, databases, customer-facing applications, intellectual property, or financial systems.

- **Business Impact Assessment**: Security teams should work closely with business units to understand the importance of each asset. Critical systems that support core business functions should be given top priority in vulnerability assessments.

Assess Vulnerabilities That Impact High-Value Assets

- **Vulnerability Scanning**: Once high-value assets have been identified, vulnerability scans should be focused on those systems. This includes using automated tools to detect vulnerabilities, such as unpatched software, misconfigurations, and security weaknesses.

- **Evaluate Severity**: Not all vulnerabilities are equal. Some may be low-severity issues that don't pose an immediate risk, while others could allow attackers to compromise critical assets. Vulnerabilities impacting high-value assets are often of higher concern due to the potential damage they could cause.

Prioritize Based on Likelihood of Exploitation and Potential Impact

- **Likelihood of Exploitation**: After identifying vulnerabilities, assess the likelihood that each one will be exploited by attackers. Factors influencing this likelihood include the availability of exploit code, the visibility of the vulnerability, and whether the vulnerability is actively being targeted in the wild.

CHAPTER 3   COMPREHENSIVE VULNERABILITY MANAGEMENT

- **Impact Assessment**: Vulnerabilities should also be assessed in terms of their potential impact. If a vulnerability were exploited, would it lead to significant data loss, financial impact, or downtime? The more severe the consequences, the higher the priority for remediation.

- **Risk Matrix**: A risk matrix is a common tool used to prioritize vulnerabilities by plotting them along axes representing impact and likelihood. Vulnerabilities that fall into the high-impact, high-likelihood category should be addressed first, while those in lower-priority categories may be remediated later or mitigated with compensating controls.

Integration with Threat Intelligence

One of the key components of risk-based vulnerability management is the integration of **threat intelligence.** Threat intelligence provides real-time information about emerging threats and vulnerabilities, helping security teams identify which vulnerabilities are most likely to be exploited. This can significantly improve the risk-based approach by ensuring that security teams focus their efforts on the most urgent and active threats.

- **Understanding Active Exploitation**: Threat intelligence feeds help security teams understand which vulnerabilities are being actively exploited in the wild. For example, if a new critical vulnerability is discovered in widely used software such as a web server or operating system, and it is actively being exploited by threat actors, it should take precedence over vulnerabilities that are not yet being targeted.

- **Contextualizing Vulnerabilities**: Threat intelligence can help provide context about the risk posed by a particular vulnerability. For example, a vulnerability in a legacy system that has no known exploits may not need immediate attention compared to a vulnerability in a widely used web application with active exploit attempts.

- **Example**: Let's say a vulnerability in a popular content management system (CMS) is disclosed, and a proof-of-concept exploit is found. Threat intelligence might reveal that cybercriminals are already using this exploit in a targeted attack. In this case, this vulnerability should be addressed immediately in comparison to another vulnerability in a non-critical, unsupported application that does not have known exploit attempts.

Risk-based vulnerability management provides a strategic framework for identifying and addressing vulnerabilities based on their actual risk to the organization. By focusing on high-value assets, evaluating the likelihood of exploitation, and considering the potential impact of each vulnerability, organizations can prioritize their remediation efforts and ensure that limited resources are allocated efficiently. Integrating threat intelligence into the process further enhances the ability to respond to vulnerabilities that are actively being exploited. By adopting a risk-based approach, organizations can significantly reduce their attack surface and improve their overall security posture while making more informed, data-driven decisions in the vulnerability management process.

Patch Management

Patch management is a critical component of maintaining a secure and resilient IT infrastructure. It involves the systematic process of acquiring, testing, deploying, and validating patches and updates to software and hardware systems to address vulnerabilities and improve functionality. Effective patch management helps prevent cyberattacks that exploit known vulnerabilities and ensures that an organization's systems remain compliant with security standards.

Role of Patch Management

The primary role of patch management is to **ensure vulnerabilities are addressed** through updates provided by software and hardware vendors. Patches are designed to fix vulnerabilities, enhance performance, and provide new features. They are essential for closing security gaps that could be exploited by malicious actors. Keeping software and hardware up-to-date with the latest patches is a proactive step in mitigating security risks, ensuring compliance with industry regulations, and maintaining the overall health of systems and applications.

Patch management also plays a pivotal role in ensuring **system stability and functionality**. Regular patching helps improve the performance of systems and applications, fixing bugs and issues that may have been present in previous versions.

CHAPTER 3   COMPREHENSIVE VULNERABILITY MANAGEMENT

Patch Management Process

1. **Patch Discovery:**

    - **Monitoring Vendor Releases:**

        Staying informed about new patches begins with consistently monitoring vendor communications. Software and hardware vendors regularly release updates, which could range from minor bug fixes to critical security patches. To stay up-to-date, organizations must actively track vendor websites, security bulletins, and subscription-based services. This ensures timely awareness of vulnerabilities that need addressing to prevent exploitation.

    - **Threat Intelligence Feeds:**

        Alongside vendor-specific updates, subscribing to threat intelligence feeds is critical for identifying vulnerabilities in real time. These feeds provide insights on newly discovered vulnerabilities, including zero-day threats and actively exploited issues. Automated tools can be integrated with these feeds to immediately identify patches that should be prioritized, helping security teams apply urgent fixes before attackers can exploit them.

2. **Patch Testing:**

    - **Compatibility Checks:**

        Before deploying patches, organizations should test them in a controlled environment to ensure compatibility with existing systems and applications. Patch testing helps identify potential conflicts with other software or hardware that might cause system instability or downtime if left undetected. This step helps organizations avoid unforeseen disruptions in production environments.

    - **Performance Verification:**

        Testing should also include performance verification to ensure that the patch doesn't negatively impact the performance of critical systems. For instance, while addressing security vulnerabilities, some patches may inadvertently affect system speed or efficiency. Performance checks help prevent these issues from affecting business operations, ensuring that patched systems perform optimally after updates.

3. **Patch Deployment:**

    - **Automated Patch Management Tools:**

        Once patches have been tested, deployment can be automated using patch management tools like Microsoft SCCM (System Center Configuration Manager) or WSUS (Windows Server Update Services). These tools simplify and streamline the patching process across large-scale IT environments, ensuring patches are consistently applied and minimizing manual intervention.

- **Deployment Strategies:**

    The deployment strategy should follow a structured approach. High-risk systems, those that are most vulnerable to attacks or most critical to business operations, should be patched first. Following the initial deployment to critical systems, patches should be rolled out to less critical infrastructure. A phased approach helps mitigate the risk of widespread issues while ensuring the security of vital systems.

4. **Validation:**

    - **Confirm Successful Application:**

        Validation is crucial to ensure that patches have been correctly applied and systems are functioning as expected. This process involves running checks to verify that all systems have received the updates and that they're operating normally. Tools like patch compliance software or automated auditing systems can help confirm that patches are successfully implemented and effective.

    - **Monitoring for Issues:**

        Continuous monitoring is essential after patch deployment to quickly detect any issues. If any systems begin showing signs of trouble after a patch is applied, it's vital to promptly troubleshoot and remediate the issue. Regular monitoring ensures that new vulnerabilities are not introduced during patch deployment and helps maintain system integrity post-update.

Challenges in Patch Management

1. **Balancing Urgency and Operational Stability:**

    - **Urgency:**

        Some patches, especially those addressing critical vulnerabilities that are actively being exploited, require immediate deployment to prevent attacks. These patches must be applied swiftly to protect the organization from potential breaches. Security teams must be prepared to act quickly, ensuring patches are prioritized and implemented without delay.

    - **Operational Stability:**

        On the other hand, applying patches too hastily can introduce unintended consequences, such as system instability or performance degradation. For example, patches might conflict with other software or disrupt ongoing operations. The key challenge is finding a balance between the urgency of patching critical vulnerabilities and maintaining the stability of production systems. A structured, tested deployment strategy minimizes the risks associated with rapid patching.

2. **Addressing Legacy Systems:**

    - **Legacy System Compatibility:**

        Many organizations still rely on outdated systems that may not be compatible with newer patches or may no longer receive support from the vendor. These legacy systems become a significant challenge in patch management because they often lack access to essential security updates, making them vulnerable to attacks. Unsupported systems require extra care, such as the implementation of compensating controls, to mitigate potential security risks.

    - **Workarounds and Mitigations:**

        For legacy systems, it may be necessary to implement workarounds, such as network segmentation, enhanced monitoring, or firewalls to reduce exposure to vulnerabilities. While these measures help protect the system temporarily, they are not long-term solutions. Ultimately, upgrading or replacing legacy systems is necessary for maintaining a secure environment.

3. **Managing Out-of-Band Patches:**

    - **Critical Vulnerabilities:**

        Some vulnerabilities are discovered outside of scheduled patch cycles, requiring immediate remediation. These out-of-band patches typically address zero-day vulnerabilities or critical flaws actively being exploited by attackers. The challenge lies in the urgency of deploying these patches quickly, which requires fast testing and deployment.

- **Unplanned Resources:**

    Responding to out-of-band patches often involves reallocating resources from other ongoing projects. Due to their immediate nature, these patches must be tested, deployed, and validated under tight timelines, which can strain resources. Organizations must have procedures in place to handle these patches promptly while minimizing the impact on other security and IT operations.

Effective patch management is a cornerstone of an organization's cybersecurity strategy, reducing vulnerabilities and maintaining the integrity of systems. By implementing a structured process that includes patch discovery, testing, deployment, and validation, organizations can efficiently address known security weaknesses and ensure systems are up-to-date. However, challenges such as balancing patch urgency with system stability, dealing with legacy systems, and managing out-of-band patches require a flexible, strategic approach. Leveraging automated tools and adhering to best practices can help organizations navigate these challenges and reduce the risk of exposure to cyber threats.

Vulnerability Management and Compliance

Vulnerability management is a critical process in ensuring both the security and compliance of an organization's IT systems. Regulatory frameworks, such as SOX, GLBA, HIPAA, HITECH, PCI DSS, NIST, and ISO, are designed to enforce policies and standards that help prevent breaches, protect sensitive data, and mitigate the risk of exploitation. Non-compliance with these regulations can result in significant financial penalties, legal consequences, and reputational damage. This section outlines the relationship between vulnerability management and key compliance regulations, illustrating how organizations can meet the necessary requirements while strengthening their security posture.

Regulatory Requirements and Vulnerability Management

1. **SOX (Sarbanes-Oxley Act):**

    - **Audit Trails and Security Controls**: SOX requires organizations to maintain robust internal controls over financial reporting systems. These controls must be designed to prevent unauthorized access to sensitive financial data. Vulnerability management is crucial in this context, as it ensures that any vulnerabilities in the financial systems are addressed promptly to protect against unauthorized access and potential financial fraud.

    - **System and Application Security:** Vulnerabilities in financial reporting systems can lead to inaccurate reporting, which may violate SOX regulations. Organizations are required to implement controls such as access management, encryption, and regular vulnerability scans to secure these critical systems.

CHAPTER 3   COMPREHENSIVE VULNERABILITY MANAGEMENT

2. **GLBA (Gramm-Leach-Bliley Act):**

    - **Data Security**: GLBA mandates that financial institutions protect nonpublic personal information (NPI). This includes taking appropriate measures to prevent security threats that could compromise consumer data. Regular vulnerability assessments and timely patch management are necessary to secure systems that store or process NPI.

    - **Risk Assessment**: GLBA requires financial organizations to conduct periodic risk assessments to identify vulnerabilities in their information security practices. Identifying weaknesses in IT systems and infrastructure that handle sensitive data is crucial to maintaining compliance.

3. **HIPAA (Health Insurance Portability and Accountability Act):**

    - **Protected Health Information (PHI) Security**: HIPAA requires healthcare organizations to safeguard patient data (PHI) from unauthorized access, alteration, or disclosure. Vulnerability management plays a vital role in this process by identifying and addressing weaknesses in systems that house PHI.

    - **Security Rule Requirements**: The HIPAA Security Rule mandates healthcare entities to implement administrative, physical, and technical safeguards, which include regular vulnerability scanning and patch management to protect against potential breaches.

- **Risk Analysis and Mitigation**: HIPAA requires healthcare organizations to perform risk analyses and implement measures to mitigate vulnerabilities identified during these assessments. Effective vulnerability management is critical to ensuring PHI is secure and that organizations comply with HIPAA's privacy and security standards.

4. **HITECH (Health Information Technology for Economic and Clinical Health Act):**

    - **Strengthening HIPAA Compliance**: HITECH expands upon HIPAA's provisions, particularly concerning the protection of electronic health records (EHRs). It emphasizes the need for improved security measures to protect patient data and requires reporting of security breaches. Vulnerability management must address vulnerabilities that could potentially expose EHR systems to threats, such as malware or hacking attempts.

    - **Breach Notification**: If vulnerabilities result in a breach of PHI, HITECH mandates timely reporting to affected individuals and the Department of Health and Human Services (HHS). A robust vulnerability management system helps identify and mitigate risks before they lead to a breach, reducing the likelihood of regulatory penalties.

CHAPTER 3   COMPREHENSIVE VULNERABILITY MANAGEMENT

5. **PCI DSS (Payment Card Industry Data Security Standard):**

    - **Vulnerability Scans**: PCI DSS requires organizations that process, store, or transmit cardholder data to conduct regular vulnerability scans. These scans must be performed by an Approved Scanning Vendor (ASV) at least quarterly and after any significant changes to the network or systems. The scans identify weaknesses that could be exploited by attackers to compromise payment card data.

    - **Remediation and Documentation**: After vulnerabilities are identified, organizations must take appropriate remediation actions. This includes applying patches, updating configurations, and implementing compensating controls, if necessary. Organizations must maintain documentation of their vulnerability management efforts to demonstrate compliance during PCI DSS assessments.

6. **NIST (National Institute of Standards and Technology):**

    - **NIST SP 800-53 and Cybersecurity Framework**: NIST provides guidelines through SP 800-53 and the Cybersecurity Framework (CSF) for vulnerability management. The guidelines cover identifying vulnerabilities, assessing the risk posed by each vulnerability, and applying appropriate controls to address them.

CHAPTER 3   COMPREHENSIVE VULNERABILITY MANAGEMENT

- **Continuous Monitoring and Risk Management**: NIST encourages a continuous approach to vulnerability management, which includes regular vulnerability scanning, patch management, and security monitoring. This continuous cycle helps organizations stay ahead of emerging threats and comply with NIST's risk management framework (RMF).

- **Risk-Based Approach**: NIST emphasizes prioritizing vulnerabilities based on their severity and potential impact on organizational assets. This approach helps organizations allocate resources efficiently and address high-risk vulnerabilities first, ensuring critical systems and data are protected.

7. **ISO (International Organization for Standardization):**

    - **ISO/IEC 27001**: ISO/IEC 27001 sets the standards for an Information Security Management System (ISMS). Under this standard, organizations are required to assess and manage risks, including vulnerabilities that could impact the security of sensitive information.

    - **Vulnerability Assessment and Risk Treatment**: ISO/IEC 27001 emphasizes conducting regular vulnerability assessments as part of a comprehensive risk management process. Organizations must document vulnerabilities, assess their impact, and apply appropriate controls or mitigations to reduce the risks to acceptable levels.

CHAPTER 3   COMPREHENSIVE VULNERABILITY MANAGEMENT

- **ISO/IEC 27002**: This standard provides a set of best practices for securing information systems. It includes recommendations on conducting vulnerability assessments and implementing appropriate countermeasures, such as patch management, to ensure ongoing compliance and minimize risks to information security.

Best Practices for Ensuring Compliance

- **Continuous Vulnerability Scanning**: Regular scans for vulnerabilities are required by many compliance frameworks. Implementing automated tools that can perform real-time scanning of systems for vulnerabilities ensures that compliance is maintained and vulnerabilities are identified promptly.

- **Patching and Remediation**: Remediation efforts, such as patching, should be a priority after vulnerabilities are discovered. Timely application of patches helps address weaknesses before they can be exploited.

- **Documentation and Auditing**: Maintaining thorough documentation of vulnerability assessments, remediation efforts, and system configurations is essential for demonstrating compliance during audits. Regular audits help ensure that vulnerabilities are properly addressed and that systems remain secure.

- **Training and Awareness**: Employees and stakeholders must be educated about the importance of vulnerability management and security best practices. Ongoing training ensures that individuals understand how to identify, report, and mitigate vulnerabilities.

- **Incident Response Planning:** Having a well-defined incident response plan in place helps organizations quickly address and remediate vulnerabilities before they lead to a security breach. The plan should include specific steps for handling vulnerabilities and coordinating efforts across departments.

Vulnerability management is a crucial component of regulatory compliance. Ensuring compliance with standards such as PCI DSS, HIPAA, SOX, GLBA, NIST, and ISO requires that organizations not only detect and address vulnerabilities promptly but also maintain comprehensive records and demonstrate adherence to security best practices. By adopting a proactive and systematic approach to vulnerability management, organizations can protect sensitive data, avoid penalties, and strengthen their overall security posture.

Auditing Vulnerability Management Processes

Regular auditing of vulnerability management processes is essential for ensuring that organizations are not only adhering to internal security policies but also meeting the requirements set forth by regulatory bodies. During an audit, vulnerability management practices are scrutinized to ensure proper documentation, risk assessments, and remediation actions are being performed.

1. **Documentation of Scans and Risk Assessments:**
    - Auditors will review the records of vulnerability scans to ensure that they are conducted regularly and cover the entire network and systems, including critical infrastructure and applications. The results of these scans must be documented

in detail, showing which vulnerabilities were identified, their severity, and which systems were affected.

- In addition to scan results, auditors will also review risk assessment documentation to ensure that vulnerabilities are being evaluated appropriately based on the potential impact they could have on the organization's security posture, assets, and data. This assessment must consider factors such as exploitability, asset value, and exposure to external threats.

2. **Documentation of Remediation Actions:**

    - For each vulnerability identified, auditors will examine the remediation actions taken by the organization. This includes reviewing patch management records, configuration changes, and any other mitigation measures applied to address vulnerabilities. Documentation should provide a clear timeline of when vulnerabilities were identified, what actions were taken, and when the issue was resolved.

    - Remediation actions must be timely and appropriate. Delays in patching, failure to mitigate known vulnerabilities, or ineffective remediation efforts can lead to compliance issues and security risks.

3. **Demonstrating Compliance During Audits:**

    - To pass audits, organizations must demonstrate that their vulnerability management processes are robust and effective. This involves not only providing evidence of compliance with regulatory requirements but also showing that the organization is proactive in managing vulnerabilities. Comprehensive reports, such as vulnerability assessment findings, risk management documents, and evidence of remediation actions, are crucial for this purpose.

    - **Continuous Improvement**: Auditors may also review how the organization learns from past vulnerabilities and applies this knowledge to improve its vulnerability management practices over time. Continuous improvement is a key component of many regulatory frameworks, such as NIST, which emphasizes the importance of adapting vulnerability management processes to meet evolving threats.

Vulnerability management is critical for ensuring that an organization complies with regulatory requirements and maintains a secure environment. Compliance frameworks such as PCI DSS, HIPAA, and NIST provide specific guidance on how vulnerabilities should be managed, from identification to remediation. Organizations must ensure they meet these requirements by conducting regular vulnerability scans, performing risk assessments, and addressing weaknesses promptly. Auditing these processes ensures accountability and demonstrates to regulators that security measures are being followed. By integrating vulnerability management with compliance efforts, organizations can strengthen their security posture and avoid costly legal and operational consequences.

Continuous Vulnerability Management

In today's rapidly changing cybersecurity landscape, vulnerabilities are constantly emerging. Threat actors continuously develop new methods of exploiting weaknesses in systems, applications, and networks. This necessitates an ongoing, proactive approach to vulnerability management. Continuous vulnerability management ensures that an organization can rapidly identify, assess, and remediate vulnerabilities before they can be exploited. This section explores why continuous vulnerability management is essential, strategies for implementing it, and how it can be integrated with modern software development practices such as DevSecOps.

Why Continuous Management Is Necessary

1. **Emergence of New Vulnerabilities:**

    - Vulnerabilities are continuously discovered in both new and existing technologies. As systems evolve and software is updated, new security holes are often identified. The National Vulnerability Database (NVD) regularly publishes new Common Vulnerabilities and Exposures (CVEs), which represent potential threats to systems worldwide. Some of these vulnerabilities can be exploited by attackers within hours of being disclosed, so organizations must be vigilant in detecting and addressing these vulnerabilities quickly.

    - Cybersecurity is a moving target, and attackers are always looking for the next weak link in the chain. For this reason, vulnerability management cannot be a one-time or periodic task—it must be a continuous process.

2. **Adapting to Evolving Threats and Environments:**
    - The threat landscape is constantly evolving. New attack techniques, such as zero-day exploits and advanced persistent threats (APTs), can exploit vulnerabilities in unforeseen ways. In addition, the rapid pace of technological change (e.g., cloud adoption, the rise of IoT devices, and the shift to remote work) means that the attack surface of organizations is constantly expanding. Continuous vulnerability management enables organizations to stay ahead of evolving threats by regularly reassessing the security of their systems, networks, and applications.
    - Changes in the environment, such as new software deployments, updates, configuration changes, or the introduction of new technologies, can introduce new vulnerabilities that were previously unknown. Ongoing vulnerability management helps identify and address these weaknesses before they become critical security issues.

Strategies for Continuous Vulnerability Management

1. **Schedule Regular Scans:**
    - To maintain an up-to-date view of their security posture, organizations should schedule regular vulnerability scans across their networks and systems. The frequency of these scans depends on several factors, including the size of the

CHAPTER 3   COMPREHENSIVE VULNERABILITY MANAGEMENT

organization, the criticality of systems, and the nature of the threats they face. Typically, scans should be performed at least weekly or monthly, but they can be more frequent in environments with high-risk assets or constantly changing infrastructures.

- Automated vulnerability scanning tools like Nessus, OpenVAS, or Qualys can help organizations schedule scans and generate reports that highlight newly discovered vulnerabilities. These scans should cover all critical assets, including external and internal networks, applications, servers, and endpoints.

2. **Automated Alerting for High-Severity Vulnerabilities:**

    - Not all vulnerabilities are created equal. Some pose an immediate risk to the organization, while others may have minimal impact. To manage vulnerabilities effectively, organizations should implement automated alerting systems that notify the security team of high-severity vulnerabilities (such as critical CVEs) that need immediate attention. Alerts can be configured based on severity scores from frameworks like CVSS (Common Vulnerability Scoring System), which categorizes vulnerabilities based on their exploitability and potential impact.

- Automation helps ensure that no critical vulnerability is overlooked. Alerts can be integrated into a Security Information and Event Management (SIEM) system for real-time monitoring and quicker response times.

3. **Regular Reviews of Vulnerability Management Policies and Processes:**

    - Continuous vulnerability management requires not just regular scans and alerts but also an ongoing evaluation of vulnerability management processes and policies. Organizations should regularly review and update their policies to ensure they reflect the latest industry best practices and compliance requirements.

    - For instance, organizations may need to adjust their remediation timelines or prioritize different types of vulnerabilities as the threat landscape changes. They should also incorporate feedback from previous vulnerability assessments to refine scanning techniques and remediation strategies, improving overall security resilience.

Integration with DevSecOps

DevSecOps (Development, Security, and Operations) is a methodology that integrates security into every stage of the software development life cycle (SDLC). By embedding security directly into the development process, organizations can identify vulnerabilities in code earlier, reducing the risk of security issues making it into production environments.

CHAPTER 3   COMPREHENSIVE VULNERABILITY MANAGEMENT

1. **Embedding Vulnerability Scanning into the Software Development Life Cycle:**

    - Vulnerability management should be integrated into the DevSecOps pipeline to ensure that security is considered at every phase of software development. This allows organizations to detect vulnerabilities early in the development process, before they can be deployed to production.

    - Developers can run automated vulnerability scans on their code as part of their regular workflow. These scans identify coding flaws, misconfigurations, and insecure coding practices that could introduce vulnerabilities into the final application. By addressing these issues during development, organizations can reduce the need for extensive patching and remediation later in the life cycle.

2. **Using Tools for Continuous Application Security Testing:**

    - Several tools can support continuous application security testing in a DevSecOps pipeline. Tools like **OWASP ZAP (Zed Attack Proxy)** can be used to perform dynamic application security testing (DAST), helping to identify vulnerabilities like cross-site scripting (XSS), SQL injection, and other web application vulnerabilities.

    - Additionally, **Static Application Security Testing (SAST)** tools like SonarQube and Checkmarx can be used to analyze source code for vulnerabilities before deployment, while **Software Composition**

Analysis (SCA) tools like Black Duck or WhiteSource can help detect vulnerabilities in third-party libraries and dependencies that might be included in the application.

Continuous vulnerability management is essential for organizations seeking to stay ahead of an ever-changing threat landscape. It ensures that vulnerabilities are identified and remediated as soon as they are discovered, reducing the window of opportunity for attackers. Regular scans, automated alerts, and continuous reviews of vulnerability management processes enable organizations to respond quickly to emerging threats. Integrating vulnerability management with DevSecOps practices further strengthens the security of applications by catching vulnerabilities earlier in the development life cycle. By adopting these strategies, organizations can maintain a strong security posture and ensure they are well-equipped to handle the dynamic challenges of modern cybersecurity.

Metrics and Reporting in Vulnerability Management

Effective metrics and reporting are crucial for tracking the progress and success of vulnerability management efforts. By using well-defined metrics, organizations can measure the efficiency and effectiveness of their vulnerability management program, ensuring that vulnerabilities are identified, remediated, and monitored in a timely and effective manner. Furthermore, actionable reporting helps communicate these results to both technical and non-technical stakeholders, driving accountability and informed decision-making.

CHAPTER 3   COMPREHENSIVE VULNERABILITY MANAGEMENT

Key Vulnerability Metrics

1. **Time to Detect:**

    - *Definition*: Time to Detect (TTD) refers to the amount of time it takes for an organization to identify a vulnerability after it has been introduced or discovered.

    - *Importance*: Reducing the Time to Detect is crucial for minimizing the exposure window of vulnerabilities. Faster detection means quicker mitigation and reduced risk of exploitation.

    - *Measurement*: This can be tracked from the moment a vulnerability is publicly disclosed (for known vulnerabilities) or detected via internal scanning tools and logs (for unknown vulnerabilities).

    - *Example*: An organization could measure TTD by looking at the time between a vulnerability's CVE release and the time it was first detected by the organization's vulnerability management tools.

2. **Time to Remediate:**

    - *Definition*: Time to Remediate (TTR) refers to the time it takes for an organization to resolve or mitigate a vulnerability after it has been identified.

    - *Importance*: A critical metric, TTR directly impacts the organization's overall security posture. The faster vulnerabilities are remediated, the lower the chances of exploitation.

- *Measurement*: TTR can be tracked from the time a vulnerability is identified (either internally or through external sources) to when it is fully addressed, typically through patching, configuration changes, or compensating controls.

- *Example*: An organization might track TTR by recording the time from vulnerability detection to the time the patch is successfully applied or remediation steps are taken.

3. **Patch Compliance Rates:**

    - *Definition*: Patch Compliance Rate refers to the percentage of systems that have received patches within the defined time frame or service level agreement (SLA).

    - *Importance*: High patch compliance rates indicate that an organization is actively keeping its systems up-to-date and addressing vulnerabilities. Low compliance rates may suggest gaps in patch management processes.

    - *Measurement*: Patch compliance can be calculated by dividing the number of systems patched on time by the total number of systems that required patches, then multiplying by 100 to get the percentage.

    - *Example*: If 90 out of 100 systems were patched within the scheduled time frame, the patch compliance rate would be 90%.

4. **Residual Risk Levels:**

    - *Definition*: Residual risk refers to the level of risk remaining after remediation efforts are applied. It is often associated with vulnerabilities that have not been fully addressed or mitigated.

    - *Importance*: Understanding residual risk is crucial for assessing whether an organization has effectively reduced its vulnerability exposure. It helps to identify areas where further work is required to achieve an acceptable risk level.

    - *Measurement*: Residual risk is often calculated by evaluating the number and severity of unaddressed vulnerabilities. This metric can be broken down into categories like critical, high, medium, and low, depending on the severity of the vulnerabilities that remain unaddressed.

    - *Example*: An organization may find that, after applying patches, ten critical vulnerabilities remain, representing the residual risk that needs attention. The severity of these remaining vulnerabilities is compared to the organization's risk tolerance.

Creating Actionable Reports

Reporting is an essential aspect of vulnerability management. The goal is to create reports that are clear, actionable, and relevant for all stakeholders, regardless of their technical expertise. Reports must provide insights into vulnerability trends, highlight key areas of risk, and guide decision-making for remediation efforts.

CHAPTER 3   COMPREHENSIVE VULNERABILITY MANAGEMENT

1. **Tailor Reports for Technical and Non-Technical Stakeholders:**

    - *Technical Stakeholders*: Technical reports should dive deep into the details of vulnerabilities, including specific CVEs, their impact on the organization's infrastructure, and recommended remediation actions. These reports may include tables, system-level breakdowns, and action plans.

    - *Non-Technical Stakeholders*: Non-technical reports should summarize the key findings and present them in an easily understandable format, using language that avoids jargon. High-level summaries, potential business impacts, and risk levels should be communicated clearly.

    - *Example*: A report for technical stakeholders may list specific patches required for critical systems, while a report for executive leadership may highlight the number of unresolved vulnerabilities and the potential business risks associated with delays in patching.

2. **Use Visualizations to Convey Key Findings:**

    - Visualizations make complex vulnerability data more accessible and actionable. Incorporating charts, graphs, and heat maps allows stakeholders to grasp trends, identify patterns, and make informed decisions more quickly.

        - **Pie Charts**: Can represent the proportion of vulnerabilities by severity (critical, high, medium, low), providing a snapshot of risk levels.

- **Heat Maps**: Can be used to show the distribution of vulnerabilities across different systems or departments, highlighting areas of high risk.

- **Trend Analyses**: Line graphs or bar charts that show how vulnerability metrics (e.g., Time to Remediate or Patch Compliance) change over time, demonstrating whether the organization is improving or falling behind.

- *Example*: A heat map could visually show that the majority of high-severity vulnerabilities are concentrated in critical customer-facing systems, allowing decision-makers to prioritize remediation efforts.

3. **Include Trend Analyses to Show Progress Over Time:**

- Trend analysis provides insights into the effectiveness of vulnerability management efforts over time. By tracking metrics like TTD, TTR, and patch compliance rates over weeks, months, or years, organizations can assess whether they are improving in addressing vulnerabilities or facing growing challenges.

- Regular trend analysis also helps to highlight recurring issues or gaps in the vulnerability management process that need to be addressed.

- *Example*: A line graph showing a downward trend in Time to Remediate over the past six months could indicate that the organization is improving in its ability to resolve vulnerabilities quickly. Conversely, if Time to Detect has been rising, it may signal a need to enhance detection capabilities.

Metrics and reporting are crucial components of a successful vulnerability management strategy. By defining and tracking key vulnerability metrics, organizations can gain visibility into the efficiency of their processes, identify areas for improvement, and take proactive steps to reduce their risk exposure. Additionally, creating actionable reports tailored to both technical and non-technical stakeholders ensures that vulnerability management efforts are well-communicated and drive informed decision-making. Visualizations and trend analyses further enhance the effectiveness of reporting by providing clear, actionable insights into the organization's vulnerability landscape. Ultimately, the combination of robust metrics and comprehensive reporting enables organizations to prioritize vulnerabilities and allocate resources effectively, ensuring a more secure and resilient environment.

Chapter Summary

This chapter has provided an in-depth exploration of vulnerability management, emphasizing its crucial role in cybersecurity. Readers have learned the significance of proactively identifying, assessing, and mitigating vulnerabilities in systems, applications, and networks to protect against potential threats. The chapter has covered the essential stages of the vulnerability management life cycle, from asset discovery and vulnerability identification to prioritization and remediation, ensuring that organizations can effectively address and manage vulnerabilities.

CHAPTER 3   COMPREHENSIVE VULNERABILITY MANAGEMENT

Key approaches like risk-based vulnerability management and the integration of patch management practices were discussed, highlighting the importance of balancing resource constraints with risk reduction efforts. Furthermore, continuous vulnerability management was presented as a necessary strategy, as new vulnerabilities emerge daily and organizations must adapt to the evolving threat landscape.

The chapter also examined popular vulnerability scanning tools, techniques for effective reporting, and metrics to measure success, offering practical insights into how cybersecurity professionals can ensure their vulnerability management processes are efficient and aligned with organizational goals. By understanding the complexities of vulnerability management and employing a structured approach, organizations can significantly reduce their attack surface, minimize potential risks, and enhance their overall security posture.

CHAPTER 4

Cybersecurity Data Analysis

In today's cybersecurity landscape, data is a critical asset. Organizations generate vast amounts of data daily, and the ability to properly collect, analyze, and interpret this data is vital for detecting threats, mitigating risks, and enhancing overall security. This chapter explores the foundational role that data plays in cybersecurity analysis and equips readers with the knowledge and skills to effectively leverage it for identifying, understanding, and addressing potential threats.

The chapter covers how cybersecurity analysts work with various types of data—including logs, network traffic, endpoint data, and more—to detect patterns of suspicious activity and identify anomalies that may indicate cyber threats. Central to the process is the ability to normalize disparate data from different sources, ensuring it is usable and comparable. The chapter dives into the tools and methodologies used to analyze and correlate this data, including security information and event management (SIEM) systems, machine learning models, and behavioral analytics.

Throughout the chapter, readers will learn about the key components of data analysis in a cybersecurity context, from data collection and preparation to advanced techniques for event correlation. They will also gain insights into how threat intelligence feeds into data analysis, providing context that enhances the ability to detect, prioritize, and respond to emerging threats. By the end of this chapter, readers will have a solid understanding of how to use data analytics to identify potential security incidents, track attacker behavior, and improve incident response strategies. The goal is to provide a comprehensive approach to cybersecurity data analysis that will empower analysts to make informed, data-driven decisions and fortify defenses against the ever-evolving threat landscape.

Data Collection and Sources

In cybersecurity, data collection is a crucial step in understanding and responding to potential threats. Effective data collection allows organizations to gather relevant information about their IT environment, network activity, and any indicators of compromise (IOCs) that could suggest a security breach. This information serves as the foundation for making informed decisions about how to respond to incidents, improve defenses, and better protect sensitive information. Data sources for cybersecurity can be varied, encompassing everything from system logs and network traffic to endpoint security tools, intrusion detection systems (IDS), and threat intelligence feeds. These sources provide valuable insights into what is happening within a network, helping security teams to detect anomalies, identify malicious activities, and even predict potential threats before they escalate.

To gather actionable and relevant data, organizations must employ a combination of manual and automated methods. Manual methods, such as reviewing logs or conducting vulnerability assessments, are often resource-intensive but can provide in-depth insights when needed. On the other hand, automated systems such as Security Information and Event Management (SIEM) tools, Security Orchestration, Automation and Response (SOAR) platforms, and threat intelligence platforms enable the continuous collection and analysis of data across large networks in real time. These systems help identify trends and patterns in cybersecurity activity, flagging potential issues for investigation. Furthermore, threat intelligence feeds provide information about emerging vulnerabilities, attack techniques, and the tactics used by cybercriminals, allowing organizations to proactively strengthen their defenses. By integrating these diverse data sources, cybersecurity teams can enhance their situational awareness, respond to incidents faster, and reduce their overall risk exposure.

Understanding Data Sources

Cybersecurity analysts gather and process a wide range of data from various sources to detect, analyze, and respond to threats. The more comprehensive and diverse the data, the better the ability to identify patterns, correlations, and anomalies indicative of potential security incidents. Each data source provides unique insights into different aspects of the organization's systems and infrastructure. By collecting data from multiple sources, analysts can develop a more complete view of the environment and improve their ability to detect, investigate, and mitigate threats.

Types of Data Sources

Understanding and utilizing various types of data sources is fundamental in cybersecurity for detecting, analyzing, and responding to threats. These sources provide critical insights into the behavior of systems, networks, and users, enabling organizations to maintain a robust security posture. Below are the key types of data sources commonly leveraged in cybersecurity, along with their unique contributions to threat detection and response.

Logs

Logs are the backbone of cybersecurity analysis, providing detailed records of events and activities within an organization's systems. They capture valuable insights that help analysts monitor, troubleshoot, and identify potential security incidents.

Network Device Logs

Logs from firewalls, routers, and switches are rich in information about the flow of network traffic and potential threats. These logs often include

- **Traffic data:** Details of inbound and outbound connections
- **Access attempts:** Successful and failed login attempts to network devices
- **Security alerts:** Detected anomalies like Distributed Denial of Service (DDoS) attacks, port scans, or attempts to exploit vulnerabilities

By analyzing network device logs, security teams can detect unusual traffic patterns, such as large volumes of traffic to uncommon ports, which might indicate reconnaissance or an active attack.

Server Logs

Server logs provide a comprehensive view of activities occurring on an organization's servers, including

- **Authentication events:** Details about user login attempts and failed authentication

- **Access patterns:** Information on which resources were accessed and by whom

- **Configuration changes:** Records of modifications to critical system settings

These logs are instrumental in identifying unauthorized access, brute force attempts, or privilege escalation by attackers.

Application Logs

Application logs capture activity and errors within software applications. They provide

- **User behavior insights:** Tracking login patterns and actions taken within the application

- **Error reports:** System messages that may indicate software vulnerabilities or ongoing exploitation attempts

- **Transaction records:** Details of completed operations or suspicious activities

Analyzing application logs can help detect signs of account compromise, abuse of application features, or data exfiltration attempts.

Telemetry Data

Telemetry data refers to the continuous flow of information from devices, endpoints, and cloud services, offering real-time insights into system behavior. This data is vital for proactive threat detection and rapid response.

Endpoint Data

Endpoint Detection and Response (EDR) tools collect telemetry from endpoints like laptops, servers, and mobile devices. They provide

- **File activity:** Logs of file executions and modifications
- **Process monitoring:** Details of running processes, including potential malware or ransomware activity
- **System actions:** Logs of actions such as registry changes or administrative tasks.

This telemetry helps analysts spot anomalies like unauthorized software installation or the use of malicious processes for lateral movement.

Cloud Activity Logs

As cloud adoption grows, cloud-based logs are essential for monitoring user and system activity within cloud environments. Examples include

- **API activity:** Logs of API calls and their parameters
- **Resource modifications:** Changes to cloud configurations or deployments
- **Administrative actions:** Records of administrator-level activities

Tools like **AWS CloudTrail** and **Microsoft Azure Monitor** enable organizations to track changes, detect unauthorized access, and mitigate misconfigurations in real time.

Threat Intelligence Feeds

Threat intelligence feeds enrich cybersecurity analysis by providing up-to-date information on known malicious activities and actors. These feeds enhance situational awareness and inform defense strategies.

Real-Time Updates on Malicious Indicators

Threat intelligence feeds deliver actionable data about

- **Malicious IP addresses:** Sources of known attacks or botnet activity
- **Suspicious domains and URLs:** Websites hosting phishing campaigns or malware
- **File hashes:** Indicators of known malware samples

By integrating these indicators into their systems, organizations can block malicious traffic or identify potential compromises faster.

Integration with SIEM Systems

Threat intelligence feeds are often incorporated into **Security Information and Event Management (SIEM)** systems to enable automated threat correlation. This provides

- **Faster detection:** Automatic matching of internal data against external threat indicators
- **Improved context:** Enhanced understanding of suspicious activity through additional threat intelligence

For instance, if a SIEM detects a login attempt from a known malicious IP address, it can trigger an alert, allowing analysts to respond quickly.

By leveraging these data sources—logs, telemetry data, and threat intelligence feeds—cybersecurity professionals gain a multifaceted view of their environment. Logs provide the foundation for retrospective and real-time analysis, telemetry data enables continuous monitoring of system behaviors, and threat intelligence feeds offer critical context for proactive threat detection. Together, these sources form the cornerstone of an effective cybersecurity strategy.

Data Collection Best Practices

Effective data collection is the foundation of cybersecurity analysis. Ensuring that data is accurate, secure, and properly managed enhances the ability to identify and respond to threats. Here are the best practices for collecting cybersecurity data:

Ensure Data Integrity

Maintaining the accuracy and trustworthiness of collected data is paramount for reliable analysis and informed decision-making.

- **Use Secure Communication Protocols:** Data collected from endpoints, network devices, and applications should be transmitted securely to prevent tampering. Protocols such as **syslog over TLS** encrypt log data during transit, safeguarding it from interception or unauthorized modification.

- **Monitor for Anomalies in Data Transfer:** Implement mechanisms to detect irregularities in data transmission, such as sudden data loss or corruption, which could signal potential interference.

- **Implement Checksums or Hashing:** Use cryptographic checksums to verify that data remains unchanged from source to destination, ensuring its integrity.

Centralized Log Collection

Centralizing data collection simplifies analysis and enhances the ability to identify correlations and patterns across the network.

- **Aggregate Logs and Telemetry:** Use centralized tools like **Splunk**, **Elastic Stack**, or **Graylog** to collect logs from diverse sources such as endpoints, servers, firewalls, and cloud platforms. Consolidating these logs in a single repository facilitates efficient querying and analysis.

- **Enable Real-Time Analysis:** Centralized systems allow for real-time monitoring and alerting by analyzing incoming data streams for anomalies or indicators of compromise (IOCs).

- **Ensure High Availability:** Set up redundant or distributed logging systems to ensure continuous data collection, even during hardware failures or maintenance.

Adhere to Regulatory Requirements

Compliance with data privacy and protection regulations is critical to maintaining trust, avoiding legal repercussions, and protecting sensitive information.

- **Understand Applicable Laws:** Identify the specific regulations your organization must comply with, such as:

  - **GDPR (General Data Protection Regulation):** Governs the handling of personal data within the European Union.

  - **CCPA (California Consumer Privacy Act):** Focuses on the protection of consumer data in California.

  - **HIPAA (Health Insurance Portability and Accountability Act):** Regulates the security and privacy of health information in the United States.

- **Minimize Data Collection:** Avoid collecting unnecessary personal or sensitive data to reduce the risk of non-compliance and minimize potential exposure during a breach.

- **Implement Data Encryption:** Encrypt sensitive data at rest and in transit to ensure it remains protected, even if accessed without authorization.

- **Document Processes and Retention Policies:** Maintain clear documentation of data collection, storage, and retention practices to demonstrate compliance during audits.

Why These Practices Matter

Following these best practices ensures that the data collected is reliable, secure, and actionable. A robust data collection process

- Improves the accuracy of threat detection and response by reducing false positives and negatives.

- Enhances the organization's ability to correlate events, identify patterns, and predict emerging threats.

- Reduces risk and demonstrates accountability in protecting sensitive information and adhering to legal obligations.

By prioritizing data integrity, centralization, and compliance, cybersecurity analysts can build a strong foundation for effective threat management and decision-making.

Data Normalization and Parsing

Data normalization is the process of transforming collected data into a consistent format, ensuring that it can be effectively analyzed and correlated across different sources. In the context of cybersecurity, data comes from a variety of sources, such as logs, telemetry, and threat intelligence feeds, and may be formatted differently depending on the device or application generating it. To make sense of this disparate data, normalization is essential. By standardizing and structuring data, analysts can more easily detect trends, patterns, and anomalies that may indicate potential security threats. Without proper normalization, raw data may be difficult to compare, analyze, or integrate, making it challenging to identify and respond to emerging risks.

Steps to Normalize Data

Normalization is a critical step in ensuring data consistency and accuracy in cybersecurity analysis. By standardizing data from diverse sources, analysts can more effectively correlate events, detect anomalies, and derive actionable insights. Below are the key steps involved in normalizing cybersecurity data:

Identify Key Data Fields

The first step in normalization is pinpointing the essential data elements needed for meaningful analysis. These fields serve as the backbone for comparing and correlating information across various systems.

- **Key Fields to Focus On:**
    - **Timestamps:** Record the exact time of events for accurate correlation and timeline construction.
    - **IP Addresses:** Identify source and destination IPs involved in network traffic, which are critical for tracing malicious activity.
    - **Event Types:** Define event categories such as login attempts, file modifications, or firewall blocks to organize and interpret events effectively.
    - **User Identifiers:** Track actions performed by individual users or accounts to identify unauthorized access or insider threats.

- **Consistent Formatting:** Once identified, ensure these fields follow a standardized format. For instance:

  - **Timestamps:** Use a uniform format, such as ISO 8601 (YYYY-MM-DDTHH:MM:SSZ), to eliminate inconsistencies.

  - **IP Addresses:** Represent in standard formats (IPv4 or IPv6) to prevent parsing errors.

Standardize Time Zones to UTC

Time zone variations are a common issue when consolidating logs from systems located in different geographical regions. Without standardization, it's nearly impossible to accurately correlate events.

- **Convert All Timestamps to UTC:** Ensure that all timestamps are aligned to **Coordinated Universal Time (UTC)**. This provides a single, consistent time reference across all data sources.

- **Automate Conversion:** Use scripts or tools to automate time zone normalization. For example:

  - Parse the local time zone metadata from logs.

  - Convert and store timestamps in UTC.

- **Benefits of Time Zone Standardization:**

  - Enables precise correlation of simultaneous events from distributed systems.

  - Reduces confusion during analysis and improves incident response accuracy.

CHAPTER 4   CYBERSECURITY DATA ANALYSIS

Eliminate Duplicate or Irrelevant Entries

Raw data often includes extraneous information that can clutter analysis, slow down processing, and increase storage requirements.

- **Filter Duplicate Records:**
    - Identify and remove multiple identical log entries.
    - Use unique identifiers (e.g., event IDs or hashes) to detect and eliminate redundancies.
- **Discard Irrelevant Logs:**
    - Focus on actionable logs by filtering out debug or verbose entries unless specifically required for a use case.
    - Exclude logs that fall outside the analysis scope, such as test environment data or benign system events.
- **Streamline the Dataset:** By removing unnecessary data, analysts can
    - Reduce noise, improving focus on critical events.
    - Enhance the speed and efficiency of automated analysis tools.

Why Data Normalization Matters

Data normalization ensures consistency, clarity, and efficiency in cybersecurity analysis. By following these steps, analysts can

- Enhance the accuracy of event correlation across systems.

- Enable seamless integration of data from disparate sources.

- Improve the reliability of automated tools, such as SIEM platforms and machine learning models.

Normalization is an essential process that transforms raw, inconsistent data into a powerful asset for detecting and mitigating cybersecurity threats.

Data Parsing Tools

After normalization, parsing is a critical step that extracts and organizes relevant data fields, making it ready for in-depth analysis. Parsing tools streamline this process, transforming raw, unstructured data into structured formats that are easier to analyze. Here are some of the most effective tools and methods for data parsing:

Log Analysis Tools

Log analysis tools are designed to handle large-scale data ingestion and parsing, particularly in environments with high volumes of logs.

- **Overview:**
  - Logstash, a key component of the Elastic Stack, is one of the most commonly used tools in cybersecurity for parsing and processing logs.
  - It ingests data from diverse sources, such as syslog servers, cloud platforms, flat files, and network devices.

- **Features:**
  - **Data Transformation:** Logstash converts raw logs into structured formats like JSON or XML, simplifying further processing and analysis.
  - **Filtering Capabilities:** Analysts can apply filters to extract key fields (e.g., timestamps, IP addresses, user activities) or to format the data consistently.
  - **Scalability:** Built to handle large volumes of logs efficiently, Logstash is well-suited for enterprise environments with extensive logging needs.
  - **Customizable Pipelines:** Logstash supports user-defined rules and filters, enabling tailored data parsing workflows.
- **Benefits:**
  - Speeds up the parsing process by automating the extraction and structuring of log data.
  - Integrates seamlessly with visualization tools like Kibana for real-time monitoring and analysis.

Scripting Languages like Python

Python is a versatile language that excels in creating custom solutions for data parsing, especially for unique or non-standardized data formats.

- **Overview:**
  - Python provides flexibility to handle complex parsing tasks that cannot be easily managed by off-the-shelf tools.

- It is particularly useful for crafting tailored parsing workflows for specific log types, telemetry data, or application logs.

- **Key Libraries:**

  - **Pandas:** Facilitates data manipulation and structuring, offering tools for cleaning and formatting data.

  - **Regex (Regular Expressions):** Allows precise pattern matching and extraction of specific data elements from logs.

  - **PyParsing:** A specialized library for constructing parsers for complex data formats.

- **Applications:**

  - Extracting specific fields from unstructured logs.

  - Automating repetitive parsing tasks across large datasets.

  - Formatting data into structured outputs compatible with SIEM systems or data analysis tools.

- **Benefits:**

  - Highly customizable and adaptable to unique data structures.

  - Provides a cost-effective solution for organizations with specific or evolving data parsing requirements.

  - Enables the automation of routine parsing processes, reducing manual effort and the risk of errors.

Why Parsing Matters in Cybersecurity

Data parsing is a vital process that ensures raw data is transformed into meaningful, structured information. By leveraging tools like Logstash for scalability or Python for customization, cybersecurity analysts can

- Quickly extract actionable insights from large datasets.
- Automate repetitive processes, improving overall efficiency.
- Prepare data for integration with threat detection systems, such as SIEM platforms or threat intelligence tools.

Choosing the right parsing approach depends on the organization's specific needs, data sources, and existing tools. With robust parsing processes in place, analysts can focus more on analyzing data and responding to threats, rather than spending time managing raw, unstructured logs.

Challenges in Data Normalization

Data normalization is a cornerstone of effective cybersecurity analysis, but several challenges can make the process complex and time-consuming. Addressing these issues is critical for ensuring accurate and actionable insights from diverse data sources.

Handling Large Volumes of Data from Diverse Sources

The sheer volume and variety of data generated by modern organizations can overwhelm even well-equipped cybersecurity teams. Logs, telemetry, and event data often originate from a wide range of sources, including

CHAPTER 4   CYBERSECURITY DATA ANALYSIS

firewalls, servers, applications, IoT devices, and cloud platforms. Each of these sources produces data in unique formats, making normalization a significant challenge.

Scalability is a key concern as organizations must manage millions or even billions of logs daily. For real-time threat detection, normalization must occur almost instantly, adding pressure on both tools and infrastructure. Additionally, storing normalized data at scale, while maintaining efficient retrieval capabilities, can require specialized database systems.

To address these issues, organizations can deploy data aggregation platforms like Elastic Stack or Splunk, which are designed to handle high-throughput data ingestion and normalization. Automating data workflows is another crucial step, as it reduces manual effort and ensures timely processing. Cloud-based solutions can help scale resources dynamically to meet growing data demands, ensuring performance and reliability even during peak loads.

Resolving Inconsistencies Caused by Proprietary Log Formats

Many devices and software systems use proprietary log formats, each with unique structures and terminology. This inconsistency makes it challenging to standardize data, as logs from different sources may use varying field names, event descriptions, or formats for timestamps. For example, a firewall might log events differently than a server or application, complicating efforts to correlate data across these systems.

Custom parsing rules are often necessary to extract meaningful information from proprietary log formats. However, creating and maintaining these rules can be labor-intensive, especially as new devices or software updates introduce changes. In addition, the lack of standardization across vendors means that even similar devices from different manufacturers may require entirely different approaches to parsing.

Flexible tools like Logstash can simplify this process by offering customizable filters and parsers for diverse log formats. Encouraging vendors to adopt standard formats, such as Common Event Format (CEF) or JSON, can also reduce the burden of normalizing proprietary logs. For organizations that frequently work with unique log formats, training analysts in scripting and log parsing techniques is essential to build in-house expertise and minimize reliance on external solutions.

Why Addressing These Challenges Matters

Overcoming these challenges in data normalization is critical for effective cybersecurity operations. Properly normalized data allows analysts to correlate events from multiple sources, identify complex attack patterns, and respond to threats more quickly. Streamlined normalization processes also enhance operational efficiency, freeing up resources for proactive security measures.

By implementing advanced tools, embracing automation, and adopting industry standards where possible, organizations can transform data normalization from a bottleneck into a strength. The result is faster threat detection, more accurate analysis, and a cybersecurity posture capable of adapting to the ever-changing landscape of cyber threats.

Data Analysis Techniques: Understanding Cybersecurity Analytics

Cybersecurity analytics is the process of examining data to identify patterns, trends, and anomalies that might indicate potential security threats or attacks. In cybersecurity, data is continuously generated from various sources, such as network traffic, system logs, user behavior, and external threat intelligence feeds. By analyzing this data, security analysts can detect malicious activity, track the progression of attacks, and respond proactively before significant damage occurs. Effective data analysis not only helps in identifying threats but also provides the insights needed for strengthening an organization's overall security posture.

Types of Analysis in Cybersecurity

In cybersecurity, analyzing data effectively requires employing various techniques that allow analysts to identify threats, uncover patterns, and respond to incidents. Each type of analysis serves a unique purpose, contributing to a comprehensive security strategy.

Trend Analysis

Trend analysis focuses on tracking data changes over time to detect patterns or deviations from normal behavior. It's a proactive approach that helps analysts identify ongoing activities or potential threats by observing metrics like login attempts, network traffic, or resource utilization.

For example:

- **Failed Login Attempts**: A gradual increase in failed login attempts over several days may signal a brute-force attack in progress, allowing analysts to intervene before the attacker succeeds.

- **Access to Sensitive Data**: An increase in access requests to restricted areas of a database could point to insider threats or data exfiltration attempts.

Trend analysis often relies on historical baselines, comparing current activity against established norms. A sudden deviation, like a spike in traffic or login failures, can act as an early warning sign, prompting further investigation. By identifying these trends early, organizations can mitigate threats before they escalate into major incidents.

Anomaly Detection

Anomaly detection identifies behaviors or activities that deviate from expected norms. This method is particularly effective for spotting unknown threats, such as zero-day attacks, that lack established signatures.

Techniques include:

- **Statistical Models**: These models create baselines of normal activity. For instance, if an organization typically sees 200 login attempts per day, a sudden surge to 1,000 attempts—especially from unusual locations—would trigger an alert.

- **Machine Learning**: Algorithms like clustering and classification adapt to evolving environments, identifying patterns and outliers. These tools can detect activities like malware communicating with command-and-control servers or users accessing systems outside of their typical behavior.

Anomaly detection is invaluable for uncovering subtle or hidden threats, such as privilege escalation, lateral movement within a network, or unauthorized access after-hours. By flagging unusual patterns, it enables faster responses to emerging threats.

Correlation Analysis

Correlation analysis connects events from multiple data sources to reveal broader patterns or attack chains. Cyber threats often involve a sequence of actions spread across different systems, making correlation crucial for identifying complex attacks.

Consider these examples:

- **Data Exfiltration**: A single event, like downloading a file, might seem benign. However, when correlated with privilege escalation and an outbound connection to an unknown server, it may indicate data theft.

- **Account Compromise**: A pattern involving multiple failed login attempts followed by a successful login, coupled with unusual system commands, can reveal an account takeover.

Correlation analysis is particularly effective against multistage attacks, such as Advanced Persistent Threats (APTs). By connecting seemingly unrelated events, analysts can uncover the entire attack path, enabling a comprehensive response that disrupts the attacker's strategy.

Why These Methods Matter

Each analysis type offers distinct advantages in strengthening cybersecurity defenses:

- **Trend Analysis** helps identify long-term patterns and emerging threats, aiding in proactive measures.

- **Anomaly Detection** uncovers unexpected behaviors, crucial for spotting new or sophisticated attacks.

- **Correlation Analysis** links disparate events, providing a holistic view of incidents and enabling faster, more accurate threat detection.

Together, these techniques form a robust framework for monitoring, detecting, and responding to cyber threats effectively. By leveraging these analytical methods, organizations can stay ahead of attackers and ensure a resilient security posture.

Visualization Tools

Visualization tools play a critical role in cybersecurity data analysis by helping analysts quickly interpret large volumes of complex data. Visualizing data allows security teams to identify trends, anomalies, and patterns more effectively, facilitating quicker decision-making and response. Several types of visualization tools are commonly used in cybersecurity:

1. **Dashboards in SIEM Platforms:**

    Security Information and Event Management (SIEM) platforms aggregate and analyze logs from multiple sources. Dashboards within these platforms provide real-time views of critical metrics, allowing analysts to monitor the security landscape of their network in an easily digestible format. These dashboards typically feature:

    - **Key performance indicators (KPIs):** Metrics that reflect the security health of the system, such as the number of security events, open tickets, or active threats.
    - **Alerts and incidents:** Visual cues (such as red or yellow warning signs) indicating potential issues like high traffic volume, multiple failed login attempts, or detected malware.

CHAPTER 4 CYBERSECURITY DATA ANALYSIS

- **Trend lines and charts:** A summary of event activity over time, helping analysts identify spikes or unusual patterns in system behavior.

Dashboards enable analysts to quickly identify areas requiring attention, investigate suspicious activity, and respond in a timely manner.

2. **Graphing Tools (e.g., Kibana):**

    Graphing tools like **Kibana** are part of the Elastic Stack and allow analysts to visualize complex relationships between various events. Kibana is particularly effective for mapping relationships between data points, such as user activity, network traffic, and system alerts. For example, an analyst might use Kibana to

    - Create **network flow diagrams** that visualize the interactions between different endpoints and servers, helping to identify unusual connections that could indicate lateral movement by an attacker.

    - Develop **heatmaps or time series plots** that show when anomalies or threats occur, allowing for immediate investigation of events that deviate from normal operating hours.

Graphing tools also provide interactive capabilities, enabling analysts to drill down into specific data points or filter events by severity, type, or source. This functionality helps to refine searches and focus efforts on the most critical incidents.

Cybersecurity data analysis relies on a variety of techniques to detect and respond to potential threats. Trend analysis helps track changes over time, anomaly detection identifies outliers using statistical models or machine learning, and correlation analysis links related events to uncover broader attack patterns. These techniques, combined with powerful visualization tools like dashboards and graphing platforms, enable cybersecurity analysts to stay ahead of evolving threats. By mastering these data analysis techniques, analysts can effectively defend against attacks, improve incident response times, and enhance the overall security posture of their organization.

Event Correlation

Event correlation is the process of connecting various data points or security events that, when analyzed in isolation, might appear unrelated but, when viewed together, form a complete picture of a potential security incident or attack. This technique helps security analysts discern patterns and relationships between events across different systems, which is critical in identifying complex threats that span multiple stages or attack vectors. By correlating data from different sources, such as network traffic logs, user behavior, and system alerts, analysts can uncover hidden threats that might not be visible through individual event logs alone.

Event correlation is essential for improving the effectiveness of Security Information and Event Management (SIEM) systems, where raw data is transformed into actionable intelligence. It allows cybersecurity professionals to recognize not just isolated incidents, but the full attack life cycle—enabling faster identification and mitigation of attacks.

Use Cases for Correlation Analysis

Correlation analysis is a critical component of cybersecurity, enabling analysts to connect seemingly unrelated events to detect and mitigate threats more effectively. Here are two key use cases where event correlation plays a pivotal role:

Detecting Multistage Attacks

Multistage attacks unfold over time, involving several distinct phases that, when viewed in isolation, may not appear malicious. Correlation analysis helps piece together these events, revealing the full attack sequence.

Example: Phishing to Malware Deployment

- **Stage 1: Phishing Email**

    A user receives an email containing a malicious link or attachment. The user clicks it, unknowingly initiating the attack.

- **Stage 2: Malware Installation**

    The link triggers the download of malware onto the user's system, which then attempts to establish communication with a command-and-control (C2) server.

- **Stage 3: Malicious Activity**

    The malware may begin lateral movement, privilege escalation, or data exfiltration.

Correlation in Action:

While each stage might generate separate logs—email delivery, file download, unusual network activity—correlating these events allows analysts to recognize the attack chain. This early detection enables them to block the malware's communication, isolate affected systems, and prevent further damage.

CHAPTER 4   CYBERSECURITY DATA ANALYSIS

Identifying Lateral Movement

Once an attacker gains a foothold within a network, they often attempt lateral movement to access higher-value targets. This behavior can be subtle and hard to spot without correlating disparate events.

Example: Tracking Unauthorized Network Access

- **Initial Compromise:**

  An attacker gains access through a compromised user account. A log records a successful login from an unfamiliar location or device.

- **Unusual Access Patterns:**

  The same account accesses sensitive systems or files not typically used by the compromised user.

- **Privilege Escalation or Remote Access:**

  The attacker uses remote tools or requests elevated permissions to gain deeper network control.

Correlation in Action:
By linking these events—unusual logins, access to sensitive data, and privilege escalation attempts—analysts can uncover lateral movement. This allows them to respond quickly, such as locking down accounts, investigating affected systems, and isolating compromised segments of the network.

The Importance of Correlation in Cybersecurity

Without correlation, these attack scenarios might go unnoticed until significant damage is done. Correlation analysis enables

- **Proactive Detection:** Recognizing the early stages of an attack chain.

- **Contextual Insights:** Understanding the broader narrative of an incident rather than isolated events.

- **Faster Response Times:** By identifying patterns and connections, analysts can respond with precision to halt attacks in progress.

By leveraging correlation tools and techniques, organizations can strengthen their defenses against both simple and complex threats, ensuring a more resilient security posture.

Correlation Rules

Event correlation is typically managed through correlation rules in SIEM systems. These rules define the patterns of behavior or conditions that should trigger alerts when detected. By setting up rules, analysts can automate the process of identifying suspicious behavior across multiple data sources, reducing the need for manual intervention and increasing the speed at which threats are detected.

For example:

- A rule could be created to flag **multiple failed login attempts** followed by a **successful login** from a different location or device, followed by **unusual file access** or data transfer. This pattern could indicate an attempted brute-force attack followed by account compromise and data exfiltration.

- Another rule might correlate network traffic to a specific **command-and-control (C2) IP address**, with internal host connections attempting to communicate with it, which could indicate a malware infection trying to reach an external server for further instructions.

SIEM platforms use these correlation rules to help filter out normal traffic and focus on genuinely suspicious activity. Rules can be fine-tuned over time based on emerging threat intelligence or specific organizational needs, ensuring that only the most relevant and high-priority incidents are flagged.

Benefits of Event Correlation

Event correlation provides significant advantages in enhancing the efficiency and effectiveness of cybersecurity operations. By connecting related data points across various systems, it enables analysts to better understand potential threats and respond more effectively. Here are two primary benefits:

Reduces Alert Fatigue

One of the most pervasive issues in modern security operations is alert fatigue. Analysts are often inundated with a high volume of alerts, many of which are false positives or low-priority events. This constant barrage can lead to missed critical alerts or delayed responses to genuine threats.

How Event Correlation Helps:

- **Streamlining Alerts:** Correlation tools aggregate related events into a single, actionable alert. For example, rather than receiving separate alerts for a failed login, a suspicious file download, and an attempt to escalate privileges, the system correlates these actions and raises a unified alert indicating potential malicious activity.

- **Prioritizing Critical Threats:** By providing more context for events, correlation helps analysts distinguish between benign anomalies and serious security incidents. This ensures that resources are focused on addressing the most urgent threats.

Real-World Impact:

Instead of investigating dozens of individual alerts, analysts can focus on fewer, high-priority incidents, reducing the cognitive load and increasing operational efficiency. For instance, an alert triggered by a single failed login might typically be ignored, but when correlated with abnormal system behavior, it points to a potentially serious threat requiring immediate action.

Enhances Situational Awareness

Situational awareness is critical for understanding the broader context of security incidents. Event correlation enables security teams to see the full narrative behind detected anomalies, rather than viewing them as isolated occurrences.

How Event Correlation Helps:

- **Building a Comprehensive View:** By connecting events across multiple systems—such as login attempts, file access, and network traffic—correlation tools create a cohesive picture of ongoing activity. For instance, several failed login attempts from different IP addresses followed by a privileged account login could signal a brute-force attack that succeeded in compromising an account.

- **Identifying Patterns:** Correlation uncovers patterns that might otherwise remain hidden, such as a coordinated attack spanning multiple systems or regions.

- **Improved Decision-Making:** With a clearer understanding of an incident's scope and context, security teams can make more informed decisions about threat mitigation and prioritize actions effectively.

Real-World Impact:

Enhanced situational awareness allows analysts to identify complex attack vectors, such as multistage or coordinated attacks. This insight enables faster responses, minimizing potential damage and reducing downtime.

Strengthening the Security Posture

The benefits of event correlation extend far beyond individual incidents:

- **Improved Detection Accuracy:** By linking related events, correlation reduces false positives and ensures analysts focus on real threats.

- **Faster Incident Response:** Context-rich alerts allow teams to act quickly and decisively.

- **Better Resource Allocation:** Analysts can concentrate on high-priority issues, optimizing team efficiency.

By reducing alert fatigue and enhancing situational awareness, event correlation empowers organizations to strengthen their defenses against increasingly sophisticated cyber threats. This results in a more resilient and proactive security posture, better equipped to protect critical assets.

Data Enrichment

Data enrichment is the process of enhancing raw data by adding additional context or information that helps to clarify its significance. In cybersecurity, raw event logs, network traffic data, or security alerts often lack the full context needed to determine whether they represent a threat. Data enrichment involves integrating external or supplementary information to make the data more actionable, enabling better detection, analysis, and response to potential security incidents. This can be done through a variety of techniques, each adding specific value to the security analysis process by improving the precision and effectiveness of threat detection.

By augmenting raw data with enriched information, security teams can better understand the nature of potential threats, correlate data from multiple sources, and make informed decisions about how to address vulnerabilities and attacks.

Enrichment Techniques in Cybersecurity

Data enrichment plays a crucial role in enhancing security by providing additional context to raw event data. This added information helps security teams detect threats more accurately, respond more effectively, and reduce false positives. Below are three key enrichment techniques:

Geo-IP Data

Geo-IP data helps cybersecurity teams pinpoint the physical location of an IP address, allowing them to determine if a connection is coming from an unusual or high-risk region. For instance, if an employee typically logs in from California but a login attempt is made from an IP address in a foreign country like Russia or China, this inconsistency raises a red flag. By linking geographic location to network activity, Geo-IP data helps detect potentially suspicious behavior faster.

Benefits:

- Identifies login attempts or access from unexpected or risky locations.

- Highlights potential threats from regions with higher rates of cybercrime.

- Adds critical context to otherwise mundane network events, enabling quicker responses.

Threat Intelligence Integration

Threat intelligence feeds provide up-to-date information on known malicious activities, such as IP addresses, domains, and file hashes associated with cyber threats. When event data is enriched with threat intelligence, analysts can immediately recognize if the activity involves known bad actors or malicious infrastructure. For example, if a network connection originates from an IP address tied to a botnet or a domain linked to ransomware distribution, security teams can prioritize these incidents and mitigate the risk before it spreads.

Benefits:

- Speeds up the identification of known threats, allowing for faster responses.

- Helps teams correlate suspicious activity with established attack patterns.

- Reduces the workload by prioritizing high-risk incidents based on historical data.

DNS Analysis

DNS analysis focuses on examining domain name queries to detect malicious behaviors like fast flux or domain generation algorithms (DGAs). Fast flux is a tactic used by cybercriminals to rapidly change IP addresses associated with a domain, making it harder to track or block malicious activity. By analyzing DNS queries, analysts can spot patterns that may indicate botnet activity or phishing campaigns.

For example, if a domain is frequently resolving to a new IP address every few minutes, it's likely employing fast flux. This behavior is often tied to phishing campaigns, and early detection can help security teams block these domains and prevent further attacks.

Benefits:

- Detects malicious domains that frequently change IP addresses to evade detection.

- Identifies botnet activity or other patterns indicative of ongoing attacks.

- Helps prevent attacks like phishing and malware distribution by blocking suspicious domains.

Benefits of Data Enrichment

Data enrichment offers several advantages that significantly improve the efficiency of cybersecurity operations. By adding context to raw data, organizations can enhance threat detection, reduce false positives, and enable more targeted responses.

Improved Threat Detection Accuracy

Enriching raw event data helps security teams identify suspicious activity with greater precision. For example, a network connection that might appear normal on its own becomes suspicious when enriched with geo-IP data showing it originates from a high-risk country. This added context ensures that security alerts are more accurate and relevant, improving the reliability of threat detection systems.

How It Helps:

- Reduces false positives by adding valuable context to raw data.

- Enables the identification of subtle threats that would otherwise go unnoticed.

- Enhances the precision of detection, making alerting systems smarter and more effective.

Actionable Insights for Incident Response

Data enrichment provides incident response teams with crucial context, enabling them to make informed decisions about how to handle a potential threat. With enriched data, teams can quickly assess if an alert is part of a larger campaign or tied to known threat actors. For instance, if a suspicious login attempt is linked with a reputation score of a malicious IP, teams can act faster, isolating a compromised system or blocking the malicious connection.

How It Helps:

- Speeds up decision-making by providing more comprehensive information.

- Allows for quicker identification of high-priority threats based on historical data.

- Improves incident handling by helping teams choose the most effective response actions, such as blocking or isolating compromised systems.

Data enrichment significantly enhances an organization's ability to detect, analyze, and respond to cybersecurity threats. By adding context to raw event data—whether through geo-IP data, threat intelligence feeds, or DNS analysis—security teams can more accurately identify malicious activities and take immediate action. The result is a more proactive and effective defense, capable of staying ahead of evolving threats and minimizing potential damage. With enriched data, organizations can detect and mitigate cyber risks faster, ultimately strengthening their overall security posture.

Machine Learning in Cybersecurity Analysis

Machine learning (ML) plays a significant role in modern cybersecurity analysis by enhancing the capabilities of traditional methods. It enables cybersecurity professionals to automate the detection of anomalies and predict potential threats, which is especially useful given the scale and complexity of today's cyber environments. ML algorithms process vast amounts of data quickly and can identify patterns that might otherwise be overlooked. The ability to automate these processes leads to more efficient and accurate identification of security risks and significantly reduces the workload on security teams.

In cybersecurity, machine learning is particularly valuable for real-time monitoring, automated threat detection, and threat prediction. ML models help security systems evolve by continuously learning from new data, adapting to emerging threats, and improving detection accuracy over time. The combination of ML's data-driven approach with human expertise results in a dynamic and responsive security infrastructure.

Common ML Applications in Cybersecurity

Machine Learning (ML) is transforming the cybersecurity landscape by enabling organizations to detect threats, predict attacks, and respond more effectively. Below are some key ML applications:

Behavioral Analytics

ML-driven behavioral analytics involves monitoring user and system activities to detect deviations from normal behavior. By continuously learning usual activity patterns, ML models can flag unusual or risky behaviors, allowing early detection of potential threats, such as insider attacks, privilege escalation, or account compromise.

Example: If an employee typically accesses their work environment from the office but suddenly logs in at odd hours from an external location, this deviation from their usual behavior can be flagged by an ML algorithm. Such behavior could suggest account compromise or unauthorized access.

Predictive Models

Predictive models use historical data to forecast potential attack trends. These models analyze past incidents to identify patterns and anticipate future threats, such as new attack techniques or emerging vulnerabilities. Predictive analytics help cybersecurity professionals prepare defenses proactively and reduce the risk of future attacks.

Example: An ML model could analyze past attack data to predict spikes in specific types of ransomware or phishing attacks based on seasonal trends or changes in industry behavior. This allows security teams to strengthen defenses before these attacks peak, potentially preventing them.

Supervised vs. Unsupervised Learning in Cybersecurity

Machine learning in cybersecurity typically falls into two categories: supervised and unsupervised learning. Each has distinct applications and advantages.

Supervised Learning

In supervised learning, ML models are trained using labeled datasets, where each input data point is already associated with the correct output. This allows the model to learn by linking inputs with known results, making it effective for tasks like phishing detection or malware classification.

Example: A supervised learning model for email filtering might be trained on a dataset containing labeled emails (e.g., phishing vs. legitimate). Using features like sender email addresses, subject lines, and content, the model can classify future emails, improving detection accuracy over time.

Unsupervised Learning

Unsupervised learning involves analyzing data without labeled examples. Instead, the model groups similar data points to find patterns, which is particularly useful for detecting unknown threats or new attack patterns. Since it does not require prior knowledge of specific attacks, it is valuable in identifying evolving or previously unseen vulnerabilities.

Example: An unsupervised learning model analyzing network traffic could detect unusual patterns, such as a sudden spike in data from a specific IP address. This could indicate a potential denial-of-service (DoS) attack or a hidden data exfiltration attempt, even if the attack technique hasn't been previously encountered.

CHAPTER 4　CYBERSECURITY DATA ANALYSIS

Challenges in ML Adoption for Cybersecurity

While ML offers significant benefits, its adoption in cybersecurity comes with some challenges that organizations must address to maximize its effectiveness.

Need for High-Quality, Labeled Data

For supervised learning to be effective, it requires high-quality, labeled data. Collecting and labeling large datasets for tasks like identifying specific malware types or phishing attempts is time-consuming and resource-intensive. Moreover, the quality of the data directly impacts the model's performance. Poor data quality can lead to ineffective models, missing threats or generating false positives.

Risk of False Positives or False Negatives

ML models can produce false positives (incorrectly flagging legitimate actions as malicious) or false negatives (failing to identify actual threats). Balancing the sensitivity of the model to avoid both types of errors is essential for effectiveness. Continuous monitoring, proper tuning, and regular updates are necessary to minimize these risks.

Example: A predictive model for detecting abnormal network traffic could flag legitimate traffic during peak business hours as suspicious (false positive) or fail to detect a sophisticated attack that mimics normal traffic patterns (false negative). Striking the right balance between sensitivity and specificity is critical for practical application.

Machine learning plays a vital role in modern cybersecurity by enhancing threat detection, anticipating future attacks, and identifying previously unknown vulnerabilities. By applying techniques like behavioral analytics and predictive models, ML empowers organizations

CHAPTER 4 CYBERSECURITY DATA ANALYSIS

to respond more effectively to a wide range of threats. While supervised and unsupervised learning offer distinct advantages for different types of analysis, challenges like the need for high-quality data and managing false positives remain. By understanding these challenges and refining ML models, organizations can leverage the full potential of machine learning to bolster their security posture and stay ahead of evolving cyber threats.

Using SIEM and Analytics Tools

Security Information and Event Management (SIEM) solutions are critical tools in modern cybersecurity defense. They aggregate, normalize, and analyze security data from various sources—such as network devices, servers, applications, and endpoints—to provide a comprehensive view of an organization's security environment. SIEM systems allow security teams to collect logs and events in real time, correlate these events to identify potential threats, and produce actionable alerts and reports. By consolidating security data from disparate sources into a unified interface, SIEM tools improve situational awareness and provide an invaluable resource for incident detection and response.

The primary goal of SIEM is to enable security teams to quickly identify, investigate, and respond to security incidents by offering a centralized platform that allows for more efficient and effective management of security events. SIEMs are typically used for compliance reporting, threat detection, and advanced incident response.

Popular SIEM Platforms

Security Information and Event Management (SIEM) platforms play a crucial role in cybersecurity by providing centralized monitoring and analysis of security events across an organization. Several leading SIEM

CHAPTER 4 CYBERSECURITY DATA ANALYSIS

platforms are widely adopted due to their features, scalability, and effectiveness in threat detection and response. Below are some of the most popular SIEM solutions:

> **Splunk:** Splunk is widely recognized as one of the most powerful SIEM platforms, offering robust capabilities for searching, monitoring, and analyzing machine data in real time. It excels in handling large volumes of log data and provides customizable dashboards, reporting, and visualization tools to help organizations monitor their IT environment. Splunk's versatility makes it suitable for organizations of all sizes, enabling them to aggregate logs from various systems, detect anomalies, and troubleshoot security incidents effectively. It also supports advanced machine learning for threat detection and automated responses, making it a top choice for organizations that require real-time insight into their cybersecurity posture.
>
> **IBM QRadar:** IBM QRadar is a comprehensive and scalable SIEM solution that integrates data collection, normalization, and analysis. It stands out for its strong event correlation capabilities, allowing security teams to link and analyze security events from disparate sources, thereby uncovering sophisticated threats. QRadar is known for its effective use of advanced analytics and artificial intelligence (AI) to detect, investigate, and respond to security incidents. It offers excellent support for compliance reporting, which is essential for industries with strict regulatory requirements.

QRadar's integration with other IBM security solutions further strengthens its ability to provide an end-to-end security operations platform, making it a popular choice for large enterprises with complex IT environments.

Microsoft Sentinel: Microsoft Sentinel is a cloud-native SIEM solution that leverages the capabilities of the Azure platform. Sentinel is designed to integrate seamlessly with Microsoft services and third-party tools, making it particularly suitable for organizations that already rely on Microsoft's cloud ecosystem. Sentinel uses machine learning to identify anomalies, detect threats, and automate responses across hybrid and cloud environments. Its integration with Azure Security Center enhances its visibility into cloud infrastructure, while its centralized data storage and analysis capabilities streamline security monitoring. Sentinel's ability to scale with organizations' cloud infrastructure makes it an attractive choice for businesses with significant cloud investments or those undergoing digital transformation.

Elastic SIEM: Elastic SIEM is an open-source solution built on the Elastic Stack (ELK Stack), which includes Elasticsearch, Logstash, and Kibana. It allows organizations to ingest, store, and analyze large volumes of security data in real time. Elastic SIEM is highly flexible and scalable, making it suitable for a variety of organizations, from small businesses to large enterprises. Because it is open-source, it offers an affordable and customizable alternative to proprietary SIEM platforms, with the added advantage of a vibrant community and strong developer support. Elastic SIEM provides powerful search and analytics capabilities, allowing security teams to monitor and respond to security events effectively.

Key SIEM Features

SIEM platforms are equipped with a range of features that enable them to collect, analyze, and respond to security incidents. Some of the most important features include

1. **Centralized Log Management:** One of the primary functions of SIEM platforms is the aggregation and management of logs from multiple sources, including servers, firewalls, endpoints, and network devices. Centralized log management simplifies the collection, normalization, and storage of log data, ensuring it is in a standardized format for easier analysis. By centralizing logs, SIEM systems can identify patterns across the network, facilitating faster detection of security incidents and enabling more effective investigations.

2. **Real-Time Alerting and Reporting:** SIEM systems are continuously monitoring the organization's environment for suspicious activity. When an event or anomaly is detected, SIEM platforms generate real-time alerts that notify security teams, enabling prompt investigation and response. Many SIEM solutions also offer robust reporting features,

allowing teams to create customizable reports for security metrics, compliance documentation, and executive summaries. These reports help inform decision-making and demonstrate compliance with regulatory frameworks such as HIPAA, GDPR, or PCI-DSS.

3. **Event Correlation and Threat Detection:** Event correlation is one of the most critical features of a SIEM solution. It allows the platform to aggregate logs from multiple sources and link seemingly unrelated events to identify potential threats. For example, a SIEM might correlate several failed login attempts followed by a successful login from a new IP address, signaling a brute-force attack. Advanced correlation capabilities help detect complex, multistage attacks that would otherwise go unnoticed, making it possible to respond to threats before they escalate into major incidents.

Implementing SIEM Effectively

While SIEM platforms provide powerful security monitoring and threat detection capabilities, maximizing their effectiveness requires careful planning, configuration, and ongoing management. Here are key considerations for implementing SIEM solutions:

1. **Tailoring Alerts to Minimize False Positives:** One of the biggest challenges organizations face when implementing SIEM solutions is managing the volume of alerts. SIEM platforms often generate a high number of alerts, many of which can be false positives or low-priority events. To address this,

organizations must fine-tune alerting thresholds and correlation rules to reflect their specific environment and threat landscape. This may involve setting severity levels for events, adding context to alerts, and using threat intelligence feeds to refine detection capabilities. Properly configured alerts allow security teams to focus on the most critical issues while minimizing distractions from less impactful events.

2. **Regularly Reviewing and Updating Correlation Rules:** The cybersecurity threat landscape is constantly evolving, with new tactics, techniques, and procedures (TTPs) emerging regularly. To ensure a SIEM system remains effective, it is crucial to periodically review and update the correlation rules that define how events are linked and analyzed. This review process should incorporate feedback from incident response teams, threat intelligence sources, and previous security events. By regularly updating correlation rules and integrating new threat data, organizations can ensure their SIEM platform stays ahead of evolving threats and maintains high detection accuracy.

SIEM platforms are essential for organizations seeking to enhance their cybersecurity posture. By leveraging the capabilities of popular platforms like Splunk, IBM QRadar, Microsoft Sentinel, and Elastic SIEM, businesses can centralize data collection, monitor their network in real time, and respond to security incidents with greater speed and precision. To maximize the effectiveness of these tools, organizations must tailor alerts to minimize false positives, regularly update correlation rules, and continuously adapt their SIEM configurations to reflect the evolving threat landscape. With proper implementation and ongoing management, SIEM solutions provide valuable insights into security operations and play a crucial role in defending against sophisticated cyber threats.

Metrics and Key Performance Indicators (KPIs)

Key Performance Indicators (KPIs) are essential tools for measuring the effectiveness of cybersecurity operations. These metrics allow organizations to gauge their performance in various areas of security, such as threat detection, response times, and operational efficiency. KPIs provide actionable insights that help security teams understand how well their security measures are working, identify areas for improvement, and ensure alignment with broader business objectives.

In cybersecurity, KPIs offer quantifiable data that can guide decision-making and strategic planning. They are invaluable for tracking the effectiveness of security controls, monitoring progress toward security goals, and optimizing resources for better threat mitigation. By establishing and regularly assessing KPIs, organizations can gain a better understanding of their security posture and continuously improve their defense mechanisms.

Examples of Key Metrics

1. **Mean Time to Detect (MTTD):**

    MTTD measures the average time it takes to identify a potential security incident after it has occurred. The ability to quickly detect threats is crucial for minimizing the impact of security breaches. A lower MTTD allows an organization to respond more promptly, reducing the window of opportunity for attackers. Improving MTTD involves optimizing monitoring systems, enhancing alerting mechanisms, and leveraging advanced threat detection technologies, such as machine learning or behavioral analytics, to identify anomalies faster. This metric is vital for any organization looking to improve its proactive security posture and prevent data breaches or other major incidents.

2. **Mean Time to Respond (MTTR):**

    MTTR tracks the average time between detecting a security threat and fully mitigating it. This metric is crucial because it highlights the efficiency of the incident response process. A lower MTTR indicates that an organization is well-prepared to quickly contain and remediate threats. Organizations can improve MTTR by establishing clear, predefined response procedures, automating incident response where possible, and investing in a well-trained security operations team. A rapid and effective response can significantly reduce the potential damage of a security incident and restore normal business operations quickly.

3. **False Positive Rate:**

    The false positive rate measures the proportion of security alerts that are incorrectly flagged as threats. High false positive rates can overwhelm security teams with unnecessary alerts, leading to alert fatigue and increasing the risk of overlooking genuine threats. Reducing the false positive rate is crucial for maintaining the efficiency of a security team. This can be achieved by fine-tuning detection rules, incorporating threat intelligence feeds, and using more precise detection technologies, like behavioral analytics or advanced machine learning models, to better differentiate between real threats and benign activity.

4. **Volume of Processed Logs:**

   This metric tracks the total number of logs processed within a specific time frame, such as daily or weekly. Logs provide invaluable insights into system and network activities, helping to detect suspicious behaviors or anomalies that may indicate a security breach. Monitoring the volume of logs is essential to ensure that the organization's security infrastructure can handle the data load, especially as the volume of data generated by modern IT systems continues to grow. High log volumes might suggest increased network activity, new security tools being implemented, or even an emerging threat. Organizations need scalable SIEM or log management systems to manage these logs effectively without compromising performance.

Using Metrics for Continuous Improvement

1. **Regularly Evaluate and Adjust KPIs to Ensure Alignment with Organizational Goals:**

   As the security landscape evolves and an organization's cybersecurity needs change, KPIs must also adapt. Regularly reviewing and adjusting KPIs ensures they remain aligned with the organization's current goals, risk appetite, and business objectives. For example, if a company is shifting to a hybrid or cloud-based infrastructure, KPIs should focus on cloud security metrics like cloud vulnerability scanning, cloud incident response, or cloud traffic analysis. KPIs should also account for emerging threats, such as new attack vectors, or business initiatives, like mergers or acquisitions, that could affect security priorities. Constant reassessment of KPIs ensures the organization's cybersecurity efforts are focused on the areas that matter most.

2. **Use Metrics to Identify Areas for Optimization in Threat Detection or Incident Response:**

    Metrics provide valuable insights into an organization's security operations and highlight areas that need improvement. For example, if MTTD is consistently high, it could indicate that the threat detection process needs to be enhanced with better tools or refined alerting mechanisms. Similarly, if MTTR is long, the incident response process might be inefficient, requiring automation, more streamlined procedures, or better coordination between teams. Metrics like these act as diagnostic tools, pinpointing bottlenecks and inefficiencies in the system. Once identified, security teams can implement changes, such as automating routine tasks, improving training, or deploying more advanced threat detection technologies, to continuously improve their performance.

3. **Measuring the Impact of Security Investments:**

    One of the most valuable uses of metrics is assessing the effectiveness of new security investments. For instance, after deploying a new SIEM system or improving threat intelligence integration, KPIs such as MTTD, MTTR, and false positive rates can provide immediate feedback on the success of the investment. Metrics help security leaders understand whether these changes are having the desired impact, such as reducing detection times, improving response efficiency, or cutting down on unnecessary alerts. Tracking these metrics over time ensures that security investments deliver measurable improvements and allows teams to justify future expenditures based on their impact on the organization's overall security posture.

Metrics are the foundation of any data-driven approach to cybersecurity. They provide actionable insights into the effectiveness of security programs, helping teams identify areas for improvement and optimize their response to emerging threats. By focusing on key metrics like MTTD, MTTR, false positive rates, and log volume, organizations can enhance their security posture and improve operational efficiency. Moreover, the continuous evaluation and adjustment of KPIs ensure that they remain aligned with evolving business needs and security challenges. Ultimately, metrics are not just about tracking performance; they are about fostering continuous improvement, empowering security teams to stay ahead of evolving cyber threats and better protect organizational assets.

CHAPTER 4   CYBERSECURITY DATA ANALYSIS

Chapter Summary

This chapter dives deeply into the critical processes and tools that form the foundation of effective cybersecurity data analysis, providing cybersecurity analysts with the knowledge and techniques necessary to proactively identify and respond to potential threats. Understanding and mastering the methods of data collection, normalization, analysis, and event correlation equips analysts with the skills to transform raw, disparate data into actionable intelligence. By leveraging a wide range of data sources—including logs, telemetry data, and threat intelligence feeds—analysts can detect irregularities, correlate events, and construct a comprehensive picture of potential security incidents.

The chapter begins by addressing the importance of data collection, emphasizing the variety of data sources available to analysts, such as logs from network devices, servers, and applications, as well as telemetry data from endpoints and cloud services. These data sources provide the raw material needed for detecting potential threats and vulnerabilities. Best practices for data collection are outlined, such as ensuring data integrity, centralizing logs for efficient analysis, and adhering to regulatory compliance standards, all of which ensure that the data is reliable and useful.

Next, the chapter explores data normalization and parsing techniques, which are essential for transforming raw, inconsistent data into a standardized format. By normalizing data, analysts can eliminate duplicates, resolve inconsistencies, and streamline the process of identifying key data points. Tools like Logstash and custom parsing scripts are introduced as solutions for dealing with large volumes of varied data, which often come from proprietary formats and systems. Overcoming the challenges of data normalization is vital for analysts to efficiently analyze and draw conclusions from diverse sources of information.

The chapter then shifts focus to the core of cybersecurity analysis: data analysis techniques. Analysts must apply sophisticated methods such as trend analysis, anomaly detection, and correlation analysis to

CHAPTER 4   CYBERSECURITY DATA ANALYSIS

identify patterns of behavior and deviations from normal activity. These techniques allow analysts to detect malicious behavior, anticipate potential security incidents, and trace the root causes of threats. Trend analysis helps identify changes over time, while anomaly detection uses statistical models or machine learning to spot outliers. Correlation analysis connects related events and actions, providing a clearer picture of how threats might unfold, such as detecting multistage attacks or lateral movement within a network.

Event correlation is then discussed as a pivotal technique in cybersecurity analysis. Correlating events involves identifying and linking disparate data points to form a cohesive picture of an attack. This is especially useful for detecting advanced persistent threats (APTs) or multistage attacks, where the threat actor's actions unfold across different phases. The chapter explores how Security Information and Event Management (SIEM) systems play a crucial role in automating the event correlation process. Analysts can set up rules within SIEMs to flag suspicious patterns, enabling faster detection and response. This automated correlation of events reduces alert fatigue and enhances situational awareness by providing additional context for detected anomalies.

Furthermore, data enrichment is highlighted as a critical component of cybersecurity data analysis. Enriching raw data with additional context—such as Geo-IP data, threat intelligence feeds, and DNS analysis—helps analysts improve the accuracy of threat detection and gain deeper insights into the nature of potential threats. Enriched data provides actionable intelligence that can support faster and more accurate decision-making during the incident response process, especially when dealing with complex threats such as fast-flux domains or known malicious IP addresses.

The chapter also addresses the role of machine learning (ML) in enhancing cybersecurity data analysis. Machine learning algorithms automate the process of detecting anomalies and predicting potential attacks. The use of behavioral analytics, predictive models, and both supervised and unsupervised learning techniques allows analysts to detect hidden threats more effectively. While supervised learning leverages labeled datasets to train algorithms (e.g., detecting phishing emails), unsupervised learning can identify unknown threats by discovering patterns in data without predefined labels. However, challenges such as the need for high-quality data and the risk of false positives or negatives are also discussed, providing a balanced view of ML's capabilities in cybersecurity.

Finally, the chapter explores the use of SIEM and analytics tools, which are central to the cybersecurity analysis process. SIEM platforms such as Splunk, IBM QRadar, and Microsoft Sentinel offer powerful features for centralized log management, real-time alerting, event correlation, and threat detection. These tools enable analysts to collect, process, and analyze vast amounts of data from diverse sources, ensuring a comprehensive view of the organization's security posture. By tailoring SIEM configurations to minimize false positives and regularly updating correlation rules, organizations can maintain a responsive and adaptive security environment.

Overall, this chapter underscores the importance of data analysis in the cybersecurity domain. By mastering the tools and techniques of data collection, normalization, analysis, and enrichment, cybersecurity analysts can uncover hidden threats, respond to incidents more effectively, and make informed decisions to strengthen an organization's security defenses. The integration of advanced tools, including SIEM systems and machine learning models, further empowers analysts to detect and mitigate evolving threats, ensuring the resilience and protection of the organization's digital infrastructure. Through a detailed understanding of these processes, analysts can turn raw data into invaluable intelligence, providing the foundation for robust and adaptive cybersecurity strategies.

CHAPTER 5

Security Operations and Monitoring

Security operations and monitoring are the foundation of an organization's cybersecurity framework, enabling the detection, response, and recovery from security incidents. This chapter provides a thorough examination of the core elements involved in security operations, with a focus on logging, monitoring, incident detection, and response. These elements play a crucial role in maintaining a secure environment by providing real-time visibility into potential threats, enabling swift action to mitigate risks.

A key focus of this chapter is the Security Operations Center (SOC), which serves as the central hub for monitoring and managing an organization's security posture. The SOC is tasked with analyzing logs, detecting anomalies, and responding to incidents promptly to minimize the impact on the organization. Through detailed discussions, readers will learn how SOCs leverage a combination of technology, processes, and skilled personnel to monitor networks, systems, and applications for signs of malicious activity.

The chapter also delves into the tools and technologies used for security monitoring, including Security Information and Event Management (SIEM) systems, intrusion detection systems (IDS), and intrusion prevention systems (IPS). These tools help SOC teams' aggregate data, correlate events, and generate alerts based on predefined rules,

CHAPTER 5 SECURITY OPERATIONS AND MONITORING

ensuring that potential threats are detected and addressed quickly. Readers will gain insight into how these systems are configured, tuned, and integrated into an organization's overall cybersecurity strategy.

Further, this chapter covers incident response techniques, emphasizing the need for preparedness and agility in the face of security incidents. Incident response involves identifying, containing, eradicating, and recovering from security events, and having a well-defined incident response plan is crucial for minimizing damage and restoring operations as quickly as possible. Additionally, the importance of continuous monitoring is highlighted, stressing that security is an ongoing process and must be actively maintained to stay ahead of emerging threats.

Through practical examples and case studies, readers will gain a deep understanding of how security operations and monitoring play a pivotal role in a proactive cybersecurity strategy. This chapter equips readers with the knowledge and tools necessary to develop effective security operations and response mechanisms, ensuring that an organization remains resilient to cyber threats.

Logging and Log Management

Logs are the cornerstone of effective cybersecurity monitoring, providing detailed records of events across systems, applications, and networks. Properly managing these logs ensures an organization can track activities, diagnose technical issues, detect anomalies, and respond swiftly to security incidents.

What Are Logs?

Logs are records of events generated by systems, applications, and devices. They serve as a historical record of activities and are instrumental in troubleshooting issues, investigating incidents, and meeting compliance requirements. Logs typically include timestamps, event descriptions, and details about the source or actor involved.

Types of Logs

Logs are a critical source of information for monitoring, diagnosing, and securing IT environments. Different types of logs offer unique insights into specific aspects of an organization's systems and networks:

1. **System Logs:**

    System logs capture events related to an operating system's core functionality, including system startups and shutdowns, hardware errors, software crashes, and user login activities. These logs help administrators monitor the stability and performance of their systems.

    - **Examples:** Windows Event Logs, Linux Syslogs

2. **Application Logs:**

    Application logs record events specific to software applications, such as transaction processing, configuration changes, user interactions, and error occurrences. These logs are indispensable for troubleshooting application issues and optimizing performance.

    - **Examples:** Logs generated by database systems, web servers like Apache or Nginx, and business applications

3. **Security Logs:**

   Security logs focus on events that pertain to the protection of systems and data. These logs include authentication attempts, access control changes, malware detections, and file access activities. Security logs are essential for identifying potential threats and ensuring compliance with regulations.

   - **Examples:** Firewall logs, intrusion detection system (IDS) logs, antivirus activity logs

4. **Network Logs:**

   Network logs document communications between devices within a network, capturing data such as traffic flow, connection requests, DNS queries, and protocol activity. These logs play a critical role in detecting anomalies like unauthorized access or data exfiltration.

   - **Examples:** Router logs, DNS logs, VPN connection logs

Log Collection and Aggregation

Effective monitoring requires collecting and centralizing logs from various sources to ensure comprehensive visibility:

- **Centralized Log Management Tools:**

  Tools such as Splunk, ELK Stack (Elasticsearch, Logstash, Kibana), and Graylog enable organizations to collect, index, and analyze logs from diverse systems in one unified platform.

- **Aggregation of Logs:**

    Logs from firewalls, routers, servers, endpoints, and cloud services should be aggregated into a single repository. This ensures that all relevant data is available for efficient analysis and correlation.

- **Automated Collection:**

    Automating log collection reduces manual effort and ensures consistent, real-time updates, enabling proactive monitoring of security events.

Importance of Log Correlation

Log correlation involves analyzing events across multiple sources to identify patterns, relationships, and unusual activities:

- **Enhanced Threat Detection:**

    Correlating logs allows security teams to uncover threats that may not be apparent when viewing logs in isolation. For example, multiple failed login attempts across different devices, followed by a successful one, could indicate a brute force attack.

- **Faster Incident Response:**

    By presenting a unified view of an incident, log correlation accelerates the process of understanding its scope and impact, enabling quicker containment and recovery efforts.

Benefits of Effective Log Management

1. **Proactive Threat Detection:**

   Logs provide the data necessary for identifying potential security issues before they escalate into serious incidents.

2. **Compliance and Auditing:**

   Many regulatory frameworks, such as GDPR, HIPAA, and PCI DSS, mandate the retention and review of logs for specified periods. Effective log management ensures adherence to these requirements.

3. **Incident Forensics:**

   Logs act as a historical record, providing insights into how incidents occurred and guiding the development of strategies to prevent similar events in the future.

Challenges in Log Management

Despite its benefits, log management faces several obstacles:

- **Data Volume:** Modern systems generate massive amounts of log data, making storage and processing challenging.

- **Retention:** Organizations must balance storage costs with compliance requirements for retaining logs over time.

- **Complex Analysis:** Logs from different sources may use varying formats, requiring skilled personnel and robust tools to parse, analyze, and correlate the data effectively.

By mastering log collection, correlation, and management, organizations can significantly enhance their ability to detect, understand, and respond to cyber threats while meeting regulatory and operational demands.

Monitoring and Detection Techniques

Monitoring and detection are essential components of a robust security strategy, enabling organizations to identify and address potential threats before they escalate into significant incidents. This section explores key techniques and approaches used to maintain visibility, detect anomalies, and respond effectively to threats.

Continuous Monitoring

Continuous monitoring involves the proactive oversight of systems, networks, and applications to ensure real-time visibility into potential security events.

- **Purpose:**

    Detect threats early, mitigate risks, and maintain compliance by consistently analyzing activities across the environment.

- **Key Features:**

    - Dashboards that provide a centralized view of security events and metrics.
    - Alerts that notify security teams of suspicious or high-risk activities.

- **Examples of Continuous Monitoring Tools:**

  SIEM platforms like Splunk, LogRhythm, or IBM QRadar, which aggregate and analyze data from diverse sources to detect patterns and anomalies.

Key Monitoring Techniques

1. **Network Monitoring:**

   Analyzes network traffic to detect unusual patterns, such as unexpected spikes in bandwidth usage or unauthorized access attempts.

   - **Tools**: Wireshark, SolarWinds, or IDS/IPS solutions like Snort
   - **Focus Areas**: Packet analysis, traffic flow, and communication patterns

2. **Endpoint Monitoring:**

   Tracks activities on user devices, including file changes, application usage, and system configurations, to detect unauthorized actions.

   - **Tools**: Endpoint Detection and Response (EDR) platforms like CrowdStrike or SentinelOne
   - **Focus Areas**: Malware detection, privilege escalation, and data exfiltration attempts

3. **Behavioral Monitoring:**

   Identifies deviations from established baselines of normal behavior, such as unusual login times, access to restricted files, or changes in system configurations.

- **Tools**: User and Entity Behavior Analytics (UEBA) solutions like Exabeam or Varonis

- **Focus Areas**: Insider threats, compromised accounts, and anomalous activities

Anomaly-Based Detection vs. Signature-Based Detection

When it comes to identifying threats in cybersecurity, two primary detection methods dominate: **anomaly-based detection** and **signature-based detection**. These approaches differ significantly in their operation, strengths, and challenges, making them complementary tools in a robust security strategy.

Anomaly-Based Detection

Anomaly-based detection relies on machine learning, artificial intelligence, or statistical models to define what "normal" activity looks like for a system or network. It continuously monitors for deviations from this baseline, flagging irregular behaviors as potential threats.

- **Strengths:**
  - **Identifies Unknown Threats:** This method shines in detecting zero-day vulnerabilities, new malware variants, and **Advanced Persistent Threats (APTs)** where attackers use unconventional tactics to avoid detection.
  - **Dynamic and Adaptive:** The system learns and evolves with changes in network activity, making it better suited for environments where standard patterns are less predictable.

- **Challenges:**
  - **False Positives:** Because legitimate activities can occasionally deviate from the baseline, anomaly detection often generates false alarms, which require human analysts to investigate.
  - **Resource Intensive:** Establishing an accurate baseline and continuously training the system can demand significant time and computational power.

Signature-Based Detection

Signature-based detection identifies threats by comparing incoming data against a library of known threat signatures. These signatures can include malware hashes, IP addresses of malicious actors, or specific attack patterns.

- **Strengths:**
  - **Highly Accurate for Known Threats:** This method excels at detecting threats that match existing signatures, offering high precision and minimal false positives.
  - **Fast and Efficient:** Scanning for matches in a pre-defined database is computationally light and provides rapid detection.
- **Challenges:**
  - **Limited Scope:** It cannot detect unknown or new threats, such as zero-day attacks or malware that has not yet been documented.
  - **Requires Frequent Updates:** The database of signatures must be continually updated to remain effective, relying heavily on external threat intelligence.

Key Differences and Practical Applications

- **Detection Scope:**

    Anomaly detection is ideal for uncovering unknown or novel threats, while signature-based methods are best suited for recognizing well-documented threats.

- **Accuracy vs. Adaptability:**

    Signature-based systems offer precision with a low false positive rate, but anomaly detection adapts to evolving threat landscapes, even at the risk of generating more alerts.

Why Use Both?

No single detection method is perfect. Combining **anomaly-based** and **signature-based detection** ensures a layered security approach that provides broad coverage. While anomaly detection serves as a proactive tool to catch emerging threats, signature detection remains a reliable and efficient line of defense against known risks. Together, they create a more resilient system capable of addressing the diverse challenges of today's cyber landscape.

Threat Hunting

Threat hunting involves proactively searching for signs of malicious activity or compromise that may have bypassed automated defenses. This technique goes beyond traditional monitoring to identify threats that remain undetected by standard tools.

- **Focus Areas:**
  - Identifying advanced persistent threats (APTs)
  - Detecting stealthy attackers who leverage zero-day exploits or custom malware
- **Methodologies:**
  - **Hypothesis-Driven**: Guided by specific questions or potential scenarios (e.g., "What if an attacker has compromised privileged accounts?")
  - **Indicator of Compromise (IOC) Search**: Focuses on identifying specific indicators, such as unusual file hashes or IP addresses
- **Tools and Techniques:**
  - Open-source tools like MISP (Malware Information Sharing Platform)
  - Specialized platforms like Carbon Black or CrowdStrike

By employing continuous monitoring, leveraging advanced detection techniques, and incorporating proactive threat-hunting practices, organizations can enhance their ability to detect and mitigate threats in real time. This multilayered approach helps protect critical assets and minimizes potential damage from emerging threats.

Incident Detection and Alerts

Incident detection and alerting are central to maintaining an organization's security posture. The ability to promptly identify and prioritize potential threats allows security teams to take swift and effective action. This section explores how incident detection works, the role of alerting systems, and strategies to reduce false positives.

Defining Incident Detection

Incident detection refers to the process of identifying potential security incidents within an organization's systems, networks, or applications. Detection relies on a combination of monitoring systems, user reports, and automated tools to uncover signs of compromise or unusual activity.

- **Common Sources of Detection:**

  - **Monitoring Systems:** Tools like SIEM platforms and IDS/IPS solutions that analyze data and flag anomalies.

  - **User Reports:** Employees or users reporting suspicious activity or behaviors.

  - **Automated Tools:** Technologies such as endpoint protection or behavioral analytics that identify and escalate risks.

Alerting Systems

Alerting systems are technologies designed to notify security teams of detected anomalies, potential breaches, or other significant events. These systems play a vital role in ensuring that identified threats are addressed promptly and efficiently.

- **Key Features of Alerting Systems:**

  - **Notifications:** Provide real-time alerts through dashboards, email, SMS, or integration with communication tools like Slack or Microsoft Teams.

  - **Prioritization Levels:** Assign severity ratings (e.g., critical, high, medium, low) to help teams focus on the most urgent threats.

- **Event Context:** Include relevant details, such as the affected system, time of occurrence, and suggested remediation actions.

• **Examples of Alerting Tools:**

  - SIEM solutions like Splunk or IBM QRadar for centralized alert management
  - EDR platforms like SentinelOne or CrowdStrike for endpoint-specific alerts

Reducing False Positives

One of the biggest challenges in incident detection is the occurrence of false positives—alerts generated for benign activities that are mistaken for threats. Excessive false positives can overwhelm security teams, delay responses to genuine threats, and reduce overall efficiency.

Strategies to Minimize False Positives

1. **Tuning Monitoring Tools:**

   - Adjust detection thresholds to better align with the organization's environment.
   - Eliminate noise by excluding known safe activities or systems.

2. **Regularly Updating Rules and Baselines:**

   - Maintain updated detection rules to reflect evolving threat landscapes.
   - Reassess and refine baselines to account for changes in normal user and system behavior.

3. **Using Contextual Data:**

    - Incorporate additional context, such as historical trends or asset criticality, to validate alerts.

    - Employ threat intelligence feeds to correlate alerts with known malicious activities.

4. **Leveraging Machine Learning:**

    - Advanced tools with machine learning capabilities can help distinguish between genuine threats and routine activities by analyzing patterns over time.

By fine-tuning detection mechanisms and implementing efficient alerting systems, organizations can ensure faster and more accurate responses to security incidents. This approach not only reduces operational overhead but also strengthens overall cybersecurity resilience.

Incident Response Process

Effective incident response (IR) is critical for minimizing the impact of security incidents and ensuring an organization's swift return to normal operations. This section provides an overview of IR, outlines its key phases, and emphasizes the roles of incident response teams.

Defining Incident Response (IR)

Incident response refers to a structured and organized approach for managing security incidents, such as data breaches, malware infections, or insider threats. The primary goal of IR is to limit damage, reduce recovery time, and prevent similar incidents in the future.

- **Core Objectives of IR:**
  - Rapidly identify and address threats.
  - Minimize disruptions to business operations.
  - Maintain compliance with regulatory and legal requirements.
  - Protect sensitive data and organizational assets.

Phases of Incident Response

The IR process is typically broken down into six structured phases, each contributing to effective incident management:

1. **Preparation:**
   - Develop and maintain an Incident Response Plan (IRP), outlining roles, responsibilities, and procedures.
   - Train staff on IR processes and conduct regular simulations (tabletop exercises).
   - Gather tools, such as forensic software, logging platforms, and communication mechanisms.

2. **Identification:**
   - Detect and analyze potential incidents through monitoring tools, user reports, or threat intelligence.
   - Assess the scope and impact of the incident, including affected systems, data, and users.
   - Classify the incident based on severity and escalate accordingly.

3. **Containment:**

    - Implement short-term measures to limit the spread of the incident, such as isolating affected systems.

    - Deploy longer-term containment solutions, such as temporary network segmentation or firewall rule adjustments.

4. **Eradication:**

    - Identify and eliminate the root cause of the incident, such as malware, unauthorized access, or configuration vulnerabilities.

    - Remove malicious files, disable compromised accounts, and address any exploited weaknesses.

5. **Recovery:**

    - Restore systems to operational status, ensuring their integrity and functionality.

    - Monitor the environment for signs of residual threats or recurring issues.

    - Verify that affected systems meet security baselines before reconnecting them to the network.

6. **Lessons Learned:**

    - Conduct a post-incident review to document what occurred, how it was handled, and what was learned.

    - Update the IRP, security controls, and training programs based on findings.

    - Share insights with relevant stakeholders to promote continuous improvement.

CHAPTER 5   SECURITY OPERATIONS AND MONITORING

Role of Incident Response Teams

Incident Response Teams (IRTs) are essential for coordinating the actions required to manage and resolve incidents effectively.

Key Responsibilities of IRTs

- **Coordination Across Departments:**

    Ensure collaboration between IT, legal, HR, public relations, and other relevant teams to address all aspects of an incident.

- **Stakeholder Communication:**

    Provide timely updates to internal and external stakeholders, including senior management, customers, and regulatory bodies.

- **Technical Expertise:**

    Analyze, contain, and remediate incidents with specialized knowledge of systems, networks, and cybersecurity threats.

- **Documentation:**

    Record all steps taken during the incident to create a detailed report for legal, compliance, and internal review purposes.

By following a structured incident response process and leveraging dedicated teams, organizations can effectively mitigate the impact of security incidents while enhancing their overall preparedness for future threats. This approach fosters resilience, protects critical assets, and supports long-term security strategies.

SIEM and Security Tools

The use of **Security Information and Event Management (SIEM)** systems and other advanced monitoring tools is a cornerstone of modern cybersecurity operations. These technologies enable organizations to proactively detect, analyze, and respond to threats by consolidating data from multiple sources into a centralized system. By doing so, organizations can enhance visibility, improve incident response times, and maintain compliance with regulatory standards.

What Is a SIEM System?

A **Security Information and Event Management (SIEM)** system is a centralized platform that collects, correlates, and analyzes security-related data from an organization's IT infrastructure. SIEM tools serve as the nerve center for monitoring and responding to threats, offering both real-time and historical insights into security events.

Primary Objectives of a SIEM

1. **Threat Detection:** Identify suspicious activities or anomalies across networks, endpoints, and applications.

2. **Incident Response:** Provide actionable insights and alerts to facilitate swift responses to security events.

3. **Compliance:** Generate reports and maintain audit trails to meet regulatory requirements.

4. **Forensic Analysis:** Investigate and trace security incidents by analyzing historical data.

Key Features of SIEM Systems

- **Data Aggregation:** Collect logs and event data from diverse sources, such as firewalls, servers, endpoints, and cloud services.
- **Event Normalization:** Standardize data from disparate formats for seamless analysis.
- **Correlation Engine:** Identify relationships between events to detect coordinated or multivector attacks.
- **Dashboards and Visualization:** Provide user-friendly interfaces for monitoring and reporting.
- **Threat Intelligence Integration:** Leverage external intelligence feeds to enhance detection capabilities.

Why Organizations Use SIEM Systems

SIEM systems play a critical role in reducing dwell time—the period between the initial compromise and detection—by enabling faster identification of threats. They also help organizations maintain compliance with frameworks like PCI DSS, GDPR, and HIPAA by providing the necessary visibility and reporting capabilities.

Core Functions of SIEM Systems

SIEM tools deliver a comprehensive suite of functions aimed at strengthening an organization's security posture:

1. **Log Collection and Normalization:**
    - Gather event data from sources like network devices, servers, applications, endpoints, and cloud environments.
    - Normalize log data into a standard format to facilitate analysis and reduce complexity.

2. **Threat Detection and Real-Time Alerting:**
    - Utilize predefined rules, machine learning algorithms, and behavioral analysis to detect anomalies and threats.
    - Provide real-time alerts to notify security teams of potential incidents, helping to reduce response times.

3. **Event Correlation:**
    - Link events across multiple sources to identify patterns indicative of coordinated attacks.
    - Example: Failed login attempts followed by an unusual file transfer could signify a brute-force attack followed by data exfiltration.

4. **Incident Investigation and Forensic Analysis:**
    - Enable security teams to perform root cause analysis by reviewing historical logs and events.
    - Help trace attack vectors and understand the scope of an incident.

CHAPTER 5   SECURITY OPERATIONS AND MONITORING

5. **Regulatory Compliance and Reporting:**

- Generate compliance-specific reports to demonstrate adherence to standards like NIST, ISO 27001, or SOX.
- Maintain audit trails for transparency and accountability.

Popular SIEM Tools

Organizations can choose from a wide range of SIEM platforms, each offering unique features to address various use cases.

- **Splunk:** Known for its scalability and advanced analytics capabilities, Splunk is a top choice for large enterprises.
- **IBM QRadar:** Offers robust threat intelligence integration and automated threat detection.
- **LogRhythm:** Combines SIEM with additional capabilities like user behavior analytics (UBA) and network monitoring.
- **Elastic Security (formerly ELK Stack):** An open-source platform offering flexibility and customization for log management and analysis.

Advanced Monitoring Tools

While **SIEM (Security Information and Event Management)** systems provide a solid foundation for centralized log management and threat detection, advanced monitoring tools enhance security operations by addressing specific layers of the attack surface. These tools add depth to an organization's ability to detect, analyze, and respond to emerging threats effectively.

Endpoint Detection and Response (EDR)

EDR solutions focus on identifying and mitigating threats that target individual devices, such as workstations, servers, or mobile endpoints.

- **Capabilities:**
  - Detects and responds to threats like malware, ransomware, unauthorized access, and suspicious activities in real time.
  - Offers endpoint visibility, enabling teams to trace the origin of incidents and analyze the attack chain.
  - Supports containment measures, such as isolating compromised devices to prevent the spread of threats.
- **Popular Tools:**
  - **CrowdStrike Falcon:** Known for its lightweight agent and robust detection capabilities.
  - **Carbon Black:** Offers comprehensive threat hunting and endpoint visibility.
  - **Microsoft Defender for Endpoint:** Provides native integration with Windows environments and advanced protection features.

CHAPTER 5   SECURITY OPERATIONS AND MONITORING

Network Detection and Response (NDR)

NDR tools focus on monitoring network traffic to detect malicious activity, anomalies, and advanced threats moving laterally within the network.

- **Capabilities:**
  - Identifies **lateral movement** by attackers, **command-and-control (C2)** communications, and attempts at data exfiltration.
  - Uses machine learning to establish baselines for normal network behavior, making it effective against unknown threats.
  - Provides deep packet inspection and analytics for investigating network incidents.
- **Popular Tools:**
  - **Darktrace:** Employs AI to detect novel threats and monitor real-time network activity.
  - **Vectra AI:** Offers comprehensive visibility into network traffic with advanced threat detection capabilities.

Security Orchestration, Automation, and Response (SOAR)

SOAR platforms enhance efficiency by automating repetitive tasks, orchestrating workflows across tools, and streamlining incident response processes.

- **Capabilities:**
  - Automates tasks such as log collection, alert prioritization, and remediation actions, reducing response times significantly.
  - Integrates with other tools like SIEM, EDR, and NDR to create a unified security ecosystem.
  - Facilitates post-incident reporting and documentation for compliance and future improvements.
- **Popular Tools:**
  - **Palo Alto Cortex XSOAR:** Known for its extensive playbook customization and integration capabilities.
  - **Splunk Phantom:** Offers powerful automation workflows and threat intelligence integration.

Why Advanced Monitoring Tools Matter

These advanced tools work together to close gaps in traditional SIEM-centric approaches. While SIEM provides centralized monitoring and correlation, **EDR, NDR, and SOAR** bring specialized capabilities to endpoint protection, network traffic analysis, and automation of incident response processes. Incorporating these tools into a security strategy ensures faster detection, reduced response times, and a proactive stance against evolving threats.

CHAPTER 5   SECURITY OPERATIONS AND MONITORING

How SIEM and Advanced Tools Work Together

By integrating SIEM systems with other monitoring tools, organizations can build a cohesive security operations framework. This combination offers:

1. **Comprehensive Visibility:** Centralized log aggregation combined with endpoint and network insights ensures a holistic view of the environment.

2. **Enhanced Threat Detection:** Correlation across SIEM, EDR, and NDR data enables the detection of complex multivector attacks.

3. **Efficient Response:** SOAR tools automate the incident response process, reducing manual effort and minimizing downtime.

Challenges in Implementing SIEM Systems

Despite their benefits, SIEM systems are not without challenges:

1. **Data Overload:** High volumes of logs and events can overwhelm teams, if not managed properly.

    - **Solution:** Use intelligent filtering and correlation to focus on actionable insights.

2. **False Positives:** Excessive or poorly tuned alerts can lead to alert fatigue.

    - **Solution:** Continuously refine detection rules and baselines to improve accuracy.

3. **Resource Requirements:** SIEM implementation can be resource-intensive in terms of cost, manpower, and expertise.

    - **Solution:** Consider hybrid or managed SIEM solutions for smaller organizations.

4. **Integration Complexity:** Ensuring compatibility with all systems and devices can be challenging.

    - **Solution:** Select SIEM platforms with robust integration capabilities and vendor support.

The Future of SIEM and Security Tools

As cyber threats evolve, so too must the tools and technologies used to combat them. The future of SIEM and advanced security tools will likely include

- Greater use of artificial intelligence and machine learning for predictive threat detection
- Deeper integration with cloud-native environments and DevSecOps workflows
- Expanded automation capabilities through SOAR and other advanced platforms

By staying ahead of these developments, organizations can ensure their security operations remain effective and adaptive to emerging threats.

CHAPTER 5   SECURITY OPERATIONS AND MONITORING

Types of Threat Intelligence

Threat intelligence is categorized into distinct types based on the depth and focus of the information, allowing organizations to tailor their strategies to operational and strategic needs. Each type serves a specific purpose, ranging from real-time detection to long-term planning.

Tactical Threat Intelligence

Tactical threat intelligence deals with specific, actionable data that helps detect and mitigate threats in real-time. It primarily targets **indicators of compromise (IoCs)** to enhance security measures.

- **Examples:**
  - Malicious file hashes or signatures
  - URLs used for phishing campaigns
  - IP addresses associated with command-and-control (C2) servers
- **Use Cases:**
  - Automatically updating firewalls, intrusion detection systems (IDS), and SIEM tools with blocklists to prevent access to known malicious entities.
  - Enhancing rule-based detection systems to identify active threats quickly.
  - Supporting frontline SOC analysts by providing precise, actionable data.

Operational Threat Intelligence

Operational threat intelligence offers insights into attackers' **tactics, techniques, and procedures (TTPs)**. It provides a deeper understanding of how attacks are carried out, enabling organizations to respond effectively to ongoing or potential threats.

- **Examples:**
  - Detailed workflows of ransomware attacks, including how malware propagates and encrypts files
  - Analysis of phishing campaigns targeting specific industries, outlining patterns and payloads used
- **Use Cases:**
  - **Incident Response:** Helps teams understand the scope and methods of active threats, aiding in containment and remediation efforts.
  - **Playbook Development:** Informs response strategies for specific attack scenarios, improving readiness for similar threats.
  - **Threat Hunting:** Guides proactive searches for signs of intrusion within an environment.

Strategic Threat Intelligence

Strategic threat intelligence takes a high-level view, analyzing global threat trends, attacker motivations, and emerging risks. It provides a foundation for shaping long-term cybersecurity policies and investments.

- **Examples:**
  - Industry reports highlighting the rise in **supply chain attacks** or new techniques employed by Advanced Persistent Threats (APTs).
  - Analysis of geopolitical events, such as conflicts or sanctions, that influence cyber threat activity in specific regions.
- **Use Cases:**
  - **Executive Decision-Making:** Equips leaders with insights to allocate budgets effectively, prioritize cybersecurity initiatives, and assess risks associated with specific ventures.
  - **Strategic Planning:** Guides the development of long-term cybersecurity strategies, including investments in technologies and staffing.
  - **Risk Management:** Assists in identifying and mitigating risks posed by geopolitical or industry-specific threats.

Integrating Threat Intelligence into Security Operations

Combining these types of threat intelligence ensures a **comprehensive approach** to cybersecurity:

- **Tactical intelligence** addresses immediate threats, bolstering defenses at the technical level.

- **Operational intelligence** bridges the gap between detection and response, offering detailed insights for active threat management.
- **Strategic intelligence** shapes overarching security policies, ensuring organizations stay ahead of evolving threats.

A robust threat intelligence program aligns these types to support both day-to-day operations and long-term resilience, empowering organizations to anticipate and neutralize threats effectively.

Benefits of Integration

1. **Enhanced Detection Capabilities:**
   - Threat feeds provide additional context, helping SOCs and SIEMs detect threats more efficiently.
   - For example, a SIEM can flag an IP address as suspicious if it matches a known threat from a feed.

2. **Improved Incident Response:**
   - With enriched intelligence, analysts can prioritize and address incidents more effectively.
   - Example: Threat intelligence helps distinguish a low-risk anomaly from a critical advanced persistent threat (APT).

3. **Automation Opportunities:**
   - Automating intelligence ingestion reduces manual effort and ensures up-to-date detection rules.

Using Threat Feeds

Threat feeds are a primary source of intelligence, offering information on ongoing or emerging threats.

- **Commercial Feeds:** Paid services like Recorded Future or FireEye, providing curated, high-quality data.

- **Open-Source Feeds:** Free options like AlienVault's OTX or MISP offer community-contributed intelligence.

- **ISACs (Information Sharing and Analysis Centers):** Industry-specific intelligence networks, such as FS-ISAC for finance or H-ISAC for healthcare.

Threat Intelligence Platforms (TIPs)

Threat Intelligence Platforms (TIPs) are advanced tools that serve as centralized systems for collecting, analyzing, and sharing threat intelligence data within an organization. These platforms are critical components of modern cybersecurity strategies, enabling organizations to gain actionable insights from vast volumes of threat data. TIPs act as integrators, pulling in threat intelligence feeds from various internal and external sources, including open-source data, commercial feeds, and proprietary information from within the organization.

Once data is ingested, TIPs apply advanced analytics and machine learning techniques to process and prioritize information. They provide security teams with structured, actionable insights by correlating threat indicators with real-time network data. This allows analysts to understand the context of potential threats, identify patterns, and evaluate risks. With this intelligence, organizations can enhance their detection and response capabilities, staying ahead of adversaries who constantly evolve their attack strategies.

One of the most significant benefits of TIPs is their ability to streamline workflows for Security Operations Center (SOC) analysts. By consolidating threat feeds into a single platform and automating routine tasks such as indicator enrichment, TIPs reduce the noise generated by false positives. This efficiency allows analysts to focus their efforts on investigating high-priority alerts and mitigating critical vulnerabilities. The integration of TIPs with other security tools, such as SIEMs (Security Information and Event Management systems) and firewalls, further enhances an organization's ability to respond to threats swiftly and effectively.

Moreover, TIPs foster collaboration and knowledge sharing within and across organizations. Many platforms support the dissemination of threat intelligence to peers or trusted networks, contributing to collective defense initiatives. By sharing insights, organizations can contribute to a broader understanding of emerging threats, improving the security posture of entire industries or communities.

In summary, Threat Intelligence Platforms are invaluable for organizations seeking to bolster their cybersecurity defenses. By automating data aggregation, enabling detailed analysis, and integrating with existing workflows, TIPs empower SOC teams to focus on proactive defense strategies. They not only reduce the complexity of managing threat intelligence but also enhance the organization's ability to anticipate, detect, and respond to evolving cyber threats.

Automating Threat Intelligence Integration

Automation is essential to manage the vast volume of threat data efficiently. Common automation techniques include

1. **Dynamic Rule Updates:**
   - Feeds can automatically update detection rules in systems like SIEMs and firewalls.
   - Example: Updating an intrusion detection system (IDS) to block malicious IPs from threat feeds.
2. **Incident Prioritization:**
   - Automating the assignment of risk scores to IoCs helps prioritize incidents for response.
3. **Response Automation:**
   - Example: A SIEM triggers an automated action to block traffic from a suspicious IP flagged by a threat feed.

Challenges in Threat Intelligence

While threat intelligence is invaluable, organizations often face challenges when utilizing it effectively.

1. **Overwhelming Data Volumes:**
   - Security teams may struggle to process the vast amounts of intelligence generated daily.
   - **Solution:** Implement filters to focus on relevant, high-priority threats.
2. **Data Quality Issues:**
   - Low-quality or outdated intelligence can lead to false positives or wasted resources.
   - **Solution:** Regularly review and validate feed sources to ensure accuracy and relevance.

3. **Integration Complexity:**

    - Aligning threat intelligence workflows with existing tools can be technically challenging.

    - **Solution:** Invest in platforms with robust APIs and pre-built integrations.

Future Trends in Threat Intelligence

Advancements in artificial intelligence (AI) and machine learning (ML) are driving the evolution of threat intelligence. Key trends include

- **Predictive Threat Intelligence:** AI algorithms analyze patterns to predict potential threats before they materialize.

- **Real-Time Intelligence:** Continuous data updates and automated analysis reduce the lag between detection and response.

- **Collaboration and Sharing:** Increased participation in ISACs and global threat-sharing initiatives enhance collective defense efforts.

By leveraging robust threat intelligence, organizations can improve their ability to detect, prevent, and respond to emerging cyber threats. When integrated effectively, it serves as a cornerstone for proactive and resilient cybersecurity operations.

CHAPTER 5   SECURITY OPERATIONS AND MONITORING

Chapter Summary

This chapter provides an in-depth exploration of security operations and monitoring, essential components in safeguarding an organization's digital infrastructure. It covers the role and function of Security Operations Centers (SOCs), detailing how they coordinate to detect, analyze, and respond to security incidents in real time. Readers gain a thorough understanding of logging practices, the importance of centralized log management, and how effective monitoring systems enhance threat visibility.

The integration of advanced tools like SIEM (Security Information and Event Management) systems, Endpoint Detection and Response (EDR) tools, and Threat Intelligence Platforms (TIPs) is explored to show how they augment threat detection and incident response efforts. The chapter emphasizes the proactive nature of security operations, highlighting the importance of continuous monitoring, real-time alerting, and threat hunting to stay ahead of evolving cyber threats.

Through a structured approach to incident response, the chapter empowers readers with the knowledge needed to mitigate and recover from security breaches, ensuring organizations can respond effectively to emerging threats and minimize potential damage. By focusing on these critical areas, readers are better prepared to build and maintain a robust security posture in the face of ever-evolving cyber risks.

CHAPTER 6

Incident Response and Recovery

Effective incident response and recovery processes are crucial for minimizing the damage caused by security breaches and ensuring that an organization can quickly return to normal operations. When a security incident occurs, how an organization responds can make the difference between a minor disruption and a major crisis. This chapter explores the methodologies, tools, and best practices involved in responding to security incidents, eliminating threats, and recovering from the impact.

We will delve into the essential phases of incident response, such as preparation, identification, containment, eradication, and recovery, highlighting the importance of each stage in the overall process. Additionally, you will learn about the role of incident response teams, key strategies for developing and executing recovery plans, and the significance of post-incident reviews for continuous improvement. Through case studies and real-world examples, we will contextualize these concepts, demonstrating their practical application in handling actual security events.

By the end of this chapter, you will have a comprehensive understanding of how to effectively manage and recover from security incidents, ensuring that your organization is prepared to respond and bounce back stronger from any potential

CHAPTER 6   INCIDENT RESPONSE AND RECOVERY

Introduction to Incident Response (IR)

Incident Response (IR) is a critical process in cybersecurity, involving a structured and coordinated approach to identifying, managing, and mitigating security incidents. An incident can range from a minor security lapse to a major breach involving sensitive data, compromised systems, or even prolonged service disruption. The goal of IR is to quickly contain and neutralize the threat, minimize the damage, and ensure that the organization can recover and resume normal operations with minimal impact. A well-executed IR process not only addresses the immediate security event but also enhances the organization's overall resilience and preparedness for future threats.

Goals of Incident Response

There are various goals that a successful incident response plan will adhere to. This is not a one-size-fits-all measure, but instead is something that will need to be catered to each organization to meet their individual needs. Keep in mind what the entity in mind is prioritizing when developing the goals at hand.

1. **Protect Organizational Assets and Sensitive Information:** The foremost objective in any security incident is to safeguard valuable resources, including intellectual property, customer data, network infrastructure, and other critical assets. The ability to quickly protect these assets from further compromise is essential to reducing long-term damage.

2. **Minimize Downtime and Operational Disruption:** An effective IR strategy aims to detect and respond to incidents swiftly to reduce the duration of

service disruptions. The faster an organization can recover from an incident, the less it will affect daily operations, revenue, and its reputation in the marketplace.

3. **Prevent Recurrence Through Post-incident Analysis:** Once an incident is resolved, a critical next step is learning from the experience. By conducting a thorough post-incident review, organizations can identify weaknesses in their security systems, refine their response strategies, and prevent similar incidents from happening in the future. This involves continuous improvement, including updates to processes, tools, and employee training.

The Importance of Preparedness

By being prepared prior to the actual event, you are able to eliminate a large portion of risk that you would otherwise face. Not only is the risk limited but the impact is greatly diminished. Similar to life itself, being properly prepared is a critical measure. Below are two highlights that outline methods of establishing a baseline level of preparedness:

- **Developing Clear Policies and Procedures:** A fundamental aspect of incident response is preparedness. Organizations must establish comprehensive, well-documented incident response policies and procedures in advance. These documents ensure that everyone, from security teams to executive leadership, understands their responsibilities and the steps they must take when a security event occurs.

- **Testing Through Simulations and Tabletop Exercises:** Preparedness goes beyond having plans on paper. Regular testing of IR protocols through simulated attack scenarios, such as tabletop exercises, ensures the team is ready for real-world situations. These exercises allow for the identification of potential gaps in procedures, coordination challenges, and communication breakdowns. Regular testing helps refine response strategies and builds confidence within the team.

By establishing a strong foundation of preparedness, organizations ensure they can act swiftly and decisively in the event of a security incident, reducing both the immediate and long-term impact on business operations.

The Incident Response Life Cycle

The Incident Response (IR) life cycle follows a well-structured, phased approach to managing and mitigating security incidents. Adhering to the National Institute of Standards and Technology (NIST) framework, the life cycle is designed to ensure that organizations can quickly detect, respond to, and recover from security breaches, while also learning from each incident to improve future response capabilities. Below are the six critical phases of the incident response life cycle.

Preparation

Preparation is the foundation for an effective incident response. This phase involves establishing a proactive and strategic approach to incident handling before an event occurs. Key activities include

- **Developing Policies and Procedures:** Organizations need clear and documented IR policies that outline roles, responsibilities, and procedures for handling incidents. This ensures that all teams understand the processes and their duties when an incident occurs.

- **Creating Incident Response Playbooks:** Incident response playbooks provide a step-by-step guide to managing specific types of incidents. These playbooks ensure a consistent and repeatable response across different scenarios.

- **Establishing Communication Protocols:** Clear communication is critical during an incident. Organizations must define how internal teams, external partners, and stakeholders will communicate, as well as escalation paths to ensure timely response.

- **Conducting Training and Simulations:** Regular training and tabletop exercises prepare teams to handle real incidents. Simulations help test readiness, improve team coordination, and uncover areas that require improvement in the IR plan.

Establishing Roles and Responsibilities

A successful incident response relies on clearly defined roles and responsibilities within an Incident Response Team (IRT). The roles are designed to ensure that the right expertise is brought in at every stage of the process.

- **Key Roles:**
  - **Incident Commander:** The Incident Commander oversees the entire incident response process. They are responsible for making high-level decisions, setting priorities, and ensuring that the response is progressing smoothly.
  - **Analysts:** These individuals assess the nature of the incident, gather data, and perform technical analysis to understand the scope and impact. Analysts may specialize in areas such as malware analysis or network traffic analysis.
  - **Forensic Experts:** Forensic experts are responsible for investigating and preserving evidence related to the incident. They use specialized tools to gather data, analyze logs, and reconstruct the sequence of events.
  - **Communication Leads:** Effective communication is crucial during an incident. The communication lead ensures that both internal and external stakeholders are informed, managing both the technical and public-facing aspects of communication.
- **Role of an Incident Response Team (IRT):** The IRT is a cross-functional team that includes members with various areas of expertise, such as IT, legal, communications, and human resources. The structure of the IRT should allow for rapid decision-making and clear communication channels during an incident.

CHAPTER 6   INCIDENT RESPONSE AND RECOVERY

Tools and Resources

Having the right tools and resources in place is critical for effective incident response. These tools allow the response team to detect, analyze, and mitigate incidents in a timely and accurate manner.

- **Incident Response Tools:**

  - **SIEM (Security Information and Event Management) Systems:** SIEM tools aggregate and analyze security data from across the network, providing real-time alerts and insights into potential threats. They are essential for identifying security incidents quickly.

  - **Endpoint Detection and Response (EDR) Platforms:** EDR platforms focus on monitoring and protecting endpoints (such as servers, workstations, and mobile devices). They help detect suspicious activity on individual devices and allow for real-time investigation and remediation.

  - **Forensic Tools:** Tools like EnCase, FTK, and X1 allow forensic experts to capture and analyze evidence from compromised systems. These tools are vital for gathering information to determine how an attack occurred and to assist in legal investigations.

- **Runbooks and Playbooks:**

  - **Runbooks:** Runbooks are step-by-step guides for responding to specific types of incidents. They offer predefined procedures that should be followed during particular scenarios, ensuring consistency and efficiency in handling similar incidents.

- **Playbooks:** Similar to runbooks, playbooks outline the actions that need to be taken during specific attack types (e.g., ransomware, DDoS, or insider threat). They provide detailed guidance on how to respond, including tools, tactics, and communication strategies.

Identification

The identification phase is focused on detecting and confirming potential security incidents. This is a critical step, as proper identification helps prevent unnecessary responses and ensures the right incidents are prioritized for investigation. Key activities include

- **Detection Tools and Alerts:** Use monitoring tools, threat intelligence feeds, and user reports to detect abnormal activities. Tools like SIEM systems, IDS/IPS, and endpoint monitoring help identify suspicious behavior and trigger alerts.

- **Validating Incidents:** Once an alert is generated, security teams validate the incident by analyzing logs, system activity, and contextual information. A clear understanding of what is happening helps prevent overreaction and ensures the right course of action is taken.

Common Indicators of Compromise

Indicators of Compromise (IOCs) are artifacts or traces left behind by malicious activities that help security teams detect potential security breaches. These can be network-related, file-related, or linked to suspicious user behaviors. Recognizing these indicators early can prevent further damage.

- **Common IOCs:**
  - **Abnormal Network Traffic:** Unusual traffic patterns, such as large data transfers to an unknown IP address or spikes in inbound/outbound traffic, can be a sign of a breach.
  - **File Changes:** Unexpected changes in critical system files or the creation of new, unfamiliar files may indicate malicious activity, especially if these changes are happening on a large scale.
  - **Unusual Login Activity:** Failed login attempts, logins at odd hours, or logins from unexpected geographic locations can suggest unauthorized access attempts.
- **Sources for Collecting IOCs:**
  - **SIEM Alerts:** Security Information and Event Management (SIEM) systems collect and analyze data from across an organization's network, providing alerts for suspicious activity based on preconfigured rules.
  - **Threat Intelligence Feeds:** External threat intelligence services provide up-to-date information on known attack patterns, malware signatures, and emerging threats.

- **Logs:** Logs from firewalls, servers, and applications provide valuable data that can help detect anomalies or confirm incidents. These logs should be continuously monitored for signs of compromise.

Initial Assessment and Triage

Once an incident is detected, the next step is to assess its nature and scope. The goal during the initial assessment is to determine whether the event is a true security incident, how severe it is, and how quickly it needs to be addressed.

- **Steps to Determine the Nature and Scope of an Incident:**
    1. **Validate the Incident:** After receiving an alert or IOC, the response team must validate whether the event is an actual incident or a false positive. This might involve reviewing logs, correlating data, and performing initial diagnostics.
    2. **Determine the Type of Incident:** Once validated, the team needs to classify the type of incident (e.g., malware, data breach, DDoS attack). The type of incident influences the response and containment strategies.
    3. **Assess the Scope:** Determine how widespread the incident is. Does it affect a single device, a group of systems, or the entire network? Understanding the scope helps prioritize resources and response efforts.

- **Assessing Severity and Prioritizing Response Actions:** The severity of the incident should be assessed based on factors like

    - **Impact on Business Operations:** If the incident is disrupting critical systems or processes, it may need immediate attention.

    - **Data Sensitivity:** If the incident involves sensitive data (e.g., customer information or intellectual property), it may require urgent escalation.

    - **Attack Vectors:** Certain types of attacks, such as those exploiting unpatched vulnerabilities, may need immediate remediation to prevent further exploitation.

The prioritization process helps ensure that limited resources are focused on the most critical incidents first, minimizing potential damage and ensuring a timely response.

Incident Documentation

Proper documentation of an incident is essential for several reasons: it ensures legal compliance, supports post-incident analysis, and enables teams to learn from past events to improve future response efforts.

- **Recording Incident Details for Legal, Operational, and Learning Purposes:** Every step of the incident response should be meticulously documented to create a detailed account of the event. This record can serve as evidence for legal and regulatory purposes, help identify areas for improvement and support forensic investigations.

Key details to document include

- **Incident Timeline:** Document key events, such as when the incident was detected, actions taken, and when the incident was resolved.

- **Scope and Impact:** Record which systems, data, and services were affected by the incident.

- **Mitigation Efforts:** Track the steps taken to contain, eradicate, and recover from the incident.

- **Tools for Incident Documentation and Case Management:**

  - **Case Management Systems:** Incident management tools (e.g., ServiceNow, JIRA) help track incidents from detection to resolution, providing a centralized repository for all case-related data.

  - **Incident Logs and Reports:** These may be generated manually or through automated processes, but the focus should be on capturing all relevant information in real time.

  - **Digital Forensics Tools:** Tools like EnCase or FTK may be used to gather and preserve evidence, ensuring it can be used in post-incident analysis or legal proceedings.

Proper documentation ensures transparency throughout the incident response process and can be essential in proving due diligence if the organization is audited or investigated post-incident.

CHAPTER 6   INCIDENT RESPONSE AND RECOVERY

Containment

Once an incident is identified, containment is necessary to prevent further damage. This phase focuses on limiting the scope and spread of the incident to reduce its impact on the organization's assets. Key containment actions include

- **Short-Term Containment:** Immediate actions are taken to limit the incident's reach. For example, disconnecting affected systems from the network, blocking malicious IP addresses, or disabling compromised accounts can quickly reduce exposure.

- **Long-Term Containment:** After short-term containment, long-term measures are implemented to stabilize the environment. This might involve applying patches, changing configurations, or adding additional monitoring to ensure the incident is fully contained and will not reoccur.

Types of Containment Strategies

Containment strategies can be broken down into two categories: **short-term containment** and **long-term containment**. Both are essential to stop the spread of the incident, but they address different aspects of the attack.

- **Short-term Containment:** Short-term containment involves taking immediate actions to stop the incident from worsening or spreading. The objective is to isolate affected systems or networks before the attacker can escalate the attack further.

- **Isolating Affected Systems:** Disconnecting compromised systems from the network (e.g., pulling the plug, disabling network interfaces) can prevent attackers from accessing additional resources.

- **Blocking Malicious Traffic:** Firewalls and intrusion prevention systems (IPS) can be configured to block traffic from suspicious IP addresses, effectively containing the attack at the network level.

- **Quarantining Malicious Files:** Anti-malware tools can isolate infected files or processes, preventing them from executing further.

These actions are usually temporary and are intended to buy time for the response team to assess the incident and implement more permanent solutions.

- **Long-term Containment:** After short-term containment has been implemented, the focus shifts to long-term containment, which involves fixing the vulnerabilities that were exploited during the attack and preventing further exploitation.

  - **Applying Patches and Fixes:** Once the attack vector is identified, applying security patches or updates to affected systems helps close vulnerabilities that could be used again.

  - **Configuration Changes:** For certain attacks, changing system configurations (e.g., disabling unnecessary services or changing admin credentials) may be necessary to lock out attackers.

- **Enhanced Monitoring:** Implementing additional monitoring can help detect any remaining malicious activity and ensure the incident is fully contained before recovery begins.

Long-term containment ensures that the systems are secured against the same attack and provides a controlled environment while full recovery and eradication efforts are ongoing.

Minimizing Impact on Business Operations

One of the biggest challenges during the containment phase is balancing the need to secure systems with the requirement to maintain essential business operations. While it's important to isolate and contain affected systems, completely shutting down operations or disrupting services can have significant business consequences.

- **Balancing Containment with Business Needs:** The primary goal is to **minimize business disruption** while containing the incident. Depending on the severity and scope of the incident, this may mean allowing some systems to continue running, even if they are partially compromised, as long as they don't pose a risk to the wider network. Conversely, in critical situations, temporary shutdowns or workarounds may be necessary to prevent further damage.

- **Using Segmentation:** Network segmentation can play a key role in minimizing impact. By isolating compromised systems or network segments from unaffected areas, you can stop the spread of the incident while maintaining access to unaffected systems. This approach allows key business functions to continue running in unaffected parts of the network, ensuring that critical operations are not halted.

- For example, isolating the finance department's network from the rest of the organization's systems may allow the finance team to continue working while the IT team contains and investigates the incident in other departments.

Communication During Containment

Effective communication is crucial during the containment phase to ensure that stakeholders are informed without compromising the security of the organization. Communication must be handled with care to prevent panic and avoid disclosing too much information, which could lead to further exploitation or insider threats.

- **Informing Stakeholders:** Communication should be transparent and timely, ensuring that all relevant stakeholders (executive teams, IT staff, legal teams, etc.) are kept in the loop. However, the level of detail shared should be appropriate to the audience. For example:
  - **Internal stakeholders** (e.g., management, IT teams) need specific details to understand the scope and action steps.
  - **External stakeholders** (e.g., customers, regulators) may only need general information, such as whether their data has been compromised and what steps are being taken to mitigate the incident.

- **Maintaining Control Over Sensitive Details:** It is crucial not to disclose sensitive information prematurely, particularly when details about the attack are still being investigated. Premature or public disclosure of an incident could

  - Alert the attackers, allowing them to adjust their tactics or exploit new vulnerabilities.

  - Lead to a loss of customer trust if the information is mishandled.

Incident communication plans should be in place to control the flow of information. Designated communications leads should coordinate public statements, and internal teams should be aligned on what can and cannot be shared at each stage of the incident response.

- **Avoiding Premature Disclosure:** There are legal and regulatory considerations to keep in mind as well. For example, organizations may be required to report breaches to regulatory bodies within specific time frames, but this must be done carefully. Public disclosure should wait until there is enough information to accurately describe the situation and the actions being taken.

In sum, effective containment not only focuses on stopping the incident but also on maintaining business operations, communicating clearly with stakeholders, and preventing further exploitation of vulnerabilities. Through short-term and long-term containment strategies, organizations can minimize damage and ensure that recovery efforts are smoother and more effective.

Eradication

Eradication focuses on completely removing the threat from the environment, addressing any remaining vulnerabilities that were exploited during the incident. This phase ensures that the threat is entirely removed to prevent a re-infection. Key activities include

- **Removing the Threat:** All traces of the incident—whether it's malware, unauthorized user accounts, or compromised systems—are completely removed from the environment.
- **Root Cause Analysis:** Identifying the root cause of the incident is crucial to understand how the breach occurred and to prevent similar incidents in the future. This analysis involves examining logs, network traffic, and security configurations.

Eliminating Threats

Once the incident is contained and the immediate threat is isolated, the next step is to **eliminate all traces of the attacker** from the environment. This ensures that the organization is not at risk of reinfection or further exploitation. Key actions during this stage include

- **Removing Malware and Malicious Code:** Any malware, backdoors, or other malicious code that the attackers may have deployed must be thoroughly removed from all affected systems. This may involve using anti-malware tools or manually scanning and deleting files that are associated with the attack.

- **Closing Exploited Vulnerabilities:** Any vulnerabilities that were exploited during the incident must be patched or fixed. Attackers often gain access through known vulnerabilities, so eliminating these entry points is critical. This includes

  - **Removing unauthorized user accounts** or changes made by the attackers.

  - **Disabling or closing open ports** or services that were used to exploit the system.

  - **Rebuilding or restoring compromised systems** to ensure that no traces of the attacker remain.

- **Neutralizing the Attacker's Presence:** Once you've isolated affected systems, it's essential to make sure the attacker has no access to your environment. This may involve

  - **Changing passwords** and resetting authentication tokens for affected systems.

  - **Expelling attackers from any remote access points** they may have used, such as VPNs or remote desktop services.

Patch Management and Security Updates

Applying **patches and security updates** is one of the most effective ways to close vulnerabilities that may have been exploited during the attack. Failure to patch systems increases the risk of recurring incidents and allows attackers to potentially re-enter the network.

- **Applying Patches to Prevent Recurrence:** Ensure that any software, firmware, or applications involved in the breach are updated with the latest security patches. It's essential to prioritize the patches based on their severity and the impact they may have on the security of the system.

  - **Operating System Updates:** Ensure all OS-level vulnerabilities are patched, particularly those that are known to be exploited in recent threats.

  - **Application Updates:** Update any third-party software or applications that were part of the attack vector.

  - **Firmware Updates:** For hardware-based attacks or vulnerabilities, ensure that firmware is up to date to close potential exploits.

- **Verifying System Integrity After Applying Updates:** After patches are applied, it is essential to verify the **integrity of systems** to ensure they are operating as expected and that the patching process did not introduce new vulnerabilities or issues. This includes

  - **Running integrity checks** to confirm that no files were altered or deleted without authorization.

  - **Testing the systems** to ensure normal operations can resume without errors or issues.

  - **Monitoring for any signs of reinfection** after patching to ensure the threat has been fully eradicated.

Collaborating with Forensics Teams

Collaboration with digital forensics teams plays a key role during the eradication phase. Forensics teams help preserve and analyze evidence to understand the full scope of the attack and determine how the incident occurred. This collaboration is particularly important when legal actions or regulatory compliance are involved.

- **Ensuring Evidence Preservation:** During eradication, it's important to preserve evidence for future investigation, legal action, or compliance requirements. Digital forensics teams can assist in

    - **Preserving logs, files, and artifacts** related to the attack.

    - **Documenting the incident** in detail to ensure the chain of custody is maintained and that evidence is not tampered with.

Evidence preservation is crucial for any potential legal or law enforcement investigation and for compliance with regulatory bodies (e.g., GDPR, HIPAA).

- **Removing Malicious Artifacts Without Compromising Evidence:** The process of removing malware and other artifacts should be carefully managed to avoid destroying potential evidence. Forensics teams often provide expertise on how to safely remove malicious files and artifacts without compromising the integrity of the investigation. This may involve

- **Isolating compromised systems** before eradicating the threat, so forensic evidence can be collected without contamination.

- **Forensic imaging** of affected systems, so that investigators can analyze the systems without further risk of data loss.

- **Coordination with Legal Teams and Law Enforcement:** If the attack is severe or criminal in nature (e.g., involving ransomware or data theft), it may be necessary to **involve legal teams or law enforcement**. This ensures that the appropriate legal actions are taken, such as filing reports with regulatory bodies or pursuing criminal investigations.

  - **Law enforcement** may help trace attackers, especially in the case of criminal breaches or data theft.

  - **Legal teams** can guide the organization on disclosure requirements and help mitigate any legal risks associated with the breach.

In summary, the **eradication phase** is all about ensuring that every trace of the threat is removed, systems are patched and secured, and evidence is preserved for future investigation. Thorough eradication is critical to prevent recurrence and to provide a solid foundation for the recovery phase. Effective collaboration between internal teams and external experts (e.g., forensics and legal teams) ensures

CHAPTER 6   INCIDENT RESPONSE AND RECOVERY

Recovery

The recovery phase involves restoring affected systems to normal operation and ensuring that the organization's business processes continue with minimal disruption. Key activities include

- **System Restoration:** Affected systems and applications are rebuilt or restored from clean backups. Systems must be tested thoroughly to ensure that they are free of any lingering threats.

- **Monitoring for Recurrence:** After systems are restored, continuous monitoring is essential to detect any signs that the incident might recur. If vulnerabilities were exploited, extra monitoring measures should be in place to detect early indicators of another attack.

System Restoration

Once all threats have been eradicated and the organization is confident that the systems are clean, the next step is to restore affected systems back to their original state. This is a critical step in ensuring that business operations can resume without compromising security.

- **Steps to Bring Systems Back Online Safely:**
  - **Restore from Clean Backups:** Begin by restoring systems from known good backups that were taken before the attack occurred. Ensure that backup data is validated and free of malware before it is restored.

- **Incremental Restoration:** Consider bringing systems back online incrementally. Start with the most critical systems, then gradually restore additional services. This minimizes the risk of spreading any hidden threats.

- **Configuration and Hardening:** Once the systems are back online, verify their configurations to ensure they are secure. Apply any security hardening measures, such as closing unnecessary ports, disabling unused accounts, and ensuring proper access controls are in place.

- **Verifying Data Integrity and Ensuring All Systems Are Clean:** After restoring systems, verify that the data has not been corrupted or altered during the attack. This is especially important for systems that store sensitive or critical data.

  - **Data Integrity Checks:** Use hashing or checksums to confirm that data remains unchanged. This can include checking database records, file system integrity, or data in cloud storage.

  - **System Cleanliness:** Run additional scans or use endpoint detection and response (EDR) tools to verify that there are no remaining indicators of compromise (IOCs). This ensures the systems are thoroughly cleansed and that no malware or malicious artifacts remain.

Testing and Monitoring Post-recovery

Even after systems have been restored, it is important to monitor and test for signs of persistence or re-compromise. Attackers often leave behind hidden backdoors or tools to maintain access to a compromised system, so continuous monitoring is key to ensuring full recovery.

- **Monitoring Systems for Signs of Persistence or Re-compromise:**

    - **Continuous Monitoring:** Implement enhanced monitoring to look for unusual behavior, signs of reinfection, or attempts to exploit any residual vulnerabilities. Use Security Information and Event Management (SIEM) systems to aggregate and analyze logs in real time.

    - **Behavioral Analytics:** Utilize behavioral analytics tools to identify anomalous activity that could indicate malicious activity is ongoing or the attacker has re-entered the system.

    - **Extended Post-incident Monitoring:** Maintain heightened monitoring for a period after recovery, as attackers may attempt to re-exploit or use compromised credentials.

- **Conducting Functionality Tests Before Declaring Full Recovery:** Before officially declaring full recovery, it is crucial to test the functionality of restored systems to ensure they are performing as expected. This includes

    - **Stress Testing:** Verify that restored systems can handle the expected workload without issues.

- **End-User Testing:** Have key users test critical applications to ensure they work as intended.

- **Performance Checks:** Ensure that there are no performance degradations in the systems, applications, or networks that could affect operations.

Communication and Reporting

Once systems are restored, it is essential to communicate incident resolution to all relevant stakeholders and document the recovery process for internal review and regulatory compliance.

- **Informing Stakeholders About Incident Resolution:**

  - **Internal Communication:** Keep internal stakeholders (e.g., executives, IT teams, and employees) informed about the incident's resolution. Share clear updates on what has been done to resolve the issue, the current status of the systems, and the steps moving forward.

  - **External Communication:** If applicable, notify customers, partners, and third-party vendors about the recovery process and any potential impact on their services or data. This is particularly important if the incident affected customer data or service availability.

- **Generating Post-incident Reports for Internal Review and Compliance:**

  - **Incident Documentation:** Compile a detailed report that outlines the full scope of the incident, including the timeline, the actions taken during the response and recovery phases, lessons learned, and any changes made to security policies or systems.

  - **Post-incident Analysis:** Conduct a post-incident review meeting with the incident response team to evaluate the effectiveness of the recovery efforts, discuss any challenges, and identify areas for improvement.

  - **Regulatory Reporting:** If necessary, prepare reports for regulatory bodies to ensure compliance with legal obligations (e.g., GDPR breach notification requirements, HIPAA, or PCI-DSS). This may include documenting the data affected, the cause of the breach, and the steps taken to mitigate the damage.

In summary, the **Recovery Phase** ensures that systems are safely restored, fully operational, and secure from further threats. It requires careful testing, continuous monitoring, and clear communication with stakeholders to prevent any further damage or recurrence. By implementing robust recovery practices and maintaining transparency, organizations can successfully navigate through the recovery process and improve their resilience against future incidents.

CHAPTER 6   INCIDENT RESPONSE AND RECOVERY

Post-incident Activities

The **Post-incident Activities** phase is critical for learning from the incident and improving the overall incident response process. It involves analyzing the event to understand what happened, identifying any weaknesses in the response, and making necessary changes to enhance preparedness for future incidents. This phase also includes ensuring legal and regulatory compliance and using the incident as an opportunity to refine policies, procedures, and training.

Lessons Learned

The final phase of the incident response life cycle is focused on improving future responses by learning from the current incident. After the incident has been resolved, the organization should conduct a comprehensive review. Key activities include

- **Post-incident Review:** Teams analyze the incident response process to identify what went well and what could have been improved. This review should involve all stakeholders and include feedback from incident response teams, IT staff, and management.

- **Updating Policies and Procedures:** Based on the lessons learned, the organization should update its incident response policies, procedures, and playbooks. This ensures that the team is better prepared for future incidents.

- **Enhancing Training:** The review should also lead to updates in employee training programs. New tactics, techniques, and procedures (TTPs) identified during the incident can be incorporated into training to ensure that personnel are better equipped for future threats.

- **Improving Security Posture:** Lastly, the lessons learned should help improve the organization's overall security posture. This might involve implementing new security controls, upgrading technology, or revising risk management strategies.

By following these six phases, organizations can ensure they are ready to handle security incidents efficiently, recover quickly, and continuously improve their security capabilities. The incident response life cycle is cyclical, and each incident serves as an opportunity for growth, helping organizations become more resilient in the face of evolving threats.

Improving Incident Response Plans

Post-incident activities should also focus on refining the organization's **Incident Response Plan (IRP)** and improving team readiness. This helps ensure that future incidents are managed more effectively.

- **Updating Policies and Procedures:**
  - **Revise the Incident Response Plan:** Based on the lessons learned, update the organization's incident response plan to address any gaps identified during the incident. This could involve improving detection mechanisms, refining containment strategies, or revising recovery procedures.
  - **Review and Adjust Security Controls:** If the incident exposed weaknesses in security controls, such as inadequate patch management or weak access controls, these should be addressed immediately. Strengthening the organization's security posture will help prevent similar incidents in the future.

- **Enhance Communication Protocols:** If communication issues arose during the incident (e.g., delays in sharing information, lack of clarity in roles), the communication protocols should be revised to ensure timely, effective, and clear communication during future incidents.

- **Enhancing Team Training and Resources:**
  - **Regular Training and Drills:** Use insights from the incident to enhance training programs for the incident response team. Conduct tabletop exercises and simulate similar incidents to test the team's response capabilities.

  - **Improving Technical Resources:** If gaps in technical resources (e.g., tools for detection, containment, or analysis) were identified during the incident, ensure the team has access to the necessary tools and resources. This could include upgrading SIEM platforms, enhancing endpoint detection and response (EDR) capabilities, or integrating threat intelligence feeds for faster decision-making.

  - **Cross-Department Collaboration:** Strengthen collaboration between teams involved in incident response, such as IT, legal, PR, and HR, to ensure that roles and responsibilities are clear and coordinated.

Incident Response Policies and Procedures

Having well-defined incident response policies and procedures is vital for organizations to respond swiftly and efficiently to security incidents. These documents outline the framework for managing incidents, ensuring a consistent and coordinated approach. Below, we break down the key components of incident response policies and procedures.

Establishing an Incident Response Policy

An effective Incident Response (IR) policy serves as the blueprint for how an organization prepares for and handles security incidents. It sets the foundation for the entire incident response life cycle and ensures that all team members understand their roles and responsibilities. Key elements to include in an IR policy are

- **Define Scope and Objectives:**

    The scope outlines what constitutes a security incident for the organization. This can include data breaches, system compromises, and service disruptions. The objectives focus on minimizing damage, restoring operations quickly, and learning from incidents to improve future responses. This section ensures that the policy aligns with organizational goals and clearly defines the purpose of incident response efforts.

- **Assign Roles and Responsibilities:**

    Every incident response effort requires clear delegation of roles to ensure the response is effective and timely. Common roles include

    - **Incident Commander:** The leader of the response effort, responsible for overall decision-making and resource allocation.

- **Communications Officer:** Manages both internal and external communication, ensuring accurate and timely information is shared with stakeholders.

- **Technical Lead:** Responsible for investigating the technical aspects of the incident, such as forensic analysis, and implementing containment measures.

- **Legal and Compliance Officer:** Ensures that the response follows legal and regulatory requirements. Clearly defining these roles ensures that responsibilities are understood and there is no confusion during a crisis.

- **Determine Thresholds for Declaring an Incident:**

    The policy should define the criteria for when an event escalates into a formal incident. These thresholds help ensure that responses are proportionate to the severity of the situation. The policy should specify what triggers an incident declaration, which could be based on factors such as the scope of impact, whether sensitive data is affected, or if there is potential for reputational damage.

Developing Incident Response Playbooks

Incident response playbooks are detailed, step-by-step guides that provide clear instructions for responding to specific types of security incidents. They are essential for ensuring a consistent, structured response to incidents and can be customized for different attack scenarios. Key components to include in an incident response playbook are

CHAPTER 6 INCIDENT RESPONSE AND RECOVERY

- **Detailed Guides for Specific Incident Types:**

    Playbooks should cover a range of potential incident types, such as ransomware, phishing attacks, data breaches, denial of service (DoS), and insider threats. For each incident type, provide a detailed guide that outlines the necessary actions to take at each phase of the incident response life cycle, from identification through recovery.

- **Tools and Resources:**

    Each playbook should list the tools and resources required to handle the incident effectively. For example, it may include specific forensic tools, network monitoring tools, malware analysis platforms, and secure communication methods. Ensuring that the team has access to the appropriate tools during an incident is crucial for minimizing response time and reducing the impact of the event.

- **Escalation Paths:**

    Clear escalation paths help ensure that incidents are handled at the appropriate level. The playbook should define what constitutes a low, medium, or high-severity incident and the appropriate escalation procedures. For example, if an incident cannot be contained within a certain time frame, it should be escalated to higher levels of management or external support teams.

- **Documentation Templates:**

    Incident documentation is vital for tracking actions taken during an incident, communicating with stakeholders, and conducting post-incident reviews.

Playbooks should provide templates for capturing key details, such as incident timelines, affected systems, response actions, and lessons learned. This documentation can also be used for compliance and auditing purposes.

Incident Response Maturity Models

Organizations can improve their incident response capabilities over time by assessing and advancing their **incident response maturity**. Maturity models provide a structured approach to evaluating how well an organization can detect, manage, and recover from cybersecurity incidents. By understanding where they stand on the maturity scale, organizations can prioritize improvements and move toward more effective, efficient, and proactive incident management.

Maturity Levels

Incident response maturity can be thought of as a journey that begins with reactive and disorganized approaches and progresses toward proactive, predictive, and automated capabilities.

- **Ad Hoc Response vs. Formalized and Repeatable Incident Management:**
    - At the **ad hoc** stage, incident response processes are typically informal, reactive, and inconsistent. Organizations may lack clear procedures, roles, and responsibilities, leading to confusion and slow response times during incidents. The response may be dependent on individual efforts and experience rather than a coordinated, structured approach.

- As an organization matures, incident response moves toward being **formalized and repeatable**. This stage involves the development of documented incident response plans, defined roles and responsibilities, and established processes for detecting, containing, and recovering from incidents. The organization may begin tracking performance metrics (e.g., mean time to detect and mean time to respond) and using these to improve its processes.

- At higher maturity levels, organizations implement continuous improvement through feedback loops, lessons learned, and regular testing of their plans. The response is agile and adaptable, ensuring that it can evolve with emerging threats and changing business environments.

- **Moving Toward Proactive Threat Hunting and Predictive Response Capabilities:**

    - As organizations progress in their incident response maturity, they move from reactive to proactive strategies. This includes actively hunting for threats within the network, identifying potential attack vectors, and uncovering indicators of compromise (IOCs) before they result in actual incidents.

    - At advanced maturity levels, organizations integrate **predictive response capabilities**. This could involve using **AI/ML-driven tools** to predict potential threats based on historical data, trends, and threat intelligence. By predicting and preventing incidents before they occur, organizations can reduce the impact and improve their overall resilience.

Frameworks for Maturity Assessment

To assess the maturity of incident response capabilities, organizations can use **maturity models** and **frameworks** that provide a structured evaluation of an organization's readiness. These frameworks typically offer defined levels of maturity, from initial stages (e.g., ad hoc) to optimized processes that are constantly evolving.

- **NIST Cybersecurity Framework (CSF):**
    - The **NIST Cybersecurity Framework** provides a comprehensive set of standards, guidelines, and best practices to manage cybersecurity risks. It can be used to evaluate and improve incident response capabilities as part of the **Respond** function in the framework, which focuses on the detection, containment, eradication, and recovery of incidents.
    - The CSF includes guidelines for establishing a structured incident response process, continuously improving that process, and ensuring resilience in the face of attacks. By aligning their processes with the CSF, organizations can evaluate where they are on the maturity spectrum and identify areas for improvement.

- **CERT Resilience Management Model (CERT-RMM):**

  - The **CERT Resilience Management Model (CERT-RMM)** is another valuable tool for assessing incident response maturity. This model provides a framework for evaluating and improving an organization's security, business continuity, and incident management practices.

  - CERT-RMM includes detailed practices and processes for responding to incidents in a manner that ensures business continuity and minimizes damage. By evaluating their capabilities using CERT-RMM, organizations can identify weaknesses in their response procedures and ensure they have the necessary resources, tools, and processes in place to handle security incidents efficiently.

These models also emphasize the need for continuous improvement. As organizations mature, they should routinely revisit their frameworks, conduct assessments, and adjust their incident response capabilities to stay ahead of evolving cyber threats.

Key Takeaways

- **Maturity levels** reflect the progress an organization has made in formalizing, optimizing, and evolving its incident response processes. Moving from ad hoc responses to proactive, predictive approaches significantly improves an organization's ability to handle cyber threats effectively.

- **Frameworks for maturity assessment** like the NIST Cybersecurity Framework and CERT-RMM provide structured methodologies for evaluating and improving incident response capabilities, guiding organizations as they move toward more mature and resilient incident management processes.

- As incident response capabilities mature, organizations can expect to handle incidents with greater speed, efficiency, and accuracy, while also mitigating the potential damage from security breaches and minimizing recovery time.

By leveraging these maturity models, organizations can take a more strategic approach to their incident response and continually evolve their practices to stay ahead of emerging threats.

Testing an Incident Response Policy

Regular testing and practice are crucial to ensuring that an incident response plan is effective when the need arises. Tabletop exercises and simulations allow incident response teams to walk through the plan in a low-stakes environment, identifying gaps in the process and refining their strategies.

- **Benefits of Testing the Plan:** Tabletop exercises help incident response teams to familiarize themselves with the procedures, practice communication protocols, and identify areas where improvements can be made. These exercises also help reinforce roles and responsibilities, ensuring that each team member is prepared for their tasks during a real incident.

- **Examples of Common Scenarios for Tabletop Exercises:**

    - **Ransomware Attack:** Teams simulate responding to a ransomware infection, from containment to recovery, while handling internal and external communications.

    - **Data Breach:** A scenario where sensitive data is exfiltrated, testing the team's ability to handle legal, regulatory, and notification requirements.

    - **Denial of Service Attack (DoS):** A test of the team's ability to detect and mitigate a large-scale DoS or DDoS attack while maintaining service continuity.

These exercises help ensure that all members of the incident response team are familiar with the tools, processes, and roles required to respond effectively when a real incident occurs.

Legal and Compliance Considerations

Incident response efforts must align with legal and regulatory requirements to ensure that the organization remains compliant and avoids potential penalties. Legal and compliance considerations must be integrated into the IR policy and playbooks. Key areas to consider include

- **Ensure Alignment with Regulatory Requirements:**

    Organizations must ensure that their incident response efforts comply with relevant regulations and standards, such as:

    - **General Data Protection Regulation (GDPR):** For organizations handling data from EU citizens, GDPR mandates specific breach notification procedures and timelines.

- **Health Insurance Portability and Accountability Act (HIPAA):** For healthcare organizations, HIPAA outlines strict requirements for protecting patient data and reporting breaches.

- **Payment Card Industry Data Security Standard (PCI-DSS):** For businesses handling payment card information, PCI-DSS requires immediate action to mitigate and report breaches involving credit card data.

The policy and playbooks should include procedures to ensure that these regulations are adhered to during the response process, such as reporting timelines, notifications to affected individuals, and coordination with relevant regulatory bodies.

- **Document Incidents Thoroughly to Meet Audit Requirements:**

    Regulatory bodies often require organizations to maintain detailed records of any incidents, including the nature of the breach, the timeline of events, and the actions taken in response. Incident response policies should include provisions for maintaining comprehensive, accurate records that document the entire incident handling process. This documentation not only supports compliance efforts but also provides valuable data for post-incident analysis and audits.

Having well-documented incident response policies, procedures, and playbooks ensures that organizations can effectively handle security incidents, comply with regulatory requirements, and minimize the impact of breaches. By defining roles, assigning responsibilities, establishing escalation protocols, and considering legal and compliance factors, organizations can build a strong foundation for incident response, improving their resilience against cyber threats.

Roles and Responsibilities in Incident Response

Effective incident response hinges on the coordination and specialization of various roles within the Incident Response Team (IRT). Each member plays a critical part in ensuring that the organization can efficiently handle and mitigate the impact of a security incident. Below is a breakdown of the key roles and responsibilities involved in incident response.

Incident Response Team (IRT)

The Incident Response Team is a specialized group of professionals with the responsibility of responding to and managing security incidents. The IRT is typically composed of various experts, each tasked with specific responsibilities to ensure a swift and effective response. The core roles within an IRT include

- **Incident Manager:**

    The Incident Manager oversees the entire incident response process. They coordinate between different teams, ensuring that all actions taken align with the overall response plan. The Incident Manager is also responsible for maintaining communication with senior management, ensuring that decisions are made efficiently, and that resources are allocated as needed. Their primary focus is on strategic direction and ensuring the incident response stays on track.

- **Forensic Analyst:**

  The Forensic Analyst is responsible for investigating the details of the security incident. This includes collecting and preserving evidence, analyzing logs, and identifying the root cause of the breach. The Forensic Analyst often works with specialized tools to uncover how the attack occurred, what vulnerabilities were exploited, and the extent of the damage. Their findings are crucial for both resolving the current incident and improving future defenses.

- **Communications Specialist:**

  The Communications Specialist plays a vital role in ensuring clear, accurate, and timely communication during an incident. This includes internal communication with stakeholders and employees, as well as external communication to customers, regulatory bodies, and the public. The Communications Specialist ensures that information is conveyed correctly and that messages are consistent across all channels. Their role also involves managing media relations and ensuring compliance with disclosure requirements, especially in cases where regulatory bodies or affected individuals need to be notified.

- **IT Support:**

    The IT Support team is essential for the technical aspects of the incident response. They implement containment and recovery measures, such as isolating compromised systems, applying patches, and restoring systems to a secure state. IT Support ensures that the organization's infrastructure is secured and operational as quickly as possible. They may also assist in the eradication of the threat by removing malware or unauthorized access points.

Third-Party Involvement

In many cases, an organization may need to engage third-party experts to support the incident response process. These external parties bring specialized knowledge and tools that may not be available internally, allowing for a more comprehensive and effective response. Common third-party partners include

- **Managed Security Service Providers (MSSPs):**

    MSSPs are external vendors that provide continuous security monitoring and management services. During an incident, they can assist with detecting anomalies, managing alerts, and providing additional expertise in threat analysis and response. MSSPs may also offer access to advanced security tools and resources that can enhance the organization's incident response capabilities.

- **Digital Forensics Teams:**

    Digital forensics teams are specialized experts in recovering, preserving, and analyzing digital evidence related to cyber incidents. These teams may be called upon to support the forensic analysis of the incident, including identifying the origin of the attack, understanding the attacker's tactics, and ensuring that evidence is preserved for potential legal proceedings. Their expertise in data retrieval and analysis helps organizations build a clear picture of the incident.

Tools and Technologies for Incident Response

A wide range of tools and technologies are available to support incident response efforts. These tools can help automate processes, analyze data, and ensure efficient handling of incidents. Below are some of the essential tools and technologies used in incident response:

Essential Tools

There is a tool for every job and some tools may hold more than one purpose, but there is no singular tool to meet every unique need. With that in mind, it is best to know what some of the core players are in respect to the incident response process. CompTIA maintains a vendor neutral policy so we will not be comparing the various brands or implementations of these products at this time.

CHAPTER 6   INCIDENT RESPONSE AND RECOVERY

Security Information and Event Management (SIEM)

SIEM systems are vital for centralized monitoring, logging, and alerting across an organization's IT infrastructure. SIEM tools collect data from a variety of sources, including network devices, servers, endpoints, and security tools, and analyze it for suspicious activity. They generate alerts based on predefined criteria, which can help incident responders quickly detect potential security breaches. Popular SIEM solutions include Splunk, IBM QRadar, and ArcSight.

Endpoint Detection and Response (EDR)

EDR tools focus on monitoring and securing endpoint devices, such as desktops, laptops, and mobile devices. These tools provide real-time monitoring and alerting on activities that may indicate a breach, such as unusual login attempts, malware activity, or changes to critical system files. EDR tools also allow for deep investigation into endpoint activity, enabling responders to identify the root cause of an attack and contain the threat quickly.

Forensic Tools

Forensic tools are used to collect and analyze digital evidence in a way that preserves its integrity for legal and investigative purposes. Tools like EnCase, FTK, and open-source platforms (e.g., Autopsy, Sleuth Kit) allow forensic analysts to retrieve deleted files, examine disk images, analyze memory dumps, and perform deep investigations into the nature of the attack. These tools play a critical role in determining how an attack occurred and ensuring that all evidence is properly handled.

CHAPTER 6   INCIDENT RESPONSE AND RECOVERY

Automation in Incident Response

Automating incident response processes can greatly improve the speed and efficiency of handling security incidents. The use of automation reduces the manual workload on responders and helps eliminate human error. Key automation tools include

SOAR (Security Orchestration, Automation, and Response)

SOAR platforms help streamline incident response by automating routine tasks, such as alert prioritization, case management, and incident documentation. These platforms integrate with other security tools and systems, such as SIEMs and EDRs, to provide a unified response. SOAR can automate actions like isolating compromised devices, blocking malicious IP addresses, or initiating an investigation workflow, allowing security teams to focus on more complex tasks. Popular SOAR solutions include Palo Alto Networks Cortex XSOAR, IBM Resilient, and ServiceNow Security Operations.

Threat Intelligence Integration

Integrating external threat intelligence into the incident response process provides valuable context that can speed up the investigation and response. Threat intelligence feeds provide real-time information about emerging threats, attack indicators, and active campaigns. This intelligence can be used to enrich SIEM alerts, EDR data, and forensic investigations. Key actions for integrating threat intelligence include

- **Enrich Investigations with External Threat Feeds:**

    Threat intelligence feeds, such as those provided by vendors like CrowdStrike or Anomali, deliver up-to-date information on the tactics, techniques, and procedures (TTPs) used by threat actors. Integrating these feeds into security systems helps responders quickly identify known threat indicators and provide context to ongoing investigations. For example, if an IP address involved in an attack is known to be associated with a specific group of hackers, the investigation can be prioritized and adjusted accordingly.

- **Indicators of Compromise (IoCs):**

    IoCs are specific artifacts or patterns of activity that indicate the presence of a security breach, such as file hashes, IP addresses, or URLs associated with malicious activity. These indicators can be incorporated into monitoring systems to help detect similar activities across the network and accelerate threat detection and remediation.

A successful incident response requires a well-coordinated team, specialized roles, and the use of advanced tools and technologies. By clearly defining the roles and responsibilities of each team member, engaging external experts when needed, and utilizing modern tools like SIEM, EDR, and SOAR, organizations can respond to incidents efficiently and minimize their impact. Integrating threat intelligence further enhances response efforts, enabling teams to stay ahead of emerging threats and respond proactively to security incidents.

CHAPTER 6   INCIDENT RESPONSE AND RECOVERY

Recovery Planning and Execution

When a security incident occurs, it doesn't end with containment and eradication. The final, crucial step is recovery—bringing systems back online while ensuring that they are secure and reliable. The recovery phase isn't just about restoring services; it's about making sure that everything functions properly and that no lingering threats remain. Below, we'll break down the key elements of recovery planning and execution in a way that's easy to understand and apply.

Key Objectives of Recovery

The goal of recovery is simple: get your organization back on its feet but do it right. It's about balancing speed with safety, making sure systems are restored quickly but also securely. The two key objectives are

- **Restore Operations Quickly and Safely:**

    The sooner critical systems are back up and running, the less disruption there is to the business. However, rushing through recovery could bring threats back into the environment. So, while speed is important, ensuring that systems are fully secured before going live again is essential. Recovery isn't just about hitting the "on" switch; it's about making sure that everything functions the way it should, without opening the door to another attack.

- **Ensure No Residual Threats Remain:**

    A fast recovery is useless if the threat that caused the incident still exists. Whether it's malware, unauthorized accounts, or hidden backdoors, it's crucial to remove all traces of the attack before systems are fully restored.

Recovery isn't complete until you're confident that everything is cleared out, and nothing can cause further damage.

Developing a Recovery Plan

A recovery plan is your roadmap for getting back to normal. It should be clear, actionable, and well-documented to avoid confusion or missed steps. Here are the essential pieces to include:

Identify Critical Systems and Prioritize Restoration

Not all systems are equal in importance. Some systems are mission-critical, meaning that without them, operations could grind to a halt. Others are secondary. A good recovery plan identifies which systems are vital to the business and sets a priority for restoring them. By focusing on the most important systems first, you minimize downtime and reduce the impact on operations.

Set Recovery Objectives: RPO and RTO

Two key metrics drive how you approach recovery:

> **Recovery Point Objective (RPO):** This defines how much data loss is acceptable during an incident. For instance, if your RPO is set to four hours, your recovery plan needs to ensure that you can restore data from no later than four hours before the incident. The smaller the RPO, the more frequent your backups will need to be.

Recovery Time Objective (RTO): This is how long you can afford for systems to be down before it negatively impacts business operations. If your RTO is four hours, then the critical systems must be restored within that window. The RTO directly influences how you prioritize and execute the recovery process.

Defining these objectives helps you set expectations and ensures that recovery efforts align with your organization's needs.

Validating Recovery

Once systems are restored, you don't want to just assume everything's back to normal. Validation is the process of making sure that recovery was successful and that all systems are functioning securely. Here's how to validate recovery:

- **Test System Integrity and Functionality:**

    After restoring systems, it's vital to run tests to confirm that everything is working correctly. This isn't just about checking if applications open or files are accessible. You need to check for performance issues, verify that security patches have been applied, and ensure that the system is stable. It's also important to confirm that data has been restored correctly and that no files were corrupted during the recovery process.

- **Monitor for Recurrence:**

    The recovery phase doesn't end once systems are up and running. You need to keep an eye on everything to make sure the incident doesn't come back. Continued monitoring is crucial, especially in the days or weeks following recovery. Keep track of logs, watch for unusual activities, and run security scans to ensure no hidden threats remain. This ongoing vigilance is key to catching any potential signs of recurring issues or overlooked risks.

Effective recovery planning and execution are vital for ensuring that your organization can bounce back after a security incident. By clearly defining your recovery objectives, prioritizing critical systems, and validating the integrity of restored systems, you can ensure a smooth and secure transition back to normal operations. And don't forget—monitoring and validation shouldn't stop once recovery is complete. With these best practices, your organization will be better prepared to handle the challenges that come after a breach, ensuring that recovery isn't just a return to business, but a chance to reinforce resilience and strengthen your security posture for the future.

Business Continuity and Disaster Recovery (BC/DR)

While Incident Response (IR) focuses on detecting, containing, and resolving immediate security threats, Business Continuity (BC) and Disaster Recovery (DR) plans ensure that operations can continue and critical systems are restored after an incident. Incident response is an essential part of BC/DR, but BC/DR plans ensure that the organization can continue to function, even if the incident causes significant disruption.

Business Impact Analysis (BIA)

BIA identifies the most critical business processes and systems that must be prioritized for recovery. It analyzes the potential impacts of disruptions to these processes and identifies dependencies between different functions and systems. This allows for prioritizing recovery efforts based on their importance to business operations.

Disaster Recovery Plans (DRPs)

DRPs outline the detailed, step-by-step procedures to restore systems, applications, and data that are vital to business functions. These plans are focused on IT systems, such as servers, networks, and data storage, and specify recovery point objectives (RPOs) and recovery time objectives (RTOs) to ensure minimal impact to operations. They also include specific actions for system restoration and the resources required to recover from an incident.

Continuity Plans

While DRPs focus on restoring IT infrastructure, continuity plans focus on maintaining essential operations. These plans outline how critical business functions can continue during recovery. For example, while IT teams restore network functionality, continuity plans ensure that customer-facing services, like support or sales, remain operational during this time.

Testing and Updating Plans

Business continuity and disaster recovery plans must be dynamic, evolving documents. They must be regularly tested, updated, and refined to ensure they remain effective:

- **Conduct Regular Disaster Recovery Exercises:**

    Disaster recovery exercises simulate a variety of disaster scenarios to assess the readiness of the recovery team, the functionality of the disaster recovery plan, and the organization's ability to execute a timely recovery. These exercises help to identify any weaknesses in the plan and ensure all stakeholders understand their roles.

- **Incorporate Lessons Learned from Incidents into BC/DR Updates:**

    After an incident or recovery exercise, it is critical to review the effectiveness of the BC/DR plan. Lessons learned from previous incidents should be incorporated into the planning process to improve recovery strategies, update procedures, and strengthen overall preparedness.

By ensuring that incident response and business continuity are aligned and continuously tested, organizations can significantly reduce the impact of disruptions and maintain operations even in the face of disaster.

CHAPTER 6   INCIDENT RESPONSE AND RECOVERY

Incident Postmortem and Continuous Improvement

Once an incident has been resolved and systems are restored, it's time to evaluate the response to understand what worked and what didn't. A thorough post-incident review helps organizations improve their incident response process for future events.

Gather Stakeholders to Evaluate Response Effectiveness

Bring together all key stakeholders involved in the response effort, including members of the incident response team, IT, legal, and management. Discuss what went well, what could have been handled better, and areas for improvement. This feedback loop helps ensure that the organization learns from each incident.

Document Findings and Recommendations

Carefully document the findings from the review. This should include details on the incident's timeline, actions taken, and outcomes. Identify any gaps in tools, procedures, or communication. Provide actionable recommendations for enhancing response efforts, such as new tools or changes to workflows.

Updating Policies and Procedures

Post-incident reviews are invaluable for uncovering weaknesses in security practices and response strategies. Once the lessons from an incident are clear, it's essential to translate those insights into actionable updates to policies and procedures, strengthening the organization's overall security posture.

Adjust Response Strategies Based on New Threats or Gaps Identified

Refine incident response processes to address newly identified threats or operational weaknesses revealed during the incident.

- **Key Actions:**
  - **Update Incident Response Plans:** Revise playbooks to include new detection rules, investigation workflows, or containment techniques tailored to the specific threat.
  - **Enhance Communication Protocols:** Streamline communication between internal teams and external stakeholders to ensure faster and more effective collaboration during incidents.
  - **Improve Escalation Paths:** Ensure that critical incidents reach the appropriate decision-makers promptly, reducing delays in response.
- **Outcome:**

  Enhanced readiness for future incidents, reducing response times and minimizing damage when threats arise.

Strengthen Security Measures

Address the root causes of the incident by improving security controls and closing exploitable gaps.

- **Key Actions:**
  - **Patch Management:** Deploy patches for vulnerabilities that were exploited and establish processes to ensure timely updates in the future.
  - **Upgrade Security Controls:** Implement advanced technologies such as Endpoint Detection and Response (EDR) or Network Detection and Response (NDR) tools to enhance threat visibility.
  - **Fortify Network Defenses:** Update firewall rules, access controls, and intrusion prevention systems (IPS) to address weaknesses exposed during the incident.
  - **User Training:** Educate employees on security best practices, especially if human error contributed to the incident.
- **Outcome:**

  A more robust and resilient security infrastructure capable of mitigating similar threats in the future.

Best Practices for Policy Updates

- **Collaborate Across Teams:** Involve all stakeholders, including SOC analysts, IT teams, and executive leadership, to ensure updates are practical and align with business objectives.
- **Regular Review Cycles:** Schedule periodic reviews of policies and procedures to keep them aligned with evolving threats and organizational changes.

- **Document Changes Clearly:** Maintain detailed records of all updates, including the rationale behind them, to support training efforts and audits.

By continuously refining policies and procedures based on real-world experiences, organizations can build a proactive and adaptive security framework, improving both prevention and response capabilities.

Training and Awareness

Incorporating lessons learned from security incidents into organizational training and awareness efforts is essential for fostering a proactive and resilient security culture. By sharing knowledge gained from real-world experiences, organizations can empower employees to better understand threats and play an active role in maintaining a secure environment.

Share Lessons Learned Across Teams to Build a Stronger Security Culture

Use post-incident insights to strengthen team collaboration and ensure all employees are equipped to contribute to the organization's security.

- **Key Actions:**
    - **Conduct Incident Debriefs:** Host cross-functional meetings to review what happened, the impact, and the steps taken to resolve the incident. Focus on areas where team actions were effective and where improvement is needed.

- **Develop Targeted Training:** Create tailored training modules based on the specific challenges identified during the incident. For example, if phishing was a factor, enhance training on recognizing malicious emails.

- **Leverage Internal Communication Channels:** Share incident insights through newsletters, bulletins, or blogs, emphasizing actionable takeaways and organizational improvements.

- **Highlight Best Practices:** Showcase examples of successful responses or preventive actions to motivate teams and encourage adherence to security protocols.

• **Outcome:**

A well-informed workforce that actively supports security measures and responds effectively to potential threats.

Promote a Culture of Continuous Improvement

Reinforce the importance of security as a shared responsibility across all levels of the organization.

- **Key Actions:**
  - **Encourage Feedback:** Allow employees to provide input on incident responses and suggest ways to improve security practices, creating a sense of ownership and involvement.

- **Gamify Security Awareness:** Introduce challenges or recognition programs to reward employees for identifying vulnerabilities or completing security training.

- **Schedule Regular Updates:** Use team meetings or company-wide forums to provide updates on new threats, security tools, or revised policies, ensuring everyone remains informed.

- **Outcome:**

  A dynamic and engaged workforce committed to staying ahead of security challenges through shared learning and continuous development.

Best Practices for Effective Training and Awareness

- **Tailor Content to Roles:** Ensure training materials are relevant to each team's responsibilities, whether it's IT staff, executives, or general employees.

- **Incorporate Real-World Scenarios:** Use examples from actual incidents to demonstrate the importance of vigilance and proper response.

- **Monitor and Measure Effectiveness:** Track metrics like training completion rates and incident reporting trends to evaluate the impact of awareness programs.

By integrating lessons learned into ongoing training and fostering open communication about security issues, organizations can create an environment where employees understand their role in safeguarding digital assets and actively contribute to preventing future incidents.

CHAPTER 6   INCIDENT RESPONSE AND RECOVERY

Metrics for Continuous Improvement

To gauge the effectiveness of the changes made and monitor progress over time, organizations should track key performance metrics:

- **Mean Time to Detect (MTTD) and Mean Time to Respond (MTTR):**

    Track how quickly security incidents are detected and how fast the team can respond. These metrics provide insight into the effectiveness of detection tools and the response efficiency of the incident response team. A shorter MTTD and MTTR indicate a more effective response strategy.

- **Number of Incidents Detected Through Proactive Measures (e.g., Threat Hunting):**

    Evaluate how many security incidents were detected through proactive measures, such as threat hunting or continuous monitoring. The goal is to identify potential threats before they cause significant harm, and tracking this metric can help assess the success of proactive security strategies.

By incorporating post-incident reviews, continuous learning, and the right metrics, organizations can build more effective incident response strategies, minimize the impact of future incidents, and enhance their overall security posture.

Chapter Summary

This chapter provides readers with a comprehensive framework for establishing an effective incident response and recovery process. By covering the entire incident response life cycle—from preparation to lessons learned—organizations will gain a clear understanding of how to minimize the impact of security incidents while ensuring business continuity. Key concepts such as developing incident response policies, assigning roles, and using essential tools are explored in detail to empower teams to respond swiftly and effectively.

The chapter also emphasizes the critical importance of recovery planning. Readers will learn how to design recovery strategies that prioritize the restoration of business operations, protect against residual threats, and validate system integrity post-recovery. The relationship between incident response and broader business continuity and disaster recovery plans is also discussed, highlighting the need for comprehensive planning to ensure resilience.

Finally, the chapter delves into continuous improvement, demonstrating how post-incident reviews, training, and proactive metrics can strengthen response efforts over time. By integrating lessons learned and regularly updating policies and procedures, organizations can enhance their preparedness for future incidents. Through practical examples and step-by-step guidance, this chapter equips readers with the tools and knowledge necessary to handle security incidents with confidence, minimize operational disruptions, and foster a culture of continuous improvement in their security practices.

CHAPTER 7

Threat Intelligence, Indicators of Compromise, and Secure Operations

Types of Indicators of Compromise (IOCs)

Indicators of Compromise (IOCs) are breadcrumbs left behind by malicious activity. Detecting and analyzing IOCs is critical for identifying threats, assessing damage, and implementing countermeasures. These indicators come in various forms, each offering a unique perspective on potential compromises.

File-Based IOCs

File-based IOCs are clues tied to specific malicious files. These indicators help cybersecurity teams identify and analyze malware artifacts.

- File Hashes:

  Every file has a unique cryptographic hash, such as MD5, SHA-1, or SHA-256, which serves as its fingerprint. Malicious files often have known hashes listed in threat intelligence databases.

  - *Example*: A malware file with the SHA-256 hash b6f456e7f8... matches a signature in a threat feed, confirming its malicious nature.

- Filenames and Paths:

  Certain filenames or directory paths are commonly associated with malware. Adversaries often hide malicious files in system folders to avoid detection.

  - *Example*: The presence of a file named malicious.exe in the C:\Windows\Temp\ directory could signal an active threat.

- File Attributes:

  Unusual timestamps, file permissions, or unexpected file types in critical directories can also serve as IOCs.

  - *Example*: Files with future timestamps or created during non-operational hours may warrant investigation.

Network-Based IOCs

Network-based IOCs reveal suspicious activities occurring over an organization's network. These indicators are crucial for identifying malicious communication and exfiltration attempts.

CHAPTER 7   THREAT INTELLIGENCE, INDICATORS OF COMPROMISE, AND SECURE OPERATIONS

- IP Addresses:

    Malicious or suspicious IP addresses often point to attacker-controlled servers. Security teams track known bad IPs using threat intelligence feeds.

    - *Example*: Traffic to the IP address 192.0.2.123, known to host a command-and-control (C2) server, raises immediate red flags.

- Domain Names and URLs:

    Attackers frequently use deceptive domains and URLs for phishing campaigns, malware distribution, or C2 operations.

    - *Example*: Access to login-securebanking.com, a domain mimicking a legitimate banking website, might indicate a phishing attempt.

- Network Traffic Patterns:

    Unusual traffic patterns, such as data spikes, connections to uncommon ports, or encrypted payloads to unknown destinations, often signal malicious activity.

    - *Example*: A workstation suddenly transmitting large amounts of data to an external server during off-hours could indicate data exfiltration.

- DNS Anomalies:

    Malicious actors may manipulate DNS queries to redirect users or mask their activities.

    - *Example*: Excessive DNS requests for a single domain, especially from multiple endpoints, may indicate botnet activity.

Behavioral IOCs

Behavioral IOCs focus on anomalies in how systems, applications, or users operate. These indicators often point to active compromises or advanced persistent threats (APTs).

- Unusual System Behaviors:

  Processes consuming excessive CPU, memory, or network bandwidth unexpectedly may be executing malicious code.

  - *Example*: A legitimate-looking process like explorer.exe suddenly spiking in resource usage might indicate process hollowing.

- Registry Modifications:

  Malware frequently modifies system registries to maintain persistence or disable security mechanisms.

  - *Example*: Changes to the registry key HKEY_LOCAL_MACHINE\SOFTWARE\Microsoft\Windows\CurrentVersion\Run to include an unknown executable may signal persistence.

- Unauthorized Privilege Escalation:

  Behavior such as a low-privileged account executing commands typically reserved for administrators is highly suspicious.

  - *Example*: An account running PowerShell scripts to modify critical configurations could indicate credential abuse.

- Scheduled Tasks or Services:

  Attackers often create or modify scheduled tasks and services to execute malicious payloads at specific intervals.

  - *Example*: A new scheduled task labeled SystemUpdate executing a script located in C:\Temp\ could be an IOC.

Why Understanding IOCs Is Critical

IOCs form the backbone of proactive threat detection. By recognizing and acting on these indicators, organizations can

- **Detect Threats Early**: Spot malicious activity before it escalates.
- **Assess and Contain Damage**: Understand the scope of the compromise and prevent further spread.
- **Enhance Threat Intelligence**: Feed newly identified IOCs into threat intelligence systems to strengthen future defenses.

In Action: The Power of IOCs

Imagine a scenario where your intrusion detection system flags a workstation communicating with malware-control.com. At the same time, endpoint monitoring detects a new file named temp12345.exe with a known malicious hash. Correlating these file-based and network-based IOCs allows you to confirm the presence of malware, isolate the infected system, and neutralize the threat before it spreads.

IOCs provide actionable intelligence, enabling cybersecurity teams to detect, respond to, and mitigate threats effectively. Understanding the different types of IOCs—file-based, network-based, and behavioral—empowers organizations to strengthen their defenses and maintain a proactive security posture.

Detecting and Using Indicators of Compromise (IOCs)

The ability to detect and use Indicators of Compromise (IOCs) effectively is a cornerstone of modern cybersecurity practices. Properly identifying, analyzing, and leveraging IOCs empowers organizations to prevent, detect, and respond to cyber threats more efficiently. This involves collecting relevant data, integrating it with security tools, and participating in collaborative threat intelligence-sharing initiatives.

Collecting and Analyzing IOCs

Accurate detection starts with gathering IOCs from diverse sources and analyzing them to extract actionable insights.

1. Collecting IOCs

    IOCs are gathered from multiple tools and processes, forming the foundation for threat detection. Common sources include

    - **Antivirus Logs**: Malicious files and behaviors flagged by antivirus tools.
    - **Endpoint Detection and Response (EDR) Systems**: Suspicious endpoint activity such as privilege escalations or unusual processes.

- **Network Traffic Logs**: Anomalous traffic patterns flagged by firewalls or intrusion detection/prevention systems (IDS/IPS).

- **Threat Intelligence Feeds**: Data from external sources offering insights into known malicious domains, hashes, and IPs.

- **Manual Incident Analysis**: Insights derived from hands-on investigations, such as forensic analysis of infected systems.

2. Analyzing IOCs

Once collected, IOCs are analyzed to assess their relevance, severity, and applicability to the organization's environment. Key techniques include

- **Pattern Matching**: Comparing IOCs against historical data or known attack signatures

- **Correlation with Incidents**: Cross-referencing IOCs with logs from multiple tools to confirm the presence of malicious activity

- **Threat Context Enrichment**: Adding contextual data to IOCs, such as associating an IP address with a known threat actor or campaign

  - *Example*: If an IOC flags the domain badexample.com, enriching this data might reveal its connection to a phishing campaign targeting financial institutions.

Integrating IOCs with Security Tools

To maximize their impact, IOCs must be integrated into an organization's security infrastructure for real-time detection and automated responses.

1. Security Information and Event Management (SIEM)

    - SIEM platforms centralize and analyze logs from multiple sources. Feeding IOCs into a SIEM enables automated alerts and correlation of events.

        - *Example*: A SIEM might trigger an alert when a flagged IP address appears in inbound traffic logs.

2. Endpoint Detection and Response (EDR)

    - EDR tools monitor endpoints for unusual behavior. Deploying IOCs allows these tools to detect and respond to threats, such as killing malicious processes or isolating compromised devices.

        - *Example*: An IOC identifying a file hash triggers the EDR system to quarantine a suspicious executable.

3. Firewalls and IDS/IPS Systems

    - Firewalls and IDS/IPS can block traffic associated with malicious IOCs. These systems are configured with rules to prevent connections to flagged IPs, domains, or URLs.

        - *Example*: A firewall rule may automatically block all traffic to the domain phishing-site.com.

Sharing and Updating IOCs

Collaboration in the cybersecurity community is critical. Sharing and updating IOCs ensures organizations stay ahead of evolving threats and contributes to a stronger collective defense.

1. Best Practices for Sharing IOCs

    Effective IOC sharing can amplify defenses while maintaining confidentiality.

    - **Share with Trusted Partners**: Collaborate with industry groups, information-sharing platforms, or government agencies.

    - **Limit Sensitive Details**: Remove identifiable information when sharing to protect organizational privacy.

        - *Example*: Share the malicious hash and behavior of a file but exclude internal details about where it was found.

2. Standards for IOC Sharing

    Standardized formats simplify and streamline the exchange of threat intelligence. Common standards include

    - **OpenIOC**: An open framework designed for defining and sharing IOCs, ensuring compatibility across platforms.

    - **STIX and TAXII**:

        - **STIX (Structured Threat Information eXpression)**: A format for describing threat intelligence in a machine-readable way.

- **TAXII (Trusted Automated eXchange of Intelligence Information)**: A protocol for sharing threat intelligence data securely and efficiently.

3. Updating IOCs

    Threat actors constantly evolve their tactics, requiring organizations to refresh their IOC databases regularly.

    - Subscribe to updated threat feeds and intelligence sources.
    - Incorporate IOCs derived from recent incidents and investigations into automated detection tools.

Benefits of Proactive IOC Management

A well-orchestrated approach to IOCs offers substantial advantages:

1. **Enhanced Detection Capabilities:** IOCs enable organizations to identify threats early and accurately.
2. **Rapid Incident Response**: Integrating IOCs with security tools automates threat detection and mitigation.
3. **Stronger Collaborative Defense**: Sharing IOCs helps defend against common threats across industries.

The effective use of IOCs is a game-changer in cybersecurity. From collecting and analyzing IOCs to integrating them into security tools and sharing them with trusted communities, these practices significantly enhance an organization's ability to detect, respond to, and mitigate threats. A proactive and collaborative approach ensures resilience against both current and emerging cyber risks.

Threat Intelligence Platforms (TIPs): Enhancing Cybersecurity Operations

In the rapidly evolving landscape of cybersecurity, Threat Intelligence Platforms (TIPs) have emerged as indispensable tools. By consolidating threat intelligence from diverse sources and automating its analysis, TIPs empower organizations to detect, mitigate, and respond to threats with efficiency and precision. These platforms streamline the threat intelligence life cycle, enhance collaboration, and optimize the utility of security infrastructures.

What Are Threat Intelligence Platforms?

Threat Intelligence Platforms (TIPs) are specialized software solutions designed to aggregate, analyze, and operationalize threat intelligence. By centralizing intelligence from multiple sources, TIPs provide actionable insights and enable organizations to address potential risks effectively.

Key Functions of TIPs

- **Aggregation**: Consolidate threat intelligence from sources like Open Source Intelligence (OSINT), commercial feeds, internal logs, and community-shared data.

- **Analysis**: Correlate and prioritize threats based on relevance, severity, and potential impact.
- **Dissemination**: Share threat intelligence with security tools, stakeholders, and teams to enable coordinated responses.

Why TIPs Are Critical

- TIPs eliminate inefficiencies caused by fragmented threat data and reduce the complexity of managing disparate sources.
- They simplify the threat intelligence life cycle, from collection and analysis to distribution and implementation, providing a unified view of the threat landscape.

Core Features and Benefits of TIPs

1. Integration with Security Tools

    TIPs serve as the central hub for threat intelligence, seamlessly integrating with

    - **SIEM (Security Information and Event Management) Systems**: Enrich threat alerts and enable real-time correlation with log data.
    - **Firewalls and IDS/IPS**: Push rules and blocklists to these systems for proactive defense.

- **Endpoint Detection and Response (EDR) Tools**: Enhance endpoint protection by detecting and responding to threats flagged by the TIP.
- **Threat Hunting Tools**: Feed intelligence into tools for proactive discovery of hidden threats.

2. Real-Time Capabilities

TIPs provide critical, time-sensitive insights for immediate action:

- **Automated Alerts**: Notify security teams of emerging threats as they are detected.
- **Threat Scoring and Prioritization**: Assign scores to threats based on factors like potential impact, prevalence, and relevance to the organization.
- **Contextual Analysis**: Offer enriched data about threat actors, their motives, techniques, and targets, helping teams make informed decisions.

3. Automation and Collaboration

TIPs significantly enhance operational efficiency and collaboration:

- **Automated Dissemination**: Ensure that updated threat intelligence is automatically distributed to relevant tools and teams.
- **Collaboration Tools**: Facilitate information sharing across internal teams and with external partners, fostering collective defense.
- **Regulatory Compliance**: Maintain detailed logs and generate reports to meet legal and industry compliance standards.

Popular Threat Intelligence Platforms

Several Threat Intelligence Platforms dominate the market, offering tailored solutions for diverse organizational needs.

1. ThreatConnect

    - **Strengths**: Renowned for advanced integration capabilities and a user-friendly interface.
    - **Use Case**: Ideal for organizations looking to align threats with operational impacts using contextual mapping.

2. Anomali

    - **Strengths**: Focuses on advanced detection, high compatibility with SIEM systems, and efficient workflows.
    - **Use Case**: Suitable for enterprises seeking operational scalability and streamlined threat intelligence management.

3. IBM X-Force Exchange

    - **Strengths**: Leverages IBM's extensive threat database and provides robust collaboration tools.
    - **Use Case**: Best for organizations needing actionable, research-backed insights into global threat activity.

How to Select the Right TIP

Choosing the ideal TIP depends on the organization's specific needs, resources, and infrastructure.

Considerations for Small-to-Mid-Sized Organizations

- **Scalability**: Ensure the platform can grow with your organization.

- **Ease of Use**: Look for simple interfaces and seamless integration with existing tools.

- **Cost-Effectiveness**: Prioritize features that meet core needs without overwhelming the budget.

Considerations for Large Enterprises

- **Advanced Analytics**: Machine learning and AI capabilities for dynamic threat detection and analysis.

- **Multisource Data Correlation**: Support for ingesting and correlating large volumes of intelligence from multiple feeds.

- **Customizable Workflows**: Flexibility to adapt to complex security operations and unique organizational requirements.

Threat Intelligence Platforms are essential for modern cybersecurity strategies. By aggregating, analyzing, and disseminating threat intelligence, TIPs empower organizations to act swiftly and decisively against evolving threats. Their ability to integrate seamlessly with security tools, automate processes, and foster collaboration makes them a cornerstone of effective cybersecurity operations.

Selecting the right TIP ensures that your organization's resources are optimized, intelligence is actionable, and defenses are robust, creating a proactive stance against the ever-changing threat landscape.

Applying Threat Intelligence to Security Operations

Incorporating threat intelligence into security operations is a critical step toward enhancing an organization's overall defense posture. By leveraging actionable insights from threat intelligence, security teams can refine detection and prevention strategies, conduct more effective threat hunting, and respond faster to active incidents.

Enhancing Detection and Prevention

Improving Signature-Based Detection

Threat intelligence plays a crucial role in improving traditional detection methods, such as signature-based detection. By integrating threat data, security teams can develop and refine signatures for known malware or attack techniques.

- **Example**: If a new malware strain is identified in the wild, threat intelligence can be used to create a signature that enables security systems to detect and block this specific threat.
- **Benefit**: This ensures that known threats are caught with precision, reducing the risk of successful attacks through recognized techniques.

Enhancing Anomaly Detection

Anomaly detection systems, which look for deviations from normal behavior, can greatly benefit from threat intelligence.

- **Learning from Emerging Threats**: Threat intelligence feeds continuously provide insights into evolving attack techniques, helping anomaly detection systems learn new patterns of malicious behavior.

- **Value in New and Evolving Attacks**: By leveraging threat intelligence, anomaly detection can flag previously unknown attack methods, such as novel malware or attack techniques, that might otherwise evade traditional signature-based methods.

Refining Security Policies

Real-time threat intelligence allows security teams to adjust security policies in response to emerging threats, ensuring that security controls remain relevant and up-to-date.

- **Example**: If new phishing campaigns are discovered, threat intelligence can prompt updates to email filtering rules, access controls, and firewall settings to prevent these attacks from succeeding.

- **Continuous Policy Adaptation**: By continuously updating policies based on the latest intelligence, organizations can stay one step ahead of attackers, minimizing their exposure to new vulnerabilities like zero-day exploits or advanced persistent threats (APTs).

Threat Hunting: Proactive Threat Detection

Threat hunting is a proactive, manual approach to detecting threats that may have already bypassed traditional security measures. By actively searching for evidence of malicious activity, threat hunters can identify and address threats before they cause significant damage.

Role of Threat Intelligence in Threat Hunting

Threat intelligence is essential to guiding the focus of threat hunters.

- **Focusing on Attack Vectors and Indicators of Compromise (IOCs)**: By providing insights into the tactics, techniques, and procedures (TTPs) used by threat actors, threat intelligence helps hunters focus on specific attack vectors and IOCs.

- **Proactive Threat Identification:** Threat hunters can leverage threat intelligence to anticipate where attacks might occur based on historical data, trends, and attack patterns, allowing them to search for signs of compromise before full-scale damage is done.

Uncovering New and Unique Threats

Beyond identifying known threats, threat intelligence helps hunters detect suspicious activities and anomalous patterns specific to their organization.

- **Tailored Hunting**: Threat intelligence can reveal unusual activity that may be overlooked by traditional security systems, helping to uncover novel threats or advanced persistent threats (APTs) that evade detection by standard defenses.

- **Faster Detection and Reduced Impact**: With threat intelligence guiding their efforts, hunters can more quickly identify emerging threats, reducing the time to detection and minimizing the overall impact of the attack.

Operationalizing Threat Intelligence for Hunting

Integrating threat intelligence into threat-hunting tools, such as Security Information and Event Management (SIEM) systems or TIPs (Threat Intelligence Platforms), can automate the collection and analysis of threat data.

- **Enhanced Automation:** By incorporating threat intelligence feeds, hunting tools can automatically correlate data and flag potential threats, allowing security teams to focus on high-priority analysis and decision-making.

- **Efficient Threat-Hunting Operations:** Automation through intelligence-driven systems speeds up the hunting process, enabling security teams to act faster and more effectively.

Incident Response and Threat Intelligence

During a security incident, every second counts. Threat intelligence provides real-time, actionable data that can accelerate both detection and remediation efforts, enabling incident response teams to act quickly and decisively.

Speeding Up Detection and Remediation

Real-time threat intelligence feeds provide immediate insights into the nature of the threat, helping teams respond quickly to an active incident.

- **Example**: When a new exploit or malware strain is detected, real-time intelligence can be used to understand the attacker's TTPs, enabling incident response teams to block malicious activity and contain the breach faster.

- **Minimizing Impact**: The more information teams have about the attack, the faster they can isolate affected systems, prevent lateral movement, and stop the spread of the attack.

Guiding Incident Response Decisions

Threat intelligence plays a critical role in guiding decisions throughout the incident response process.

- **Contextual Decision-Making**: Knowledge of the malware, its variants, and how it spreads allows teams to implement specific countermeasures. For example, if a known attack is leveraging a vulnerability in a specific software, teams can isolate or patch those systems first.

- **Coordinated Response**: By collaborating with external intelligence providers, teams can stay up-to-date with the latest developments, ensuring that responses are informed by the most current and relevant threat data.

- **Post-Incident Analysis**: After the incident, threat intelligence can be used to conduct root cause analysis, identify missed vulnerabilities, and strengthen defenses against future attacks.

Integrating threat intelligence into security workflows is essential for building a proactive, responsive, and adaptive cybersecurity strategy. By enhancing detection capabilities, refining security policies, and empowering threat hunters, organizations can ensure that they are prepared for both known and emerging threats. Additionally, during incidents, threat intelligence speeds up detection and remediation, guiding response teams to make informed, efficient decisions.

Incorporating threat intelligence into every aspect of security operations—from prevention and detection to incident response and post-incident analysis—ensures that organizations can stay ahead of cyber threats and continually strengthen their defenses.

Threat Intelligence in the Context of Emerging Threats

As the cybersecurity landscape continues to evolve, organizations face an increasing number of sophisticated threats. Threat intelligence is critical in helping organizations stay ahead of emerging threats, such as advanced persistent threats (APTs), ransomware, supply chain attacks, and zero-day exploits. By continuously monitoring, analyzing, and applying threat data, cybersecurity teams can improve their ability to detect, prevent, and mitigate these evolving threats.

Evolving Threat Landscape: Staying Ahead of Emerging Threats

The cybersecurity threat landscape is constantly evolving, with attackers developing new tactics, techniques, and procedures (TTPs) to bypass traditional security measures. Threat intelligence plays a crucial role in identifying and understanding these evolving threats, enabling organizations to take proactive measures.

- **Advanced Persistent Threats (APTs):** APTs are highly targeted and sustained attacks by well-resourced and skilled threat actors, often state-sponsored. These threats can go unnoticed for long periods, as attackers remain within a network for extended periods. Threat intelligence provides insights into the tactics and tools used by APT actors, allowing organizations to better detect and respond to these threats. By tracking the patterns and behaviors of known APT groups, intelligence helps security teams anticipate and mitigate potential attacks.

- **Ransomware:** Ransomware attacks continue to grow in frequency and sophistication. By using threat intelligence, organizations can track ransomware trends, identify indicators of compromise (IOCs), and understand emerging ransomware variants. Intelligence can help prevent these attacks by alerting organizations to new strains of ransomware and advising on preventive measures, such as patching vulnerabilities and strengthening endpoint defenses.

- **Supply Chain Attacks:** Attackers are increasingly targeting third-party vendors or partners in supply chain attacks to gain access to larger organizations. Threat intelligence helps organizations identify vulnerabilities within their supply chain and stay informed about threats affecting their partners. By leveraging external intelligence sources and sharing threat data with vendors, organizations can protect themselves from attacks that exploit trusted relationships.

- **Zero-Day Exploits:** Zero-day vulnerabilities are flaws in software that are unknown to the vendor or security community. Threat intelligence provides valuable data about new vulnerabilities and exploits, often before they are publicly disclosed. This allows organizations to take immediate action to patch systems or implement mitigations before the vulnerabilities can be exploited.

Case Study Examples:

- **Example 1: The SolarWinds Supply Chain Attack:** In late 2020, a sophisticated APT group used a supply chain attack to compromise SolarWinds software, which was then used to infect thousands of organizations worldwide. Threat intelligence played a critical role in identifying the breach early, providing key IOCs and TTPs that helped organizations detect the attack and respond before it caused widespread damage.

- **Example 2: Ransomware Response:** In 2021, several high-profile organizations fell victim to ransomware attacks, including the Colonial Pipeline attack, which disrupted the US fuel supply chain. Threat intelligence gathered from both internal and external sources helped identify the attacker's tactics, the ransomware variant used, and the infrastructure involved. This intelligence allowed affected organizations to quickly implement defensive measures and share information with law enforcement, helping to prevent further attacks.

CHAPTER 7   THREAT INTELLIGENCE, INDICATORS OF COMPROMISE, AND SECURE OPERATIONS

AI and Machine Learning in Threat Intelligence

As the volume of threat data continues to grow, artificial intelligence (AI) and machine learning (ML) are increasingly being used to automate the analysis and interpretation of this data. These technologies enable security teams to process large amounts of threat intelligence, identify patterns, and predict potential threats with greater speed and accuracy than traditional methods.

- **Automated Data Analysis:** AI and ML algorithms can sift through vast amounts of raw data, identifying anomalies and patterns that may indicate an emerging threat. For example, AI can be used to analyze network traffic and spot irregularities that might suggest a malware infection, even if the malware has not yet been identified. By automating this process, AI can significantly reduce the time it takes to detect threats, allowing security teams to respond more quickly.

- **Predictive Threat Analysis:** One of the most valuable applications of AI and ML in threat intelligence is in predictive analysis. By analyzing historical attack data and identifying patterns, machine learning models can predict future attack vectors or emerging threats. These predictions can help organizations proactively adjust their security measures and focus their resources on the most likely threats. For instance, AI systems can analyze the TTPs used by threat actors over time and predict which attack methods will be used in the near future.

- **Early Threat Detection:** AI and ML can enhance early threat detection by continuously monitoring systems for signs of malicious activity. For example, ML-based intrusion detection systems (IDS) can learn what constitutes normal network behavior and flag deviations from that baseline as potential threats. These systems can detect attacks in their early stages, often before the threat is fully realized.

Applications in Threat Intelligence

- **Automated Threat Hunting:** AI and ML algorithms can be used to assist in threat-hunting efforts by automatically scanning for indicators of compromise (IOCs) or anomalous behaviors that might indicate an attack. These systems can help identify hidden threats or slow-moving APTs that might otherwise go undetected.

- **Enhanced Incident Response:** In the event of a cyberattack, AI-driven threat intelligence can help incident response teams quickly analyze the attack and identify the threat actor's tactics. For example, AI can be used to analyze malware samples and determine the tools and techniques used by attackers, allowing security teams to respond more effectively.

- **Real-Time Threat Intelligence Feeds:** AI systems can continuously monitor threat intelligence sources for real-time data, ensuring that organizations have the latest information about emerging threats. This can help security teams stay ahead of new attacks and apply mitigations before a threat becomes widespread.

CHAPTER 7   THREAT INTELLIGENCE, INDICATORS OF COMPROMISE, AND SECURE OPERATIONS

Threat intelligence is essential for navigating the complex and ever-changing landscape of cybersecurity threats. By leveraging intelligence to stay ahead of emerging threats like APTs, ransomware, supply chain attacks, and zero-day exploits, organizations can better anticipate and mitigate potential risks. Furthermore, AI and machine learning are transforming threat intelligence by automating data analysis, enhancing predictive capabilities, and improving early detection. Together, these tools provide a comprehensive and proactive approach to safeguarding against modern cyber threats.

Threat Intelligence Sharing and Legal Considerations

Sharing threat intelligence is a critical component of modern cybersecurity strategies. It enables organizations to stay ahead of evolving threats by collaborating with industry peers, government agencies, and other stakeholders. However, while the benefits of sharing intelligence are vast, there are inherent legal and compliance challenges involved. It is crucial for organizations to understand how to share intelligence effectively while adhering to privacy laws, data protection regulations, and managing potential liability. This section provides a comprehensive guide on how to navigate the landscape of threat intelligence sharing with a focus on collaboration, benefits, and the legal complexities involved.

Collaboration and Information Sharing: The Importance of Collaboration

In today's interconnected world, cybersecurity threats do not respect organizational boundaries. A cyberattack that affects one organization can easily extend to others, especially with the rise of targeted, sophisticated

CHAPTER 7 THREAT INTELLIGENCE, INDICATORS OF COMPROMISE, AND SECURE OPERATIONS

attacks such as ransomware and phishing campaigns. Collaboration and sharing threat intelligence between businesses, industry groups, and government agencies are vital for mitigating these risks and staying ahead of cyber adversaries.

- **Peer Collaboration**: One of the most powerful ways organizations can benefit from threat intelligence sharing is through peer collaboration. Networking with other companies or organizations facing similar threats allows security teams to stay informed about new attack techniques and indicators of compromise (IOCs). By sharing threat intelligence, organizations can collectively build a stronger defense posture. Peer networks also provide valuable insights into new vulnerabilities, methods of exploitation, and tactics used by cybercriminals.

- **Industry Groups and Government Agencies**: Many industry-specific groups exist to facilitate the sharing of threat intelligence. These include **Information Sharing and Analysis Centers (ISACs)**, which are designed to help organizations within the same sector (e.g., finance, healthcare, energy) share information regarding common cybersecurity threats. Additionally, government entities such as **Computer Emergency Response Teams (CERTs)** provide broader intelligence-sharing platforms, especially for national-level threats. Government agencies, like the Department of Homeland Security (DHS) in the United States or Europol in the EU, may offer valuable insights on state-sponsored cyberattacks, emerging threat trends, and even resources for threat mitigation, including incident response and training.

- **The Information Sharing Environment (ISE)**: The ISE is a crucial initiative aimed at facilitating secure and efficient sharing of threat intelligence across public and private sectors. Initiatives like the ISE allow both organizations and government bodies to share cybersecurity information in a way that respects confidentiality while enhancing collective defense. For example, through platforms like the **Automated Indicator Sharing (AIS)** initiative or the **National Cyber Awareness System**, participants can exchange real-time data on emerging threats.

The Benefits of Threat Intelligence Sharing

Sharing threat intelligence is not only about exchanging information; it is about building stronger defenses against cyberattacks and improving overall cybersecurity resilience. Here are some key benefits organizations can derive from sharing intelligence:

- **Improved Early Detection**: One of the most significant advantages of threat intelligence sharing is the ability to detect cyber threats earlier. Organizations that participate in information-sharing networks gain access to a larger pool of intelligence, increasing the likelihood of detecting emerging threats. For example, when one organization identifies a new ransomware variant or zero-day vulnerability, sharing this information within a network like an ISAC allows other organizations to proactively defend against the same attack before it spreads. This early detection is crucial for mitigating potential damage.

- **Faster Response to Incidents**: During a cyberattack or security breach, timely and accurate information can make all the difference. Real-time threat intelligence sharing allows organizations to act quickly, contain the damage, and initiate the appropriate defensive measures. Coordinated, rapid responses can reduce the overall impact of the attack, minimize downtime, and prevent further damage across other connected organizations. For instance, during a widespread Distributed Denial of Service (DDoS) attack, organizations sharing intelligence on attack vectors and mitigation techniques can reduce the collective impact.

- **Collaboration for Threat Mitigation**: Cybercriminals are becoming more sophisticated, often leveraging advanced attack techniques and collaborating across borders. By sharing intelligence, organizations can pool their resources and work together to defend against shared threats. This collaboration can lead to the development of more coordinated and effective defense strategies, such as joint threat hunting or creating sector-specific mitigation playbooks that address the tactics, techniques, and procedures (TTPs) of adversaries.

Legal and Compliance Issues

While the benefits of threat intelligence sharing are clear, it also introduces several legal and regulatory challenges. Organizations must be mindful of privacy laws, regulatory compliance, and the potential for legal liability when sharing intelligence. This section explores the legal considerations that organizations must navigate when participating in threat intelligence programs.

Privacy Concerns

The sharing of threat intelligence often involves sensitive data, including personally identifiable information (PII), proprietary business information, or metadata that could reveal confidential operational details. Therefore, privacy concerns must be addressed when sharing threat intelligence.

- **Anonymization of Threat Data**: To mitigate privacy risks, organizations should ensure that any personal or sensitive data is anonymized before sharing. Anonymizing or redacting data helps to protect the privacy of individuals and ensures compliance with data protection laws. This is particularly important when sharing attack metadata that may inadvertently contain PII, such as email addresses, IP addresses, or other identifying details related to the victims of a cyberattack.

- **Avoiding Over-Disclosure**: Organizations must also ensure that they are not sharing more information than necessary. Over-disclosure of sensitive data, such as detailed network configurations or proprietary business information, could inadvertently expose vulnerabilities or compromise competitive advantage. Ensuring that only relevant and non-sensitive data is shared is key to maintaining privacy and security.

Regulatory Compliance

Organizations must ensure that their threat intelligence sharing efforts comply with relevant laws and regulations. Different jurisdictions have varying rules governing the sharing of personal and sensitive data.

- **General Data Protection Regulation (GDPR)**: In the European Union, the **GDPR** imposes stringent requirements on the handling and sharing of personal data. For instance, organizations sharing data across borders may need to obtain explicit consent from individuals or ensure that adequate safeguards are in place. Sharing data without proper legal grounds or failing to anonymize data may result in heavy fines and legal consequences. GDPR's extraterritorial scope means that even organizations outside the EU could be subject to its rules if they handle data belonging to EU citizens.

- **California Consumer Privacy Act (CCPA)**: Similarly, the **CCPA** in California imposes data protection regulations that organizations must adhere to, especially when sharing personal data of California residents. The act includes provisions on how data should be collected, used, and shared, as well as the rights of consumers to access, delete, or opt out of the sale of their data.

- **Cross-Border Data Sharing**: Threat intelligence often requires sharing data internationally. However, different countries have different regulations regarding cross-border data transfers. For example, while the GDPR places strict restrictions on transferring data outside the EU, countries like the United States may not have the same level of protection for personal data. Organizations sharing intelligence across borders must ensure compliance with both domestic and international data protection laws.

Liability

Organizations that share threat intelligence may also be exposed to legal liability, particularly if the intelligence is inaccurate or results in harm to another party.

- **Incorrect or Harmful Information**: If an organization shares inaccurate intelligence that leads to another organization's wrongful targeting or mishandling of sensitive data, it could face legal repercussions. For example, sharing a false report about a malware variant could lead to unnecessary security measures being implemented or damage to a third party's reputation.

- **Formal Agreements to Manage Risk**: To mitigate these risks, many organizations use formal agreements such as **Non-Disclosure Agreements (NDAs)** and **Information Sharing Agreements (ISAs)**. These agreements help clarify the roles, responsibilities, and liabilities of each party involved in intelligence sharing. They also provide clear guidelines on how shared intelligence should be used and what the consequences are if the information is misused or proves inaccurate.

Best Practices for Sharing Intelligence

Organizations can follow several best practices to ensure secure, effective, and compliant threat intelligence sharing:

1. **Ensure Anonymization**: Where possible, organizations should remove identifying information from threat intelligence before sharing it. This step helps protect individual privacy and reduces the risk of non-compliance with data protection regulations.

2. **Follow Data Protection Laws**: Stay updated on relevant data protection regulations, such as GDPR and CCPA, and ensure that intelligence sharing complies with these laws. Organizations should conduct regular audits of their data-sharing practices to ensure compliance.

3. **Establish Clear Policies and Agreements**: Formal agreements, including NDAs and ISAs, are essential for clarifying expectations, roles, and legal responsibilities when sharing threat intelligence. These agreements should clearly state how shared data will be handled, who will have access, and how liability will be managed in the event of misuse.

4. **Limit Data Sharing to Relevant Parties**: Limit the sharing of intelligence to trusted partners who can use the data effectively and securely. This includes industry peers, government agencies, and security vendors who are familiar with the data-sharing processes and the risks involved.

5. **Use Secure Platforms**: Always use secure platforms and encrypted communication channels for sharing threat intelligence. Organizations should also ensure that the data is properly stored, tracked, and protected throughout its life cycle.

Threat intelligence sharing is a vital practice for strengthening cybersecurity and enhancing collective defense across organizations and sectors. By collaborating with trusted partners and participating in initiatives like ISACs and CERTs, organizations can improve early threat detection, enhance incident response, and build stronger defenses. However, sharing intelligence requires navigating a complex legal landscape that involves privacy concerns, regulatory compliance, and potential liability. By following best practices, ensuring compliance with applicable laws, and adopting secure sharing protocols, organizations can maximize the benefits of threat intelligence while minimizing the associated risks.

The Importance of Proactive Threat Intelligence

Proactive threat intelligence is not just a reactive tool for incident response, but an integral part of an organization's overall cybersecurity strategy. By continuously gathering and analyzing threat data, organizations can detect and mitigate potential threats before they escalate into major incidents. This proactive approach allows security teams to understand the tactics, techniques, and procedures of threat actors, giving them the insights needed to fortify their defenses and prevent attacks. As cybercriminals and nation-state actors become more sophisticated, anticipating their movements and identifying vulnerabilities before they are exploited becomes a crucial element of risk reduction.

Continuous Improvement and Adaptation

Threat intelligence is not a one-time task but an ongoing process. As the cyber threat landscape constantly shifts with new attack techniques, evolving technologies, and emerging vulnerabilities, threat intelligence programs must be dynamic and adaptable. This chapter emphasized the need for continuous improvement by integrating feedback from real-world incidents, refining intelligence collection, and adjusting analysis methods. Security teams must remain vigilant, regularly update their threat intelligence tools, and embrace new technologies like artificial intelligence and machine learning to enhance their analytical capabilities. This continuous evolution ensures that organizations stay one step ahead of cyber adversaries.

Key Takeaways

- **Proactive Defense**: Threat intelligence is a cornerstone of a proactive cybersecurity strategy, enabling organizations to anticipate and mitigate potential threats.

- **Adaptability**: As the threat landscape evolves, so must the threat intelligence programs, with continuous refinement and adaptation to emerging trends and technologies.

- **Comprehensive Understanding**: This chapter provided readers with a comprehensive understanding of how threat intelligence fits into the modern cybersecurity ecosystem. It covered the critical aspects of collecting, analyzing, and applying threat data effectively to improve security posture.

By incorporating these insights, cybersecurity professionals are better equipped to use threat intelligence not only to respond to attacks but also to anticipate and prevent them, making their organizations more resilient to the ever-changing cyber threat environment.

Chapter Summary

In this chapter, we explored the critical role that threat intelligence plays in modern cybersecurity. By leveraging both tactical and strategic intelligence, organizations can build a proactive defense posture, anticipate emerging threats, and enhance their overall security operations. The dynamic nature of the threat landscape demands that security teams remain agile and continually adapt their threat intelligence programs. This ensures that they stay ahead of evolving attack vectors, such as advanced persistent threats, ransomware, and other sophisticated cyberattacks.

CHAPTER 8

Security Operation Centers and Managing Security Incidents

In this chapter, we will explore the critical practices and processes that make up effective security operations and incident response. From the detection of potential security events to the coordinated efforts required to respond, recover, and mitigate the impact of cybersecurity incidents, this chapter provides a comprehensive overview of how to manage these complex and high-stakes situations.

Security operations are foundational to maintaining the integrity and resilience of an organization's IT infrastructure. These operations are responsible for monitoring, detecting, and responding to any signs of potential security breaches or attacks. When an incident occurs, a structured and timely response is crucial to containing the threat and minimizing its impact.

Incident response, on the other hand, is a critical component of cybersecurity that directly influences how quickly and effectively an organization can recover from a breach. By employing proven frameworks, strategies, and best practices, security teams can respond to incidents in an efficient and organized manner, ensuring that systems are restored, evidence is preserved, and the organization is protected from further harm.

Through the guidance provided in this chapter, cybersecurity professionals will gain the necessary tools and knowledge to manage real-time security events, respond effectively to threats, and implement recovery measures that help to restore normal business operations as quickly as possible. By combining strategic insights with hands-on procedures, this chapter will help bridge the gap between theory and practice, ensuring professionals are ready for the complexities and challenges posed by modern cybersecurity incidents.

Introduction to Security Operations

Security operations are the ongoing activities and processes designed to maintain the **confidentiality, integrity, and availability** of an organization's information systems. By actively monitoring, analyzing, and responding to threats, security operations ensure that an organization's digital assets are protected from potential attacks, breaches, or disruptions. This discipline is critical in today's cybersecurity landscape, where threat actors continuously evolve their tactics to exploit vulnerabilities and bypass defenses.

Defining Security Operations

At its core, security operations encompass a range of tasks aimed at safeguarding organizational systems, networks, applications, and data. These tasks involve identifying, mitigating, and recovering from cyber threats to ensure uninterrupted operations. Security operations are a proactive and reactive function, balancing prevention measures with the capability to address incidents when they occur.

Goals of Security Operations

The goals of security operations are deeply intertwined with an organization's overarching cybersecurity strategy, ensuring proactive and effective defense against ever-evolving cyber threats. Key objectives include

- **Detecting and responding to incidents:** The primary purpose of security operations is to identify and mitigate threats promptly, minimizing the time attackers have to exploit vulnerabilities and preventing potential escalations.

- **Reducing potential damage:** By swiftly addressing security incidents, organizations aim to limit the impact on critical business operations, sensitive data, and overall productivity.

- **Maintaining compliance:** Security operations play a vital role in adhering to regulatory requirements like GDPR, HIPAA, or PCI DSS, and aligning with recognized security frameworks such as ISO 27001 or NIST CSF.

By focusing on these goals, security operations not only enhance an organization's ability to withstand and recover from cyberattacks but also safeguard its reputation, ensure trust with stakeholders, and support seamless business continuity.

Key Components of Security Operations

Effective security operations rely on a combination of processes, tools, and strategies that work cohesively to fortify an organization's cybersecurity posture. These components include

CHAPTER 8   SECURITY OPERATION CENTERS AND MANAGING SECURITY INCIDENTS

1. **Centralized Monitoring and Alerting:**

   A cornerstone of security operations is the ability to continuously observe network activity, system logs, and user behavior through centralized platforms like a Security Operations Center (SOC). These systems generate alerts when suspicious activities or anomalies are detected, enabling immediate action.

2. **Incident Detection and Response:**

   This involves tools and methodologies designed to identify, assess, and respond to threats. Key steps include investigating incidents, containing malicious activities, eradicating threats, and recovering systems to a secure state.

3. **Log Collection and Analysis:**

   Security operations depend on the aggregation and examination of log data from sources like servers, firewalls, and endpoint devices. Analyzing these logs reveals patterns, correlations, or anomalies that may indicate a security event.

By integrating these components into daily operations, organizations establish a resilient framework capable of addressing modern cyber threats. Security operations form the backbone of a proactive cybersecurity strategy, equipping businesses with the tools and expertise needed to safeguard their assets and operations.

Introduction to Security Operation Centers

Security operations are the comprehensive suite of activities and practices designed to protect an organization's digital infrastructure and data from cybersecurity threats. These operations go beyond reactive responses to incidents and emphasize proactive measures aimed at preventing attacks before they occur. The scope includes monitoring, threat detection, prevention, response, and the ongoing management of security technologies, systems, and personnel. Effective security operations require constant vigilance, with the ability to identify vulnerabilities, monitor system activities, and ensure the security of critical assets at all times.

Role of Security Operations Centers (SOCs)

Security Operations Centers (SOCs) are central hubs in an organization where security professionals work around the clock to safeguard digital assets and data. A SOC's core mission is to monitor, analyze, and respond to security incidents in real time, ensuring that any potential threats are detected and neutralized as quickly as possible. The SOC is responsible for gathering, analyzing, and correlating data from various sources to provide visibility into the security landscape. These centers often utilize advanced technologies, such as SIEMs (Security Information and Event Management) systems, to identify suspicious activities, investigate potential incidents, and support the overall security health of the organization.

Key Components of Security Operations

Security operations involve a variety of essential components, all of which contribute to building a robust defense strategy. These include

- **Continuous Monitoring:** Constant surveillance of networks, systems, and applications to detect any potential security issues before they escalate into significant incidents.

- **Threat Detection:** Leveraging technologies like intrusion detection systems (IDS), threat intelligence feeds, and behavioral analytics to identify abnormal activities or attacks.

- **Vulnerability Management:** Identifying, assessing, and addressing vulnerabilities within systems to reduce the risk of exploitation by threat actors.

- **Risk Management:** Evaluating and prioritizing risks based on the organization's critical assets, ensuring that resources are allocated effectively to mitigate the most severe threats.

- **Incident Response:** Having a structured and well-practiced approach to responding to incidents to minimize damage, recover quickly, and ensure business continuity.

- **Recovery:** Ensuring systems and data are restored quickly and securely after an attack, including maintaining backup systems and disaster recovery protocols.

The integration of tools such as **SIEM systems**, **network monitoring software**, and **endpoint detection tools** is crucial for streamlining and enhancing these activities, ensuring that security operations are carried out efficiently and effectively across the organization. These components collectively provide the foundation for a well-rounded security posture that can detect, prevent, and respond to cyber threats in a timely manner.

CHAPTER 8   SECURITY OPERATION CENTERS AND MANAGING SECURITY INCIDENTS

Types of Security Incidents

There are various types of security incidents, each with distinct characteristics and potential impacts on an organization's operations, data, and reputation. Understanding these incidents and knowing how to respond to them is critical for ensuring robust security practices. Below is an overview of the most common types of security incidents:

1. Malware Incidents

- Malware refers to malicious software designed to damage, disrupt, or gain unauthorized access to computer systems. It encompasses a variety of types, including viruses, worms, Trojans, ransomware, and spyware. Each type has unique characteristics but typically aims to compromise the integrity, confidentiality, or availability of data.

    - **Viruses**: Self-replicating programs that attach themselves to legitimate files and spread to other files and systems.

    - **Worms**: Self-replicating malware that spreads across networks without needing to attach to files.

    - **Trojans**: Malicious software disguised as legitimate programs, used to gain unauthorized access to systems.

    - **Ransomware**: Malware that locks or encrypts data and demands payment for its release.

    - **Spyware**: Software designed to secretly monitor and collect user information, often for malicious purposes.

- **Detection and Analysis:**
  - **Antivirus Software**: Used to detect known malware signatures and block malicious files from executing.
  - **Network Traffic Monitoring**: Helps identify unusual traffic patterns that could be associated with malware activity, like data exfiltration or communication with known malicious IP addresses.
  - **Forensic Tools**: Used to analyze affected systems and identify malware persistence mechanisms, entry points, and impact.
- **Response:**
  - Quarantine infected systems or files.
  - Analyze and remove the malware using malware removal tools or system re-imaging.
  - Restore affected systems from backups and deploy patches to prevent reinfection.

2. Phishing and Social Engineering

- **Phishing:**

  Phishing involves deceptive attempts to acquire sensitive information such as passwords, credit card details, or personal data by posing as a trusted entity. It often comes in the form of emails, fake websites, or phone calls that seem legitimate.

- **Social Engineering:**

  Social engineering attacks exploit human psychology and behavior to bypass security measures. Techniques include

  - **Impersonation**: Pretending to be someone else, such as a trusted colleague or vendor, to gain access to systems or data.

  - **Pretexting**: Creating a fabricated scenario (e.g., pretending to be from IT support) to trick a target into providing sensitive information.

  - **Baiting**: Offering something appealing (e.g., free software or hardware) to lure victims into taking actions that lead to a security compromise.

- **Detection and Response:**

  - **Investigating Email Headers**: Analyzing the metadata and source of the email can reveal phishing attempts.

  - **User Behavior Analysis**: Identifying suspicious patterns, such as employees clicking on links from unknown or unusual sources.

  - **Network Logs**: Monitoring for unusual outbound traffic or failed authentication attempts that might indicate a phishing attack is in progress.

3. Denial of Service (DoS) and Distributed Denial of Service (DDoS)

- **DoS and DDoS Attacks:**

  Denial of Service (DoS) and Distributed Denial of Service (DDoS) attacks aim to overwhelm a system's resources, making it unavailable to legitimate users. DoS attacks are typically launched from a single source, while DDoS attacks use multiple systems, often in a botnet, to target the victim simultaneously.

- **Impact:**

  These attacks can render websites, services, or entire networks unusable by flooding them with excessive traffic or requests, consuming all available resources like bandwidth or processing power.

- **Response:**

  - **Traffic Analysis**: Monitoring network traffic patterns to identify DDoS signatures (e.g., sudden spikes in traffic from certain regions or IP addresses).

  - **Rate Limiting**: Configuring firewalls and load balancers to limit the number of requests from a single source.

  - **Cloud-based Mitigation**: Using cloud services such as Cloudflare or AWS Shield to absorb large-scale DDoS traffic and mitigate the attack.

  - **Traffic Filtering**: Implementing advanced filtering techniques to block malicious traffic while allowing legitimate traffic to pass.

4. Data Breaches

- A data breach occurs when unauthorized individuals gain access to confidential or sensitive information. This may involve data exfiltration, tampering with files, or unauthorized access to databases, resulting in the theft, loss, or exposure of data.

- **Types of Data Exposed**:
    - Personally identifiable information (PII)
    - Financial data
    - Health records
    - Intellectual property

- **Response:**
    - **Identify Exposed Data**: Investigate which files or systems were accessed and what data was exposed or exfiltrated.
    - **Notification**: Notify affected individuals, regulators, and stakeholders about the breach, as required by laws such as GDPR or CCPA.
    - **Forensic Investigation**: Conduct a detailed forensic analysis to determine how the breach occurred (e.g., exploiting vulnerabilities or using stolen credentials) and who is responsible.
    - **Remediation**: Patch vulnerabilities, update access controls, and take necessary steps to prevent similar breaches in the future.

5. Insider Threats

- Insider threats involve individuals within the organization (e.g., employees, contractors, or vendors) who misuse their authorized access to cause harm, such as stealing data, sabotaging systems, or facilitating external attacks.

- **Types of Insider Threats:**

    - **Malicious Insider**: An employee or contractor intentionally misuses their access for personal gain or to harm the organization.

    - **Negligent Insider**: An employee who unintentionally causes harm by failing to follow security protocols, such as accidentally sharing passwords or downloading malicious attachments.

    - **Compromised Insider**: An individual whose credentials have been stolen or exploited by an external attacker.

- **Response:**

    - **Investigate Access Logs**: Review system access logs and network activity to identify unusual behavior or unauthorized access by insiders.

    - **User Behavior Monitoring**: Implement user behavior analytics (UBA) to detect anomalies in employee activity that may indicate malicious intent.

- **Communication Channels**: Analyze communication patterns (emails, chat messages, file-sharing activities) to detect suspicious actions.
- **Security Awareness**: Conduct regular training to ensure employees are aware of security best practices and the risks of insider threats.

By understanding these types of security incidents and the appropriate response actions, organizations can better prepare for and mitigate the effects of these threats, improving their overall security posture. Each incident type requires a tailored approach to detection, analysis, containment, and recovery to ensure the best possible outcome in protecting organizational assets and data.

Security Monitoring and Detection

Effective security monitoring and detection are critical components of an organization's security operations. These tools and technologies work together to identify potential threats in real time, enabling the security team to take swift action before damage occurs. Below are key tools and technologies used in monitoring and detecting cybersecurity threats:

SIEM (Security Information and Event Management)

SIEM systems serve as the backbone of an organization's security monitoring strategy. By aggregating log data from various sources, including network devices, servers, and applications, SIEM tools provide a centralized view of security events. This integration and analysis help organizations detect, respond to, and mitigate security incidents in real time.

- **Real-Time Alerts:** SIEM platforms continuously analyze incoming log data and generate real-time alerts when suspicious patterns are detected. These alerts are often based on predefined rules that highlight behaviors such as failed login attempts, abnormal access to sensitive resources, or unauthorized changes to system configurations. The speed at which these alerts are triggered is crucial, as it allows security teams to investigate and respond before an attack can escalate.

- **Incident Investigation and Reporting:** In addition to real-time alerts, SIEM platforms offer the ability to store and index large volumes of historical log data. This allows security teams to perform post-incident analysis, identifying the timeline and potential impact of attacks. By analyzing historical data, SIEM systems also help in identifying recurring security trends, vulnerabilities, and gaps in the security infrastructure.

- **Examples:**
  - **Splunk**: A popular SIEM platform known for its advanced data analytics capabilities, allowing security teams to gain deep insights into network and system activity.
  - **IBM QRadar**: Provides comprehensive security intelligence and automated incident responses, focusing on threat detection and compliance.
  - **ArcSight**: A long-standing SIEM tool that excels in integrating with other security solutions and provides robust threat detection capabilities.

CHAPTER 8   SECURITY OPERATION CENTERS AND MANAGING SECURITY INCIDENTS

Intrusion Detection and Prevention Systems (IDS/IPS)

IDS and IPS systems are essential for network security, providing real-time monitoring and protection against malicious traffic that could compromise the network. While IDS focuses on detecting threats and alerting security teams, IPS takes proactive action to block or mitigate those threats.

- **IDS:** Intrusion Detection Systems (IDS) passively monitor network traffic to identify suspicious activities. They analyze network traffic patterns, logs, and system behavior to detect known attack signatures or anomalous activities. IDS tools do not interfere with the network traffic itself but send alerts when malicious activity is detected.

    - **Example: Snort** is a widely used open-source IDS that analyzes network traffic for malicious content. **Suricata**, another popular IDS, also includes capabilities for intrusion prevention and network monitoring.

- **IPS:** Intrusion Prevention Systems (IPS) go a step further than IDS by actively blocking or mitigating attacks. When a potential threat is detected, IPS systems act by blocking malicious IP addresses, dropping packets, or applying firewall rules to prevent further harm.

    - **Example: Cisco Firepower** integrates network intrusion prevention with advanced threat protection capabilities. **Palo Alto Networks** provides both IDS and IPS functionalities through its next-generation firewall solutions.

- **Configuration and Tuning:** For IDS/IPS to be effective, they require fine-tuning to avoid generating false positives. This process involves defining attack signatures, setting thresholds for detection, and regularly updating detection rules. Well-configured IDS/IPS systems help reduce the risk of missing genuine threats or overwhelming security analysts with too many alerts.

Endpoint Detection and Response (EDR)

EDR tools focus on protecting endpoints like workstations, servers, and mobile devices. Since endpoints are often the initial targets of cyberattacks, EDR tools are designed to detect, investigate, and respond to threats directly on these devices. These solutions play a crucial role in identifying and mitigating threats that bypass traditional perimeter defenses.

- **Real-Time Monitoring:** EDR solutions offer continuous monitoring of endpoint activities to identify malicious behavior such as malware infections, unauthorized access attempts, or abnormal system activity. If a threat is detected, the EDR system can take immediate action, such as isolating the affected device or blocking the malicious process.

- **Forensic Analysis:** In the aftermath of an incident, EDR platforms provide detailed forensic capabilities that allow security teams to investigate the scope of the attack. Analysts can trace the attack's origin, determine which systems were compromised, and understand how the threat propagated across the network.

CHAPTER 8   SECURITY OPERATION CENTERS AND MANAGING SECURITY INCIDENTS

- **Examples:**

  - **CrowdStrike Falcon**: A cloud-based EDR solution known for its advanced AI-driven threat detection and response capabilities.

  - **SentinelOne**: Provides automated endpoint protection through its AI-driven EDR system, offering real-time detection and remediation.

  - **Microsoft Defender for Endpoint**: A comprehensive EDR solution built into the Microsoft ecosystem, offering integrated protection against various endpoint threats.

Network Traffic Analysis

Network traffic analysis tools provide insight into the traffic flowing through an organization's network. By analyzing this traffic, security teams can detect and respond to attacks that may not be immediately apparent, such as data exfiltration, lateral movement, or malware communication. These tools offer a more granular level of monitoring than traditional network security solutions.

- **Traffic Anomalies:** Anomalies in network traffic, such as unexplained data spikes, unexpected communication with external servers, or unusual outbound traffic, are red flags for potential attacks. Monitoring for these anomalies helps identify activities such as data exfiltration, botnet communication, or distributed denial-of-service (DDoS) attacks.

- **Protocol Analysis:** Tools like **Wireshark** and **Zeek** enable deep packet inspection, allowing security teams to analyze network protocols in real time. By capturing and inspecting individual data packets, these tools provide insights into the types of traffic traversing the network. This helps identify suspicious protocols, data flows, or communication patterns that could indicate a cyberattack.

- **Tools:**
  - **Wireshark**: An industry-standard packet capture and network protocol analyzer that allows in-depth inspection of network traffic.
  - **NetFlow**: Offers visibility into network traffic patterns, helping identify deviations from normal behavior.
  - **Zeek** (formerly Bro): A powerful network monitoring tool used for security analysis and incident detection, with a focus on network traffic behavior and security-related activities.

These tools work together as part of a layered security approach, enabling organizations to detect, respond to, and mitigate cyber threats more effectively. By implementing a combination of SIEM, IDS/IPS, EDR, and network traffic analysis, security teams can enhance their ability to protect against evolving cyber threats.

Importance of Monitoring and Detection in Security Operations

Continuous monitoring and detection are essential for identifying threats early and taking proactive measures to mitigate their impact. By implementing SIEMs, IDS/IPS, EDR, and network traffic analysis tools, organizations can enhance their ability to detect and respond to a wide range of security incidents, ensuring a faster and more effective incident response. The integration of these tools into a holistic security operations framework is key to building a resilient defense posture against evolving threats.

Forms of Threat Hunting

Proactive Threat Detection

Threat hunting is a key practice for those willing to go beyond traditional reactive measures. Unlike conventional security monitoring, which waits for alerts to trigger based on predefined rules, threat hunting involves actively looking for potential compromises. Security teams assume the role of investigators, continually searching through systems and networks for signs of sophisticated, hidden threats that bypass existing defenses.

Hypothesis-Driven

Threat hunters use their knowledge of adversarial behaviors, environments, and threat intelligence to create hypotheses for potential attack scenarios. These could include possibilities such as lateral movement within the network or an insider attack designed to steal sensitive data. These hypotheses guide the hunting efforts, helping analysts focus their searches on the most likely attack vectors.

Manual Investigation

Instead of depending on automated detection, threat hunters conduct manual investigations. They comb through logs, examine system activity, and look for Indicators of Compromise (IOCs) that automated tools may have missed. IOCs could be anomalous network traffic, unusual user activity, or suspicious file changes. Threat hunters are looking for early indicators of a breach before they escalate into larger, more visible attacks.

Threat Hunting Methodologies

TTP (Tactics, Techniques, and Procedures) Analysis: TTP analysis is at the core of threat hunting. Using frameworks like MITRE ATT&CK, threat hunters can categorize and understand the different ways adversaries may infiltrate and move through a network. This structured approach provides a comprehensive view of attack techniques, helping hunters predict and identify malicious activities based on known patterns.

- **Tactics:** Broad goals of an adversary (e.g., Initial Access, Lateral Movement, Exfiltration).

- **Techniques:** Specific methods used by attackers to achieve those tactics (e.g., phishing, exploiting software vulnerabilities).

- **Procedures:** Concrete methods used by attackers to implement their techniques (e.g., specific malware strains or tools).

Behavioral Analysis

Rather than focusing on signature-based detection (which looks for known threats), behavioral analysis aims to spot irregularities in typical system or network behavior. Attackers may use slow, subtle movements to avoid detection, so this methodology tracks deviations such as:

- Unusual login times or locations
- Unexplained outbound traffic
- Unexpected file access patterns

Data-Driven Hunting

This methodology leverages historical data to uncover potential threats. By analyzing

- Log Data: Security teams look for signs of suspicious activity across logs from systems and applications.

- Network Traffic: Any unusual traffic patterns, such as high data volume to an unfamiliar server, may indicate an attack.

- File System Activity: Abnormal file changes or unusual files in critical locations can be a red flag.

By analyzing trends in past data, hunters may detect previously undetected incidents or confirm an ongoing campaign that hadn't yet triggered automated alerts.

Tools for Threat Hunting

Threat hunters use a range of tools to aid in their investigations. These tools help streamline the hunting process by providing visibility, correlation, and detailed analysis.

EDR (Endpoint Detection and Response)

EDR tools monitor endpoint devices like computers and servers for suspicious activities, such as unauthorized file execution or changes in system settings. They offer real-time alerts and forensic capabilities, which are invaluable for tracking down threats that are actively in progress or have already compromised endpoints.

- Examples: CrowdStrike Falcon, SentinelOne, Microsoft Defender for Endpoint

CHAPTER 8   SECURITY OPERATION CENTERS AND MANAGING SECURITY INCIDENTS

SIEM (Security Information and Event Management)

SIEM platforms aggregate logs and data from various security tools and systems across the organization. By analyzing these logs, SIEMs help detect incidents that span multiple systems, giving hunters a bird's eye view of potential threats. They provide crucial correlation capabilities to detect complex attacks.

- Examples: Splunk, IBM QRadar, LogRhythm

YARA (Yet Another Recursive Acronym)

YARA is a tool used for identifying malicious files and malware by matching patterns and signatures. Hunters create custom YARA rules to search for known malware and suspicious behavior patterns in files and network traffic. This tool aids in signature-based detection and is particularly useful for finding malware across large datasets.

- Example: Writing YARA rules to detect a specific malware strain across your network

Volatility

This tool focuses on memory forensics. Some threats, such as rootkits or certain forms of malware, can hide themselves in the system's memory rather than leaving traces on the hard drive. Volatility helps extract and analyze memory dumps to uncover these hidden threats, which are otherwise invisible to traditional log-based detection.

- Example: Analyzing memory dumps to detect hidden malware or running processes not captured by file logs

Wireshark

A network protocol analyzer that allows security teams to inspect network traffic in detail. It can capture network packets and analyze data transmissions, making it particularly useful for spotting attempts to exfiltrate data, unusual connections, or communications with known malicious IP addresses. It's an essential tool for identifying and analyzing attacks that use network-based techniques, such as data exfiltration.

- Example: Analyzing HTTP traffic for signs of data being siphoned off to an external server

Threat hunting is a proactive, manual approach to cybersecurity that allows security teams to stay ahead of attackers who evade automated defenses. By using methodologies like TTP analysis, behavioral analysis, and data-driven hunting, threat hunters can uncover subtle threats before they escalate. The effective use of tools like EDR, SIEM, YARA, Volatility, and Wireshark enhances these efforts by providing detailed insights into endpoint, network, and memory activities. For organizations aiming to stay ahead of evolving threats, integrating threat hunting into their cybersecurity strategy is an essential step in reducing the likelihood of a successful attack.

Effective Communication During a Cybersecurity Incident

During a cybersecurity incident, clear, structured communication is critical to ensure a coordinated and efficient response. Effective communication helps minimize the incident's impact, protects the organization's reputation, and ensures compliance with legal and regulatory obligations. The following outlines the key elements of incident response coordination and communication:

Internal Communication During Incidents

Internal communication within the organization is essential during a cybersecurity incident. Keeping all relevant parties informed—leadership, technical teams, and support staff—ensures that the response is timely, organized, and effective.

Incident Reports

Incident reports are vital for documenting the specifics of the event. These reports should include details such as the initial discovery, an assessment of the incident's impact, and the steps being taken to contain and mitigate the threat. By providing leadership with clear, actionable information, incident reports help ensure decision-making is based on accurate and up-to-date data.

Escalation Protocols

Clearly defined escalation protocols ensure that incidents are promptly escalated to the right teams or individuals. A structured escalation process allows for a quick response to evolving incidents, ensuring that the necessary expertise and resources are engaged as the situation progresses.

Communication Plans

An effective communication plan is essential for maintaining a steady flow of information during an incident. This plan should clearly outline what information needs to be shared, who will receive it, how it will be communicated, and the frequency of updates. Having a clear communication strategy ensures consistency and accuracy in the information shared across teams.

Best Practices

- Use centralized, secure communication channels for incident updates.

- Ensure that incident reports and updates are concise, clear, and provide actionable next steps.

- Avoid overwhelming teams with excessive information; focus on critical updates and key action items.

External Communication

In the case of major incidents, communication with external parties—such as law enforcement, regulators, third-party vendors, and customers—becomes critical. External communication should be handled thoughtfully to ensure compliance with regulations while safeguarding the organization's reputation.

Law Enforcement

When criminal activity is suspected, such as data breaches, ransomware attacks, or other malicious acts, involving law enforcement is essential. Promptly notifying law enforcement ensures that investigations are launched in a timely manner and provides the organization with necessary legal support.

Regulators and Compliance

Many industries are governed by regulations that require the prompt notification of regulators and affected individuals when a security breach occurs. For example, GDPR mandates that data breaches be reported within 72 hours. Organizations must be well-versed in the regulations that apply to them and ensure that external communications are compliant with these laws to avoid fines and legal repercussions.

Third-Party Vendors

If external vendors or partners are affected, especially those involved in cloud hosting, data storage, or other key services, it is essential to keep them informed. Collaborating with vendors helps to ensure that they can take immediate action to address the risks on their side, minimizing further exposure.

Affected Customers

Transparency with customers is vital. While customer communication must be handled carefully to avoid causing unnecessary panic, it's crucial to inform them about the breach's nature, the organization's efforts to resolve it, and any protective steps they need to take. Clear, calm, and precise communication will help maintain trust.

Best Practices

- Designate a single, trusted point of contact for all external communications to ensure consistency and avoid mixed messages.

- Be transparent with external stakeholders but avoid disclosing sensitive or technical details that could jeopardize security.

- Provide timely and regular updates to customers, regulators, and other stakeholders as new information arises.

Public Relations and Crisis Management

The impact of a cybersecurity incident is often magnified by how the organization communicates with the public, media, and stakeholders. A well-managed public relations and crisis response strategy can help preserve the organization's reputation and manage the incident's public perception.

Managing Reputation

The manner in which an organization handles an incident has a direct impact on its reputation. A well-executed response, demonstrating control and proactive action, reassures the public, customers, and partners. Conversely, poor communication can lead to long-term reputational damage.

Strategies for Media Communication

Media coverage can greatly influence how the incident is perceived. A pre-planned media strategy should outline key messaging that focuses on the steps being taken to address the issue while safeguarding sensitive or proprietary information. The goal is to keep the media and the public informed without disclosing too much technical detail, which could inadvertently worsen the situation.

Internal Coordination

To ensure consistency, all internal teams—including marketing, customer support, and technical staff—should be aligned on the organization's public stance. Clear internal coordination prevents mixed messages and ensures that everyone is on the same page when responding to media or customers.

Crisis Management Plans

A crisis management plan should include guidelines on how to address public relations challenges, including key talking points, FAQs, and media training for spokespersons. This plan ensures that the organization is ready to respond quickly and professionally, mitigating any reputational harm and protecting key stakeholders.

Best Practices

- Appoint a trained spokesperson to handle all media communications to maintain consistency and professionalism.

- Prepare a set of predefined statements or FAQs to address common media inquiries, ensuring rapid and accurate responses.

- Maintain transparency in communication but avoid oversharing information that could compromise security or legal standing.

- Monitor public sentiment and media coverage regularly to adjust the response as needed and stay ahead of potential issues.

Effective communication during a cybersecurity incident is just as important as the technical response itself. Clear and consistent communication—internally and externally—ensures that the organization can manage the incident efficiently, comply with legal requirements, and protect its reputation. A robust communication strategy provides clarity, keeps stakeholders informed, and minimizes the potential damage caused by the incident. By prioritizing communication, organizations can effectively navigate the challenges of a cybersecurity event and emerge stronger from the experience.

Role of Forensics in Incident Response

Forensic analysis plays a critical role in incident response by providing a methodical and systematic approach to investigating security breaches. Digital forensics focuses on collecting, preserving, and analyzing electronic evidence to understand the attack's origins, methods, and impact. This analysis is essential not only for mitigating the immediate incident but also for identifying weaknesses in security measures that could be exploited in future attacks. Key forensic activities include

- **Disk Imaging**: Creating bit-by-bit copies of storage devices to preserve evidence while ensuring that the original data remains intact.

- **Memory Forensics**: Analyzing volatile memory (RAM) to identify running processes, network connections, and other data that may have been lost when a system is powered down.

- **Log Analysis**: Reviewing system logs, event logs, and network logs to reconstruct the timeline of the attack and trace the actions of the attackers.

- **Network Traffic Analysis**: Examining captured network packets to identify malicious communication patterns, data exfiltration, or communication with command and control servers.

Forensic Tools

Forensic tools enable analysts to collect, preserve, and analyze data in a way that ensures its integrity and reliability in an investigative context. These tools are designed to support detailed forensic examination and investigation of systems involved in security incidents. Some prominent tools include

- **EnCase**: A widely used tool for disk imaging and forensic analysis of files and metadata. EnCase provides detailed data recovery and analysis capabilities, with an emphasis on creating a detailed audit trail for legal purposes.

- **FTK (Forensic Toolkit)**: A powerful forensic software suite that provides evidence gathering, file analysis, and reporting. FTK excels at data indexing, making it easier to search and filter large datasets.

- **Volatility**: A memory forensics tool used for analyzing system memory (RAM) dumps. It helps investigators find hidden malware, running processes, and traces of sophisticated attacks that are not stored on disk.

- **Autopsy**: An open-source digital forensics platform that supports disk and file system analysis, timeline analysis, and more. It integrates with other forensic tools and allows investigators to collaborate effectively.

Forensic tools ensure the systematic and legal handling of evidence, preserving its chain of custody and integrity, critical for use in court or regulatory reporting.

Chain of Custody

Maintaining a clear and documented **chain of custody** is essential for ensuring that the collected evidence remains untampered with and admissible in legal or regulatory proceedings. The chain of custody refers to the documentation that tracks the handling and movement of evidence from the point of collection to its use in analysis or in court. This involves

- **Detailed Records**: Every interaction with the evidence must be logged, including who handled it, when, and why.

- **Physical Security**: Evidence should be stored securely, often in tamper-evident bags or containers, to prevent any unauthorized access.

- **Integrity Verification**: The use of cryptographic hash functions (e.g., MD5, SHA-1) ensures that the data hasn't been altered. If hashes change between collection and analysis, it indicates potential tampering, compromising the investigation.

Proper chain of custody ensures the integrity of the investigative process and supports legal and regulatory compliance, making it indispensable in forensic analysis during incident response.

Post-Incident Analysis and Reporting

Once an incident is contained and recovery is underway, conducting a **post-incident review** becomes essential. This review serves as the foundation for evaluating the effectiveness of the response and identifying areas that need improvement. It is crucial to learn from each incident to strengthen future incident response and defense mechanisms.

Key components of a post-incident review include

- **Incident Assessment:** What worked well during the response? Was the team able to contain the incident in a timely manner? How effectively were the security measures put in place before and during the incident?

- **Lessons Learned:** Which aspects of the incident response could have been handled better? Were there any communication gaps or delays? Was there an area of the system or network that was overlooked, leading to prolonged exposure or damage?

- **Process Refinement:** What changes can be made to existing procedures? Were there any gaps in the incident response plan that became apparent during the incident? How can training and awareness programs be improved to address these deficiencies?

The review process should involve all stakeholders, including IT, security, legal, and communication teams, as well as leadership. This collaboration ensures a holistic evaluation of the response and provides a clear understanding of the lessons learned.

Creating Incident Reports

A comprehensive **incident report** is a vital artifact of the post-incident process. This report serves as both documentation and analysis, providing a clear record of the incident and the response taken. The documentation should be detailed, accurate, and structured in a way that makes it useful for both internal and external audiences (such as auditors or legal teams).

CHAPTER 8 SECURITY OPERATION CENTERS AND MANAGING SECURITY INCIDENTS

Key elements of an effective incident report:

- **Incident Overview:** A high-level summary that includes the type of incident, the impact on the organization, and the timeline of events. This section should also highlight the incident's severity and any immediate actions taken.

- **Timeline of Events:** A chronological list of actions taken from the discovery of the incident to its resolution. This timeline is critical for understanding the incident's progression, delays, and key decisions made throughout the response.

- **Root Cause Analysis:** A thorough investigation into what caused the incident. Was it a vulnerability that was exploited, human error, or a failure in the security infrastructure? Identifying the root cause helps in addressing the source of the problem, not just the symptoms.

- **Response Actions and Outcomes:** A detailed list of the steps taken to contain, mitigate, and recover from the incident. This section should also discuss the effectiveness of these actions and any adjustments made during the process.

- **Lessons Learned:** A reflective analysis on what went well and what could have been improved during the response. This section will help inform future response strategies and processes.

- **Recommendations:** Based on the findings, what steps should be taken to prevent similar incidents in the future? This may include policy changes, technical improvements, or increased training for staff.

Creating standardized **incident report templates** is useful for ensuring consistency in reporting. These templates should include predefined fields for the most critical information, making it easier to collect and analyze data across different incidents.

Continuous Improvement and Feedback Loop

The ultimate goal of post-incident analysis is **continuous improvement**. Every incident presents an opportunity to improve response strategies, strengthen defenses, and enhance organizational security posture. This can be achieved by establishing a robust feedback loop where the insights gained from each incident are used to refine processes, policies, and security measures.

Key elements of continuous improvement:

- **Updating Incident Response Plans:** Use the findings from the post-incident review to update the organization's incident response plan. For example, if there was a delay in detection, adjustments may need to be made to monitoring systems or response protocols to reduce time to detection in the future.

- **Enhancing Defenses:** If the root cause of the incident was a vulnerability in a specific system or process, take steps to patch or replace the vulnerable components. Regularly conduct vulnerability assessments and penetration testing to ensure that systems are fortified against emerging threats.

- **Training and Awareness:** Use lessons learned to enhance security training programs. If human error was a factor, consider implementing more targeted training or awareness campaigns to address specific issues.

- **Automation and Tools:** Investigate opportunities to automate incident detection, reporting, and response. Tools like Security Information and Event Management (SIEM) systems can provide real-time insights and automate many aspects of incident handling, allowing security teams to respond more efficiently.

The feedback loop should also extend to the broader security community. Sharing insights and lessons learned with peers, vendors, and industry groups can help strengthen the overall cybersecurity ecosystem.

Incident Response and Legal/Compliance Considerations

In any cybersecurity incident, adhering to legal and regulatory requirements is crucial. Failure to comply with laws and regulations can result in severe financial penalties, loss of trust, and even legal action. During an incident, cybersecurity professionals must be aware of the various laws and regulations that apply to their organization and jurisdiction.

Some of the key **legal and regulatory requirements** include

General Data Protection Regulation (GDPR)

GDPR applies to organizations that process personal data of individuals in the European Union (EU). Under GDPR, organizations must ensure that personal data is protected and that individuals' privacy rights are respected. If an incident involves a breach of personal data, GDPR mandates that the organization must notify the relevant supervisory authority within 72 hours and inform affected individuals if their data is at high risk.

Key considerations for GDPR compliance: Understanding the type of data involved, notifying authorities on time, and ensuring that data breaches do not result in further harm to individuals' rights and freedoms.

Health Insurance Portability and Accountability Act (HIPAA)

HIPAA applies to the healthcare sector in the United States, safeguarding sensitive patient information. If an incident involves a breach of protected health information (PHI), HIPAA requires organizations to notify affected individuals within 60 days of discovery and report the breach to the Department of Health and Human Services (HHS).

Key considerations for HIPAA compliance: Incident responders should ensure that PHI is properly protected and that all notifications are made in a timely manner. Failing to do so could result in substantial fines.

Payment Card Industry Data Security Standard (PCI DSS)

PCI DSS applies to any organization that processes, stores, or transmits credit card information. During a breach involving payment card data, organizations must notify the card brands and affected financial institutions. They must also assess the breach's scope and take corrective actions to prevent future incidents.

Key considerations for PCI DSS compliance: Proper identification of affected payment systems, timely notification to relevant entities, and a thorough forensic investigation to determine the extent of the breach.

Breach Notification Responsibilities

Regardless of the regulatory framework, incident responders are often required to notify affected individuals, regulators, or authorities about the breach. This could include notifying data subjects, the Federal Trade Commission (FTC) in the case of consumer data breaches, or law enforcement in cases of criminal activity.

Key considerations for breach notification: Being clear, transparent, and timely with communication to minimize the impact on affected individuals and comply with legal requirements.

Data Protection During an Incident

A key element in legal compliance is protecting sensitive data during the incident. Organizations must ensure that their incident response efforts do not inadvertently compromise the privacy or security of sensitive information.

Key considerations for data protection: Safeguarding evidence during the investigation, preventing unauthorized access, and ensuring that all data is handled in accordance with applicable privacy laws.

In order to comply with these requirements, organizations should have an established process for identifying the legal and regulatory obligations that apply to specific types of data, industries, and geographical regions.

Ethical Considerations in Incident Response

In addition to legal compliance, **ethical considerations** play a significant role in incident response. Security professionals must balance their efforts to address threats while ensuring that they do not infringe upon privacy or civil liberties.

Some key **ethical considerations** include

Protecting Privacy Rights

Even during an incident, organizations must respect the privacy of individuals. For example, during a data breach investigation, it is important to limit access to personal data and ensure that any sensitive information is only viewed by authorized personnel. Ethical conduct requires transparency about what data is being accessed and why.

Example: If an employee's email account is compromised, investigators should ensure that they only access emails relevant to the investigation and avoid unnecessary access to private communications.

Balancing Transparency and Confidentiality

Ethical considerations often require that sensitive information is handled with care. While transparency is necessary for reporting breaches and sharing information with stakeholders, it is equally important to maintain confidentiality where it pertains to private data or proprietary information.

Example: Reporting the breach to affected individuals or regulatory bodies is essential, but sharing too much information in public forums (e.g., media) may harm individuals or the organization unnecessarily.

Civil Liberties During Investigations

When responding to incidents that involve individuals or employees, it is important to respect their rights. Investigations should be conducted fairly, and personnel should not be unjustly targeted or have their activities scrutinized without cause. Ethical incident response means ensuring that internal investigations, such as those involving employee misconduct, are conducted in a way that respects due process.

Example: If an employee is under suspicion for causing the incident, the investigation should focus on the facts of the breach rather than assuming guilt without evidence, and employees should be treated with fairness throughout the process.

Avoiding Conflicts of Interest

Ethical incident responders must avoid situations where their actions may conflict with their personal interests or the interests of their employer. They should not take advantage of privileged information, and decisions should be made with the organization's best interests in mind, rather than personal gain.

Example: If a third-party vendor is involved in the breach, the investigation should remain impartial, and there should be no pressure from the vendor to skew findings or cover up faults.

Incident Transparency and Responsibility

Ethical behavior during and after an incident also involves taking responsibility for actions taken or not taken. If mistakes were made during the response or if certain steps were missed, acknowledging these shortcomings and striving for improvement reflects an ethical approach to cybersecurity.

Example: If certain critical systems were overlooked during containment, reporting these mistakes honestly to leadership and implementing corrective measures will help prevent future errors.

Reporting and Accountability

Ethical incident responders must ensure that they report all findings and actions accurately, without falsifying records or selectively omitting information. Transparency in reporting ensures that the organization can take appropriate corrective actions and avoid future incidents.

By adhering to ethical guidelines, incident responders can maintain trust, respect privacy, and ensure that the investigation is carried out with integrity. Ethical standards should be part of an organization's broader cybersecurity policies, and responders should be regularly trained on ethical conduct during incident management.

CHAPTER 8   SECURITY OPERATION CENTERS AND MANAGING SECURITY INCIDENTS

Adapting to the Evolving Threat Landscape

As **cyber threats become more sophisticated**, so too must the strategies and tools used to combat them. The threat landscape is constantly changing, with attackers adopting new **tactics**, **techniques**, and **technologies** to bypass traditional defenses. It is no longer enough to rely solely on reactive measures; organizations must be agile and capable of adapting quickly to these shifting threats.

Incident response strategies must evolve in tandem with these changes. Security teams should continuously monitor the latest threat intelligence and stay informed about emerging attack vectors, from advanced persistent threats (APTs) to new ransomware strains. **Threat hunting**, leveraging cutting-edge **security technologies** (such as AI, machine learning, and automation), and investing in advanced detection and response tools will be key to staying ahead of cybercriminals. Additionally, **collaboration with industry peers** and sharing intelligence through trusted networks can enhance situational awareness and improve response times.

By fostering a culture of continuous learning and adaptation, organizations can stay one step ahead of cybercriminals and ensure their security measures remain robust in the face of evolving threats.

Continuous Improvement

In cybersecurity, there is no such thing as "set it and forget it." **Security operations and incident response** are not static functions but require constant **evaluation, training**, and **improvement** to ensure that organizations can respond effectively to the next challenge. Even after an incident is resolved, the work is far from over.

After each incident, teams should conduct a **postmortem analysis** to evaluate what went well, what could have been improved, and what new gaps or vulnerabilities have been exposed. This analysis should feed into a cycle of **continuous improvement**, driving adjustments to security policies, response plans, and security infrastructure. Regular training and simulated incident response exercises can help ensure that teams are well-prepared and familiar with the latest tactics and tools.

Organizations should also invest in developing **incident response metrics** that allow them to measure performance, track progress, and identify areas of improvement. This can help in determining response time effectiveness, identifying recurring issues, and ensuring that teams can make data-driven decisions to enhance overall incident response strategies.

Chapter Takeaways

This chapter has equipped you with a solid understanding of **security operations**, **incident response processes**, and the **tools** necessary to effectively manage and mitigate cybersecurity incidents. You have learned that an effective response relies on a combination of well-prepared personnel, robust incident response plans, and the ability to adapt to an ever-changing cybersecurity environment.

By embracing a **proactive, adaptable, and continuously improving approach**, organizations can not only recover from incidents but also strengthen their defenses to prevent future breaches. Your understanding of these principles will help you contribute to building a resilient and secure environment for your organization's information systems.

As the cybersecurity landscape continues to evolve, so too must our response strategies. By remaining vigilant, adaptive, and committed to improvement, we can better protect our organizations from the ever-present threat of cyberattacks.

CHAPTER 8   SECURITY OPERATION CENTERS AND MANAGING SECURITY INCIDENTS

Chapter Summary

In the face of an ever-evolving threat landscape, **proactive incident response** is not just a good practice—it's a necessity. Organizations must prepare for cybersecurity incidents before they occur, rather than reacting in the heat of the moment when systems are compromised and damage is already done. Having a well-structured, **tested incident response plan** is crucial for minimizing the impact of these incidents, restoring operations swiftly, and protecting valuable assets.

A proactive approach involves more than just creating an incident response plan. It means establishing a **cybersecurity culture** that prioritizes vigilance, awareness, and preparedness at all levels of the organization. It also includes regular updates to the plan to reflect new risks, technologies, and threats. Testing the plan through **tabletop exercises**, **simulated attacks**, and post-incident reviews ensures that the organization is ready when an actual incident occurs. The lessons learned from each incident only serve to strengthen this foundation and better prepare teams for future challenges.

CHAPTER 9

Governance, Risk, and Compliance (GRC)

In today's interconnected world, cybersecurity is not just a technical issue—it is a critical component of overall business strategy. As cyber threats evolve and regulatory landscapes tighten, organizations must ensure that their cybersecurity efforts are aligned with their broader governance, risk management, and compliance (GRC) strategies. This chapter delves into the essential intersection of **Security Governance, Risk Management, and Compliance (GRC)**, which are foundational to managing cybersecurity effectively.

Security governance defines how cybersecurity aligns with business objectives, ensuring leadership and accountability. Risk management addresses how organizations identify, assess, and mitigate cybersecurity risks to protect valuable assets. Meanwhile, compliance ensures that organizations meet legal, regulatory, and industry-specific requirements to avoid penalties and maintain stakeholder trust. Together, these three pillars form a robust framework for building resilient and secure systems that can adapt to the dynamic threat landscape.

CHAPTER 9   GOVERNANCE, RISK, AND COMPLIANCE (GRC)

Throughout this chapter, we will explore the principles and processes that underpin GRC, the frameworks that guide cybersecurity governance, and the methodologies for risk assessment and compliance management. By understanding and implementing effective GRC strategies, organizations can not only reduce risks but also create a security culture that fosters trust, transparency, and continuous improvement.

Introduction to Security Governance, Risk, and Compliance (GRC)

Governance, Risk Management, and Compliance (GRC) are interconnected pillars that form the foundation of a strong cybersecurity strategy. Together, these elements guide how an organization manages its security operations, mitigates risks, and ensures it meets legal and regulatory obligations. Effective GRC practices enable organizations to not only protect sensitive data and systems but also align their cybersecurity efforts with broader business goals, ensuring a comprehensive and sustainable approach to risk management.

- **Governance** refers to the processes and structures used to direct and manage an organization's security functions. This involves leadership, oversight, and strategic decision-making to ensure that cybersecurity objectives are aligned with the broader organizational goals. Cybersecurity governance provides the framework for accountability and decision-making, ensuring that security efforts are prioritized, resources are appropriately allocated, and policies are effectively implemented.

- **Risk Management** is the identification, evaluation, and prioritization of risks that could threaten an organization's assets, followed by the implementation of measures to mitigate or manage these risks. Effective risk management helps organizations minimize vulnerabilities and prevent potential security breaches, making it a vital component of any cybersecurity strategy. This proactive approach to risk ensures that organizations can respond quickly to emerging threats and protect critical data.

- **Compliance** involves ensuring that an organization adheres to the various laws, regulations, and standards that govern its industry and operations, particularly in relation to data protection and cybersecurity. Compliance is crucial for avoiding legal penalties, maintaining customer trust, and ensuring that an organization operates within the bounds of the law. It requires an organization to stay updated on ever-changing regulatory requirements and implement the necessary controls to maintain compliance.

The Importance of GRC cannot be overstated. Together, these three elements ensure that an organization has a clear and structured approach to managing cybersecurity risks, responding to threats, and maintaining compliance with applicable laws and regulations. A strong GRC framework helps organizations achieve a balanced approach to cybersecurity—one that not only minimizes risk but also enables operational efficiency and ensures legal compliance. In an increasingly complex threat landscape, integrating governance, risk management, and compliance strategies is crucial for safeguarding an organization's assets, reputation, and future growth.

CHAPTER 9   GOVERNANCE, RISK, AND COMPLIANCE (GRC)

Cybersecurity Governance Frameworks

Governance frameworks provide structured approaches for managing and overseeing an organization's cybersecurity activities. They ensure that policies, strategies, and practices are effectively implemented and monitored to protect critical information assets. These frameworks are essential in guiding organizations to create a robust cybersecurity strategy that aligns with their overall business goals while also helping to meet regulatory requirements. By establishing clear guidelines for governance, they provide accountability and ensure that cybersecurity efforts are integrated into broader risk management and business operations.

NIST Cybersecurity Framework (CSF)

The **NIST Cybersecurity Framework (CSF)** is one of the most widely adopted frameworks globally, known for its flexibility and risk-based approach to managing cybersecurity. The CSF is structured around five core functions: **Identify**, **Protect**, **Detect**, **Respond**, and **Recover**. These functions offer a comprehensive and systematic approach to cybersecurity that helps organizations manage their risks effectively.

- **Identify**: Understand cybersecurity risks to systems, assets, data, and capabilities.

- **Protect**: Implement appropriate safeguards to ensure delivery of critical services.

- **Detect**: Develop activities to identify the occurrence of a cybersecurity event.

- **Respond**: Take action to contain the impact of a detected cybersecurity event.

- **Recover**: Plan for resilience and restore any impaired services due to cybersecurity events.

This framework encourages organizations to assess their cybersecurity posture regularly, identify gaps, and implement the necessary protections, detection measures, and recovery plans.

COBIT (Control Objectives for Information and Related Technologies)

COBIT is a comprehensive framework for IT governance and management that ensures the alignment of IT with business goals. It emphasizes the importance of managing IT risks and security in a way that supports business objectives. COBIT focuses on control objectives, performance management, and auditing. By aligning IT and cybersecurity practices with organizational goals, it helps mitigate cybersecurity risks while optimizing IT governance and performance. COBIT's flexibility allows it to be applied to various types of organizations, including both large enterprises and smaller businesses.

ISO/IEC 27001 and 27002

The **ISO/IEC 27001** standard is widely recognized for its role in establishing, implementing, operating, monitoring, reviewing, and improving an **Information Security Management System (ISMS)**. It provides a systematic approach to managing sensitive information, ensuring its confidentiality, integrity, and availability through a comprehensive risk management process.

ISO/IEC 27002 complements this by providing a set of best practices for information security controls. This standard helps organizations manage and protect sensitive data, including risk assessments and controls for managing the security of information. Both ISO/IEC 27001 and 27002 are essential for organizations looking to establish a formal security management system and adhere to recognized international security standards.

CHAPTER 9   GOVERNANCE, RISK, AND COMPLIANCE (GRC)

The Role of Senior Leadership in Cybersecurity Governance

Cybersecurity governance requires strong leadership and active involvement from senior management. It is essential that senior leaders set the vision and direction for cybersecurity strategies, ensuring that these strategies align with the organization's overall business goals. They must allocate appropriate resources, empower teams, and ensure that the necessary processes, controls, and monitoring mechanisms are in place.

Moreover, senior leaders are responsible for establishing accountability throughout the organization and fostering a culture of security awareness. By ensuring that cybersecurity is a priority at the highest levels of management, organizations can better mitigate risks, respond to threats, and adapt to evolving cybersecurity challenges.

Risk Management in Cybersecurity

Risk management in cybersecurity is the process of assessing potential threats, vulnerabilities, and impacts to an organization's assets and implementing appropriate strategies to mitigate those risks. This ongoing process involves the identification, analysis, evaluation, and prioritization of risks, with the ultimate goal of reducing or eliminating the likelihood and impact of cyber threats.

Effective risk management helps organizations make informed decisions on how to protect their information, systems, and infrastructure. By understanding the potential risks and their implications, cybersecurity professionals can take proactive measures to defend against potential breaches, reduce vulnerabilities, and ensure business continuity. It's important to note that risk management is not a one-time effort; it is a continuous cycle that evolves as new threats and vulnerabilities emerge.

Qualitative Risk Assessment

A qualitative risk assessment is based on subjective analysis. It typically involves evaluating risks based on descriptions of their potential impact and likelihood, rather than numerical data. This method often uses terms like **low**, **medium**, or **high** to represent the severity of a risk.

Examples of qualitative methods include

- **Brainstorming sessions** to identify potential threats

- **Expert judgment**, where experienced professionals assess risks based on their knowledge

- **Scenario-based analysis**, where potential threats are evaluated by simulating various attack scenarios

While qualitative assessments are useful for gaining a quick understanding of risks, they can lack the precision of quantitative methods.

Quantitative Risk Assessment

A quantitative risk assessment uses numerical data to assess risks, focusing on calculating the financial or other measurable impacts of a risk event. This approach often involves the use of formulas and data to estimate the cost of potential security breaches or the impact of identified vulnerabilities.

Key metrics used in quantitative assessments include

- **Annual Loss Expectancy (ALE):** The expected annual monetary loss due to a specific risk.

- **Single Loss Expectancy (SLE):** The cost incurred from a single occurrence of a risk event.

- **Exposure Factor (EF):** The percentage of asset loss due to a specific threat.

Quantitative risk assessments provide more precise estimations of potential impacts and are often useful for making data-driven decisions, especially when it comes to allocating resources for risk mitigation.

Risk Treatment and Mitigation

After risks have been assessed, the next step is to determine how to handle them. There are several strategies for treating and mitigating risks, including

- **Avoidance**: Changing business practices or processes to eliminate the risk entirely. For example, discontinuing a high-risk service or product could eliminate the associated cybersecurity risks.

- **Mitigation**: Reducing the impact or likelihood of the risk through security controls, such as implementing stronger firewalls, encryption, or access control measures.

- **Transfer**: Sharing the risk by purchasing insurance or outsourcing specific functions to a third party, thereby offloading some of the financial or operational burden if the risk materializes.

- **Acceptance**: Acknowledging the risk and deciding to accept its potential consequences, often due to the cost of mitigation outweighing the potential impact. This is often the case for low-likelihood, low-impact risks.

Cybersecurity Risk Management Life Cycle

The cybersecurity risk management life cycle is a systematic approach to managing and mitigating cybersecurity risks. It involves four key stages:

- **Risk Identification**: The first step is to identify the organization's assets, vulnerabilities, threats, and the potential impacts of these risks. This process involves gathering information about systems, data, and infrastructure that need protection.

- **Risk Analysis**: After identifying risks, the next step is to assess the likelihood and impact of each risk. This stage helps in determining which risks pose the greatest threat to the organization's assets and operations.

- **Risk Evaluation**: Once risks have been analyzed, they are evaluated and prioritized based on their potential consequences. Risks with the highest likelihood and most severe impact are given higher priority for treatment and mitigation.

- **Risk Treatment**: The final stage involves selecting and implementing strategies to mitigate, transfer, or accept the risks. This may involve applying security controls, updating policies, or taking other actions to reduce the organization's exposure to cyber threats.

CHAPTER 9   GOVERNANCE, RISK, AND COMPLIANCE (GRC)

Regulatory Compliance Standards and Frameworks

Regulatory compliance plays a critical role in ensuring that organizations adhere to legal and regulatory standards regarding data privacy, cybersecurity, and other key areas necessary for maintaining operational integrity, public trust, and business success. Non-compliance can lead to hefty fines, reputational damage, and legal consequences. Therefore, it's crucial for organizations to understand and implement the relevant regulatory requirements that govern their industry and operations.

Compliance not only involves adhering to specific regulations but also creating a culture of security and privacy within the organization. Compliance efforts are ongoing, requiring regular monitoring, documentation, and audits to ensure that security practices evolve in line with changing regulations and emerging threats.

General Data Protection Regulation (GDPR)

The GDPR is one of the most comprehensive data protection regulations in the world, applicable to any organization that processes the personal data of residents of the European Union (EU). It imposes strict requirements on how personal data is handled, including the right to access and delete data, obtaining explicit consent for data collection, and reporting data breaches within 72 hours.

Organizations subject to the GDPR must ensure that their cybersecurity practices support the principles of data protection, such as minimizing data use, ensuring accuracy, and safeguarding the data against unauthorized access or breaches.

Health Insurance Portability and Accountability Act (HIPAA)

HIPAA sets the standards for safeguarding protected health information (PHI) in the US healthcare sector. It applies to healthcare providers, insurers, and business associates that handle PHI. HIPAA mandates that organizations implement stringent security measures, such as encryption, access controls, and audit trails, to protect the confidentiality, integrity, and availability of health data. Non-compliance with HIPAA can lead to significant penalties and loss of trust among patients and business partners.

Payment Card Industry Data Security Standard (PCI DSS)

PCI DSS is a set of security standards aimed at ensuring that all companies processing, storing, or transmitting credit card information maintain a secure environment. The standards cover aspects such as encryption, access controls, and vulnerability management to prevent data breaches involving payment card information. Compliance with PCI DSS is mandatory for businesses that handle cardholder data, and failure to comply can result in fines, reputational damage, and loss of business.

Federal Information Security Modernization Act (FISMA)

FISMA is a US law that requires federal agencies and contractors to secure their information systems. The law mandates the implementation of cybersecurity measures to protect federal information from cyber threats. FISMA compliance involves meeting the standards set by the National Institute of Standards and Technology (NIST) and conducting regular assessments to ensure the effectiveness of security controls.

CHAPTER 9   GOVERNANCE, RISK, AND COMPLIANCE (GRC)

ISO/IEC 27001 and 27002

ISO/IEC 27001 provides a framework for establishing, implementing, operating, monitoring, reviewing, and improving an Information Security Management System (ISMS). The standard helps organizations manage the confidentiality, integrity, and availability of their information.

ISO/IEC 27002 complements 27001 by offering a set of best-practice controls for information security management. These frameworks help organizations demonstrate compliance with security requirements and ensure that sensitive data is protected against unauthorized access and cyber threats.

NIST SP 800-53

NIST Special Publication 800-53 provides a catalog of security and privacy controls designed to help organizations meet federal information security requirements. It covers a wide range of topics, including access control, incident response, and system and communications protection. NIST 800-53 is widely used by federal agencies and contractors to comply with FISMA, but its controls can also be applied to other sectors to enhance cybersecurity and compliance efforts.

The Role of Audits and Assessments

Regular security audits and assessments are vital for ensuring that an organization is compliant with legal, regulatory, and security standards. Audits can take several forms, including

- **Internal reviews**, where organizations evaluate their own compliance with security policies and controls.

- **External assessments** conducted by independent third parties to provide an objective evaluation of compliance.

- **Self-assessments**, in which organizations perform a self-check to ensure their cybersecurity practices align with regulatory standards.

These assessments help organizations identify gaps in their cybersecurity practices, ensure they are meeting regulatory requirements, and enhance their overall security posture. Additionally, audit findings can be used to inform ongoing improvements in both security and compliance strategies.

Creating Effective Cybersecurity Policies

Cybersecurity policies play a crucial role in defining how an organization manages and mitigates security risks. These policies set the framework for consistent and effective cybersecurity practices across the organization, ensuring that everyone adheres to a unified approach. By establishing clear guidelines, policies help create a shared understanding of the organization's cybersecurity objectives and the roles and responsibilities of employees, contractors, and other stakeholders in safeguarding assets.

When creating effective cybersecurity policies, it is essential to align them with the organization's overall security goals and regulatory requirements. Policies should be clear, concise, and adaptable to evolving threats, with regular reviews and updates as needed. Well-crafted policies can significantly reduce the risk of human error and ensure that security measures are consistently followed.

Some examples of common cybersecurity policies include

- **Password Management Policy**: Ensures strong password practices are followed across the organization to prevent unauthorized access.

- **Data Encryption Policy**: Dictates how sensitive data is encrypted, both at rest and in transit, to protect it from unauthorized access during storage or transfer.

- **Remote Access Policy**: Establishes secure methods and protocols for remote employees to access the organization's network, ensuring that these connections are properly secured.

Common Types of Cybersecurity Policies
Acceptable Use Policy (AUP)

An Acceptable Use Policy (AUP) defines the rules and expectations for users regarding the use of organizational resources such as computers, the Internet, email, and software. It helps to ensure that employees understand the boundaries of acceptable behavior when using company devices and networks. This policy is designed to prevent misuse of resources, such as accessing inappropriate websites, downloading malicious software, or engaging in activities that could compromise security.

Data Protection and Privacy Policy

A Data Protection and Privacy Policy outlines how personal, confidential, and sensitive data should be managed, protected, and shared to comply with relevant privacy laws and regulations. This policy is essential for ensuring that the organization meets its obligations under data protection regulations such as GDPR, HIPAA, or CCPA. It specifies how data is collected, stored, transmitted, and disposed of, as well as how employees should handle data to avoid unauthorized access, leaks, or breaches.

Incident Response Policy

The Incident Response Policy provides a structured approach for handling cybersecurity incidents, ensuring that the organization can respond effectively and efficiently to breaches, cyberattacks, or other security events. This policy details the roles and responsibilities of the incident response team, steps to identify and contain the threat, communication protocols, and recovery measures. A well-documented incident response policy helps minimize damage and ensures a swift return to normal operations.

Access Control Policy

An Access Control Policy defines the processes and rules for managing user access to organizational systems and data. It specifies who can access what resources, under what circumstances, and with what level of permissions. The policy is designed to enforce the principle of least privilege, ensuring that users only have access to the information and systems necessary to perform their roles. This minimizes the risk of unauthorized access and reduces the potential for data breaches.

Business Continuity and Disaster Recovery

Business continuity is a crucial element of any organization's overall risk management strategy. It ensures that essential business functions can continue operating or be quickly restored during and after an unexpected disruption, such as a cyberattack, natural disaster, or system failure. Business continuity planning (BCP) is not just about having backup systems in place but also ensuring that processes, personnel, and resources are ready to maintain operations during challenging times.

In the context of cybersecurity, a BCP is vital for ensuring that even if critical systems are compromised or lost, an organization can still deliver key services or products, mitigate financial losses, and protect its reputation. For example, in the case of a ransomware attack that locks vital business systems, a well-designed business continuity plan would ensure that the organization can operate with minimal disruption by relying on backup systems, manual processes, or cloud-based solutions.

A BCP includes defining which functions are critical to the organization's survival, setting recovery priorities, and developing procedures to maintain or restore operations quickly. These procedures can include setting up temporary workspaces, identifying alternative communication channels, and making sure that data can be accessed even if primary systems go down.

Disaster Recovery (DR) and its Relationship to Cybersecurity

While business continuity is about keeping the business running, disaster recovery (DR) focuses specifically on the restoration of IT systems and data after a disaster. DR ensures that the organization can quickly recover from cyberattacks, data breaches, or infrastructure failures with minimal downtime and data loss. A strong DR plan is an integral part of the overall cybersecurity strategy, as it helps minimize the impact of security incidents like ransomware or data breaches.

Key components of a DR plan include identifying critical IT assets and systems, establishing clear recovery objectives, and developing processes for restoring services. Two important metrics for DR planning are

- **Recovery Time Objective (RTO):** This is the targeted duration of time within which critical systems must be restored after a disruption to avoid significant harm to the organization.

- **Recovery Point Objective (RPO):** This refers to the acceptable amount of data loss in terms of time. For example, an RPO of four hours means that the organization can tolerate losing up to four hours of data if systems go down.

Effective disaster recovery planning also includes setting up mechanisms for data backups, creating failover procedures for systems, and ensuring that there are clear communication protocols in place for both internal and external stakeholders during an incident.

The Role of Testing and Drills

One of the most effective ways to ensure that business continuity and disaster recovery plans are ready to be activated during an actual incident is through regular testing and drills. Without testing, organizations may be unaware of gaps in their plans or challenges they may face during a real crisis.

Testing and drills can vary in complexity and scope, but they all play a crucial role in validating the organization's preparedness. Common types of tests include

- **Tabletop Exercises:** These are scenario-based discussions that simulate a cyberattack or disaster. They allow the team to walk through the incident response and recovery procedures in a controlled environment, identifying weaknesses and areas for improvement.
- **Simulation Drills:** These are more hands-on exercises that replicate real-world incidents, allowing teams to practice their response under more realistic conditions.

- **Full-Scale Recovery Tests:** These are comprehensive tests where the organization runs through an actual recovery scenario, often involving the restoration of systems from backups, failover procedures, and the coordination of resources. These tests are typically done periodically to ensure all systems and processes work as planned.

Regular testing and drills help to ensure that employees understand their roles and responsibilities, systems work as expected, and the organization can restore operations within the defined RTO and RPO. They also provide an opportunity to refine the plan and address any issues before an actual disaster occurs.

Building a Strong Cybersecurity Culture

A robust cybersecurity strategy goes beyond just technology and tools. It requires an organizational culture where cybersecurity is deeply embedded in daily practices. Every employee, from the executive team to frontline staff, must be aware of the risks and responsibilities associated with maintaining secure systems and data. Leadership support is crucial in setting the tone for security, while regular training and awareness programs empower employees to act as active participants in defending against cyber threats. By fostering this security-first mindset, organizations can reduce vulnerabilities and create a more resilient security posture across all levels of the business.

Continuous Improvement and Adaptation

Cybersecurity governance, risk management, and compliance (GRC) are not static processes. As the cyber threat landscape constantly evolves, so must the strategies and practices used to protect sensitive data and business operations. New technologies, such as artificial intelligence (AI) and machine learning, are changing the way threats are detected and mitigated, while changes in regulations and industry standards demand ongoing updates to compliance frameworks. This dynamic environment requires organizations to continuously assess and adapt their cybersecurity governance and risk management strategies. Regular reviews and improvements ensure that cybersecurity efforts remain aligned with organizational goals and resilient to emerging risks.

The Future of GRC in Cybersecurity

As technology advances, so will the demands placed on cybersecurity governance, risk management, and compliance frameworks. With the rise of AI, automation, and other cutting-edge technologies, the future of GRC will involve more intelligent, responsive systems that can predict, detect, and mitigate threats in real time. Regulations will continue to evolve, particularly with respect to data privacy and protection, as businesses become more global and interconnected. The future of GRC will see greater integration between business strategy and cybersecurity practices, ensuring that security is not just a technical requirement but an essential component of organizational success.

This chapter has provided a comprehensive overview of how to manage cybersecurity governance, risk management, and compliance. By integrating effective frameworks and aligning organizational processes with legal and regulatory requirements, cybersecurity professionals can build defenses that meet both business needs and regulatory expectations. A proactive, continuously improving approach to GRC ensures that organizations are not only secure today but also prepared for the challenges of tomorrow.

CHAPTER 10

Final Review and Exam Preparation

Successfully passing the **CompTIA Cybersecurity Analyst (CySA+)** exam requires more than just theoretical knowledge, demands a **strong analytical mindset, hands-on skills, and strategic preparation**. As an intermediate-level cybersecurity certification, the CySA+ validates your ability to **proactively detect, analyze, and respond to security threats** in modern enterprise environments. Unlike entry-level certifications, this exam emphasizes **practical application, threat intelligence, and security operations**, making a structured study approach essential.

This chapter serves as your **final checkpoint** before test day, helping you **reinforce core concepts, develop test-taking strategies, and manage time effectively**. The CySA+ exam consists of **multiple-choice questions, performance-based simulations, and scenario-driven analysis**, requiring a blend of **technical expertise and problem-solving skills**. Understanding the exam format and preparing with **real-world cybersecurity scenarios** can significantly enhance your confidence and performance.

Throughout this chapter, we will cover **key review topics, exam strategies, and practical study techniques** to ensure you are fully prepared. Whether you're refining your knowledge or focusing on last-minute details, these insights will help you approach the exam with clarity and confidence, setting you up for success in your cybersecurity career.

CHAPTER 10   FINAL REVIEW AND EXAM PREPARATION

To effectively prepare for the **CompTIA Cybersecurity Analyst (CySA+)** exam, it's essential to reinforce the following core concepts:

1. **Security Operations:**

    - **System and Network Architecture**: Understand log ingestion, operating system concepts, infrastructure, network architecture, identity and access management, encryption, and sensitive data protection.

    - **Malicious Activity Analysis**: Identify and analyze indicators of potentially malicious activity across network, host, and application layers.

    - **Threat Intelligence and Hunting**: Differentiate between threat intelligence and threat hunting concepts and apply appropriate tools and techniques.

    - **Incident Response**: Develop and implement effective incident response plans and procedures.

    - **Data Analysis and Interpretation**: Collect, analyze, and interpret security data from multiple log and monitoring sources to identify vulnerabilities, threats, and risks.

2. **Vulnerability Management:**

    - **Vulnerability Assessment**: Conduct network, host, and web application vulnerability assessments using appropriate tools.

    - **Prioritization and Mitigation**: Prioritize identified vulnerabilities and recommend effective mitigation strategies.

- **Remediation Processes**: Understand and implement processes to remediate identity management, authentication, and access control issues.

3. **Incident Response and Management:**

    - **Preparation and Planning**: Establish and maintain incident response capabilities, including communication plans and stakeholder engagement.

    - **Detection and Analysis**: Recognize signs of an incident, analyze relevant data, and determine the incident's scope and impact.

    - **Containment, Eradication, and Recovery**: Implement strategies to contain the incident, eliminate the threat, and restore systems to normal operations.

    - **Post-Incident Activities**: Conduct lessons learned sessions, update response plans, and implement improvements based on incident findings.

4. **Compliance and Assessment:**

    - **Regulatory Requirements**: Understand key regulations and standards affecting cybersecurity practices, such as GDPR, HIPAA, and PCI-DSS.

    - **Risk Management**: Perform risk assessments to identify potential threats and vulnerabilities and develop strategies to manage and mitigate risks.

- **Security Audits**: Conduct security audits to ensure compliance with organizational policies and regulatory requirements.
- **Policy Development**: Develop and enforce security policies and procedures to guide organizational cybersecurity efforts.

Create a Study Plan

A well-structured study plan is essential for mastering the material and increasing your chances of passing the **CompTIA CySA+** exam. Rather than passively reading through topics, an effective plan ensures steady progress, reinforces key concepts, and helps you stay on track. Whether you're balancing study time with a full-time job or dedicating yourself entirely to exam preparation, a strategic approach will maximize efficiency and retention.

1. Assess Your Starting Point

Before diving into the material, evaluate your current knowledge of **CySA+ exam domains**. Identify areas where you feel confident and those that require more attention. If you're experienced with **log analysis** but struggle with **vulnerability scanning and assessment**, prioritize those weaker areas. Consider taking a **practice test** at the beginning of your studies to highlight strengths and gaps in knowledge.

2. Set Clear and Achievable Goals

Breaking your study sessions into **manageable milestones** will prevent information overload. Set realistic weekly goals, such as mastering **one or two domains per week** while allocating additional time for **review and practice exams**. A structured approach might look like this:

- **Week 1-2:** Focus on **Threat and Vulnerability Management**
- **Week 3-4:** Cover **Security Operations and Monitoring**
- **Week 5-6:** Study **Incident Response and Forensics**
- **Week 7-8:** Review **Compliance, Assessments, and Exam Readiness**

By setting measurable objectives, you'll create a roadmap that keeps you motivated and ensures you cover all critical areas before exam day.

3. Stick to a Consistent Study Schedule

Consistency is key to retaining information and building long-term knowledge. Set aside **dedicated, uninterrupted study blocks** that fit your lifestyle—whether it's an hour each morning, a few hours on weekends, or a mix of both. Use **active learning techniques** such as:

- **Flashcards** to reinforce technical terms and concepts
- **Mind maps** to connect related security concepts
- **Hands-on labs** to gain practical experience with SIEM tools, log analysis, and network monitoring

Staying engaged with the material rather than passively reading will improve comprehension and recall.

4. Reinforce Learning with Practice Exams

Regularly test yourself with **practice exams, scenario-based questions, and simulated assessments** to gauge your understanding and track progress. Aim to complete at least **two full-length practice exams** before your actual test date, reviewing any incorrect answers to reinforce weak areas.

5. Adapt and Refine Your Plan

As you progress, adjust your study plan based on your performance in **practice tests and topic reviews**. If certain areas require extra attention, allocate additional study time.

By following a structured, goal-oriented plan, you'll not only increase your chances of passing the **CompTIA CySA+** exam but also build the practical skills necessary for a successful career in cybersecurity.

Use a Variety of Study Materials

A well-rounded study approach ensures deeper comprehension and retention of the **CompTIA CySA+** material. Since everyone absorbs information differently, using a mix of resources can reinforce learning and keep you engaged. By incorporating **text-based materials, visual aids, hands-on practice, and peer discussions**, you'll develop a stronger grasp of exam objectives and real-world applications.

1. Official Study Guides and Books

Using an **up-to-date CySA+ study guide** is essential, as it provides structured explanations of key concepts, domain breakdowns, and practice questions. Look for books that align with the latest exam objectives to ensure you're studying the most relevant material. Some trusted options include

- **CompTIA CySA+ Official Study Guide**
- **CySA+ Exam Cram**
- **Other reputable cybersecurity books covering SIEM, threat intelligence, and vulnerability assessment**

2. Video Tutorials and Online Courses

For **visual and auditory learners**, video tutorials provide a dynamic way to understand complex security concepts. Platforms like **LinkedIn Learning, Udemy, Cybrary, and YouTube (Professor Messer, John Hammond, and other cybersecurity educators)** offer in-depth explanations, demonstrations, and real-world examples that enhance comprehension.

3. Hands-on Labs and Simulations

Practical experience is crucial for the CySA+ exam, which focuses heavily on **real-world cybersecurity tasks**. Utilize platforms that provide **virtual labs, SIEM tools, and threat analysis scenarios**, such as:

- **CompTIA CertMaster Labs**
- **TryHackMe & Hack The Box (Blue Team paths)**
- **RangeForce & CyberSecLabs for defensive security training**
- **Security Onion & Splunk for log and SIEM analysis**

4. Practice Questions and Mock Exams

Regularly testing yourself with **practice exams** is one of the most effective ways to prepare. They help you **familiarize yourself with the question format, identify weak areas, and build confidence** before the actual exam. Use multiple resources for practice questions, including

- **Official CompTIA Practice Tests**
- **Boson Practice Exams**
- **Exam-specific question banks from study guides and online platforms**

Aim to complete at least **two to three full-length practice exams** before your test date and thoroughly review any incorrect answers to reinforce your understanding.

5. Online Forums, Study Groups, and Discussion Boards

Engaging with **cybersecurity communities** allows you to **discuss key topics, clarify doubts, and gain insights from other learners and professionals**. Consider joining

- **CompTIA's official forums**
- **Reddit (r/CompTIA, r/cybersecurity, and other study groups)**
- **Discord servers or LinkedIn groups dedicated to CySA+**

Actively participating in discussions, asking questions, and even explaining concepts to others will solidify your knowledge and expose you to different perspectives.

By combining multiple study resources, you'll create a **comprehensive and engaging learning experience** that enhances both your theoretical knowledge and practical skills, ensuring you're fully prepared for the **CompTIA CySA+** exam.

Focus on Hands-on Practice

Cybersecurity is a hands-on field, and while theoretical knowledge is essential, **practical experience is what truly solidifies your understanding**. The CompTIA CySA+ exam includes **performance-based questions (PBQs)** that assess your ability to apply security concepts

CHAPTER 10   FINAL REVIEW AND EXAM PREPARATION

in real-world scenarios. To develop these critical skills, it's important to practice using security tools, analyze threats, and troubleshoot vulnerabilities in simulated environments.

1. Set Up a Home Lab

Building a **home lab** is one of the best ways to gain real-world experience with cybersecurity tools and techniques. You can create a virtual environment to test security configurations, analyze traffic, and simulate attacks. Here's how to get started:

- Use **VMware Workstation, VirtualBox, or Hyper-V** to run multiple operating systems simultaneously.

- Install **Linux distributions** such as **Kali Linux** (for security testing) and **Ubuntu** (for general system administration).

- Experiment with **Windows Server and client versions** to understand enterprise security configurations.

- Deploy and configure key security tools like **Snort (IDS/IPS), Suricata, Security Onion, Wireshark, Splunk, and Metasploit**.

- Simulate real-world scenarios such as **log analysis, malware detection, and SIEM integration**.

2. Use Simulation and Cloud-Based Labs

For those who may not have access to hardware resources for a home lab, cloud-based and virtualized cybersecurity labs provide an excellent alternative. These platforms offer pre-built cybersecurity exercises that allow you to practice **threat detection, network defense, and forensic analysis** without needing complex setups. Some valuable resources include

- **CompTIA CertMaster Labs**: Interactive labs aligned with CySA+ objectives.

- **TryHackMe & Hack The Box (Blue Team Paths)**: Hands-on cybersecurity challenges for defensive security training.

- **RangeForce & CyberSecLabs**: Interactive security training environments focusing on SOC operations and incident response.

- **AWS, Azure, and Google Cloud Free Tiers**: Explore cloud security configurations and IAM policies in enterprise settings.

3. Engage in Open-Source Threat Intelligence and Incident Response

Practicing with **real-world security incidents and open-source threat intelligence feeds** will help you develop **SOC analyst skills** and prepare for **real-time cyber defense scenarios**. You can

- **Monitor and analyze live attack data** using sources like **MalwareBazaar, VirusTotal, and AlienVault OTX**.

- **Engage with SIEM tools** like **Splunk, ELK Stack (Elasticsearch, Logstash, Kibana), or Graylog** to process and analyze security logs.

- **Investigate cyber incidents** using forensic tools like **Autopsy, Volatility (for memory analysis), and Wireshark (for packet analysis)**.

By combining **hands-on practice with theoretical study**, you will reinforce your knowledge, **gain confidence in security operations**, and be better prepared for both the **CySA+ exam and real-world cybersecurity roles**.

Take Practice Exams and Review Mistakes

One of the most effective ways to **gauge your readiness** for the **CompTIA CySA+** exam is by taking **full-length practice tests**. These exams simulate real test conditions, helping you become familiar with the **question format, timing, and complexity**. Simply memorizing concepts isn't enough, you need to apply your knowledge to different scenarios, just like in the actual exam.

1. Understand the Exam Format

The **CySA+ exam** includes **multiple-choice, drag-and-drop, and performance-based questions (PBQs)**. PBQs are particularly challenging because they require you to **perform tasks such as analyzing logs, identifying threats, and configuring security settings** in a simulated environment. Taking practice exams that include PBQs will help you **get comfortable with the interactive format** and **develop strategies for managing time efficiently**.

2. Identify Weak Areas and Adjust Your Study Plan

Practice exams reveal your strengths and weaknesses, allowing you to **focus on areas that need improvement**. After completing a test, carefully analyze your results:

- **Which domains did you score lowest in?** These are your priority areas for review.

- **Which question types gave you the most trouble?** Did you struggle with PBQs, scenario-based questions, or theoretical concepts?

- **Did you misinterpret any questions?** Sometimes, questions are worded in a tricky way. Learning how to **identify keywords** and **understanding what's really being asked** is a crucial test-taking skill.

3. Improve Exam Stamina and Time Management

The **CySA+ exam lasts up to 165 minutes**, and staying focused for the entire duration is a challenge. Taking **full-length practice exams under timed conditions** helps you **develop the endurance needed to maintain concentration** throughout the test. Here's how to maximize your practice sessions:

- **Simulate real exam conditions** by taking the test in a quiet space, without distractions.

- **Stick to time limits** to ensure you can complete the exam within the allocated time.

- **Learn to pace yourself**—don't spend too long on a single question. If you're unsure, mark it for review and move on.

4. Review Your Mistakes and Reinforce Key Concepts

Taking practice exams isn't just about answering questions, it's about **learning from mistakes**. After each test, go through every incorrect answer and ask yourself

- **Why did I get this wrong?** Did I misunderstand the concept, misread the question, or second-guess my answer?

- **What is the correct answer, and why?** Understanding the reasoning behind the correct response helps reinforce your knowledge.

- **How can I avoid this mistake in the future?** Take notes on challenging topics and revisit them in your study sessions.

By consistently **practicing under exam conditions, analyzing mistakes, and refining your understanding**, you'll gain the confidence needed to **approach the CySA+ exam with a strong strategy and a higher chance of success**.

Master Time Management

Time management is a crucial skill when taking the **CompTIA CySA+ exam**, as you'll need to **complete up to 85 questions in 165 minutes**. While this provides a bit more time per question compared to some other CompTIA exams, the **complexity of the questions, especially the performance-based ones—can be time-consuming**. Having a solid time management strategy ensures that you maximize your chances of answering every question effectively.

CHAPTER 10   FINAL REVIEW AND EXAM PREPARATION

1. Set a Realistic Pace

To stay on track, you should aim to spend an **average of 1.5 to 2 minutes per question**. However, some questions, especially **multiple-choice ones—can be answered more quickly**, while others, such as **performance-based questions (PBQs), may take significantly longer**.

- **PBQs first or last?** Some test-takers prefer to tackle PBQs at the beginning while they're fresh, while others skip them initially and return later. Choose whichever approach works best for you.
- **Keep an eye on the clock.** If you find yourself spending too much time on a single question, move on and revisit it later if time permits.

2. Prioritize Easy Wins

- **Start with what you know.** Quickly answering the questions you're confident about ensures you rack up easy points early on.
- **Mark difficult questions for review.** Instead of wasting valuable time agonizing over a tough question, flag it and return later if time allows.

3. Use the Process of Elimination

If you're unsure about a question:

- **Eliminate obviously incorrect answers** to improve your odds of guessing correctly.
- **Look for keywords** that hint at the correct response.
- **Trust your training.** Overthinking can sometimes lead to second-guessing correct answers.

4. Manage PBQs Efficiently

Performance-based questions can be time-consuming, so approach them wisely:

- **Read instructions carefully.** Misinterpreting the task can cost you valuable minutes.
- **Don't get stuck troubleshooting minor details.** Answer to the best of your ability and move on if needed.

5. Leave Time for Review

If possible, set aside the last **10-15 minutes** to review marked questions. Double-check your answers but avoid unnecessary second-guessing unless you have a strong reason to change an answer.

By **pacing yourself, prioritizing easy points, and strategically tackling complex questions**, you'll optimize your time and increase your chances of success on the CySA+ exam.

Review Key Concepts the Day Before the Exam

The last day before your **CompTIA CySA+ exam** should focus on reinforcing key concepts rather than cramming new information. At this stage, your priority is to **solidify your understanding, boost confidence, and prepare mentally for exam day**. Here's how to make the most of your final review:

CHAPTER 10   FINAL REVIEW AND EXAM PREPARATION

1. Focus on High-Yield Concepts

- **Revisit your notes and summaries** instead of diving into full chapters or long study sessions.

- **Review key security frameworks and methodologies**, including **NIST, ISO 27001, MITRE ATT&CK, and the Cyber Kill Chain**.

- **Refresh your knowledge of attack techniques and mitigation strategies**, such as **SQL injection defenses, privilege escalation prevention, and risk management best practices.**

- **Go over essential acronyms and terminology** to ensure you understand industry jargon and can quickly recall their meanings during the test.

2. Use Quick-Recall Tools

- **Flashcards or cheat sheets** can help you reinforce key definitions, formulas, and concepts.

- **Mind maps and diagrams** are great for reviewing network security, incident response, and threat intelligence concepts.

- **Practice a few questions** but avoid taking a full practice exam—focus on reinforcing weak areas instead.

3. Optimize Mental Readiness

- **Avoid last-minute cramming.** Trying to learn new topics at the last minute can cause confusion and unnecessary stress. Stick to reviewing what you already know.

- **Get a good night's sleep.** Fatigue can significantly impact your cognitive performance, so aim for **at least 7-8 hours of sleep** the night before.

- **Stay relaxed and confident.** Stress and anxiety can affect your recall ability, so take breaks, breathe deeply, and trust your preparation.

By following these steps, you'll ensure that you walk into your **CySA+ exam feeling well-prepared, focused, and ready to succeed**.

Stay Calm and Confident on Exam Day

The **CompTIA CySA+ exam** can feel challenging but staying composed and focused will help you perform at your best. By following these strategies, you can minimize stress and **approach the exam with confidence**:

1. Arrive Early and Be Prepared

- **For in-person exams:** Arrive at the testing center at least **30 minutes early** to allow time for check-in procedures. Bring the required identification and ensure you understand the testing center's rules.

- **For online exams:** Set up your **exam environment ahead of time**. Ensure a stable Internet connection, test your webcam and microphone, and clear your workspace to meet the proctoring requirements.

2. Stay Focused and Manage Stress

- **Take deep breaths before starting** to calm your nerves and improve concentration.
- **Read each question carefully**, don't rush, and watch out for tricky wording.
- **Use the flagging feature** to mark difficult questions and return to them later if needed.

3. Trust Your Preparation

- **You've put in the time and effort**—believe in your knowledge and problem-solving skills.
- **If unsure, use elimination techniques** to rule out incorrect answers and make an educated guess.
- **Stay positive**—a confident mindset can help you think more clearly and avoid second-guessing yourself.

By following these best practices, you'll be well-equipped to tackle the **CompTIA CySA+ exam** successfully. With a structured study plan, consistent practice, and smart test-taking strategies, you can maximize your performance and **take the next step in your cybersecurity career**.

Glossary of Key Terms

1. **Access Control**: Security measures that restrict access to systems and data based on user roles or permissions.

2. **Access Control List (ACL)**: A list of rules that specify who can access an object and what actions they can perform on it.

3. **AES (Advanced Encryption Standard)**: A widely used encryption standard for securing data.

4. **Agile**: A project management methodology that emphasizes flexibility, collaboration, and iterative development.

5. **Antivirus Software**: Programs designed to detect and remove malicious software from a computer system.

6. **API (Application Programming Interface)**: A set of protocols for building and interacting with software applications.

7. **AppLocker**: A security feature in Microsoft Windows that controls which applications can run on a computer.

8. **APT (Advanced Persistent Threat)**: A prolonged and targeted cyberattack, often carried out by skilled adversaries to gain unauthorized access to an organization's networks.

9. **Asset**: Anything of value to an organization, such as hardware, software, data, or intellectual property.

10. **Attack Surface**: The total sum of all points (e.g., network ports, devices, or applications) where an attacker can try to enter or extract data.

11. **Authentication**: The process of verifying the identity of a user, system, or entity.

12. **Authorization**: The process of granting or denying access to resources based on verified identity.

13. **Backup**: The process of copying and storing data to ensure it can be restored in case of data loss or corruption.

14. **BIOS (Basic Input/Output System)**: Firmware that initializes hardware during the booting process of a computer.

15. **Black Hat**: A term used for hackers or cybersecurity professionals who use their skills for malicious purposes.

16. **Blended Threat**: A type of attack that combines multiple attack techniques, such as viruses, worms, and trojans.

17. **Botnet**: A network of infected computers or devices controlled remotely to carry out cyberattacks.

18. **Buffer Overflow**: A type of vulnerability where a program writes more data to a buffer than it can handle, potentially allowing malicious code execution.

GLOSSARY OF KEY TERMS

19. **Business Continuity**: The ability of an organization to maintain its essential operations during and after a disaster.

20. **Business Continuity Plan (BCP)**: A strategic plan that outlines how an organization will continue operations in the event of a major disruption.

21. **CIA Triad**: A foundational concept in cybersecurity that emphasizes the importance of Confidentiality, Integrity, and Availability.

22. **Cloud Security**: The practice of securing data, applications, and services hosted on cloud platforms.

23. **CISSP (Certified Information Systems Security Professional)**: A globally recognized certification for information security professionals.

24. **CVE (Common Vulnerabilities and Exposures)**: A public database of known cybersecurity vulnerabilities in software and hardware.

25. **Cybersecurity**: The practice of protecting systems, networks, and data from digital attacks.

26. **Cybersecurity Framework**: A structured approach to managing cybersecurity risks, often consisting of policies, procedures, and standards.

27. **Data Encryption**: The process of converting data into a coded format to prevent unauthorized access.

28. **Data Loss Prevention (DLP)**: A set of tools and processes designed to prevent the unauthorized sharing or loss of sensitive data.

29. **Data Masking**: The process of obfuscating sensitive data to prevent unauthorized access while maintaining its functionality.

30. **Data Protection**: The practice of safeguarding sensitive information from unauthorized access, use, or destruction.

31. **Denial of Service (DoS)**: A type of cyberattack where an attacker attempts to make a system or network unavailable by overwhelming it with traffic or requests.

32. **Disaster Recovery (DR)**: The process of restoring IT systems and data after a catastrophic event to minimize downtime and data loss.

33. **Disaster Recovery Plan (DRP)**: A set of procedures to recover IT systems, applications, and data after a disaster or disruption.

34. **Distributed Denial of Service (DDoS)**: A type of DoS attack where the traffic is generated from multiple sources, making it harder to defend against.

35. **Endpoint Security**: The practice of securing end-user devices, such as computers, smartphones, and tablets, from threats.

36. **Encryption**: The process of converting data into an unreadable format to protect its confidentiality during transmission or storage.

37. **Ethical Hacking**: The practice of probing systems for vulnerabilities to improve security, typically performed by security professionals with permission.

GLOSSARY OF KEY TERMS

38. **Exfiltration**: The unauthorized transfer of data from a computer or network.

39. **Firewall**: A network security system that monitors and controls incoming and outgoing network traffic based on predetermined security rules.

40. **Governance, Risk, and Compliance (GRC)**: A framework that combines governance, risk management, and compliance to ensure that an organization meets its cybersecurity and legal obligations.

41. **Incident Response**: The process of identifying, managing, and mitigating cybersecurity incidents.

42. **Incident Response Plan (IRP)**: A documented set of procedures to follow when responding to a cybersecurity incident.

43. **Intrusion Detection System (IDS)**: A security tool that monitors network traffic for signs of suspicious or malicious activity.

44. **Intrusion Prevention System (IPS)**: A security tool that not only detects but also blocks malicious activities in real time.

45. **ISO/IEC 27001**: An international standard for managing and securing sensitive information through an Information Security Management System (ISMS).

46. **ISO/IEC 27002**: A code of practice that provides guidelines for information security controls within an ISMS.

GLOSSARY OF KEY TERMS

47. **KPI (Key Performance Indicator)**: A measurable value that demonstrates how effectively an organization is achieving its cybersecurity objectives.

48. **Malware**: Malicious software designed to damage, disrupt, or gain unauthorized access to a computer system or network.

49. **Multi-Factor Authentication (MFA)**: A security process that requires users to provide two or more forms of authentication before gaining access to a system.

50. **NIST Cybersecurity Framework (CSF)**: A risk-based framework developed by NIST to guide organizations in managing and reducing cybersecurity risks.

51. **Penetration Testing**: A controlled, simulated cyberattack performed to identify and exploit vulnerabilities in a system.

52. **Phishing**: A type of cyberattack where attackers impersonate legitimate entities to trick individuals into disclosing personal information.

53. **Privileged Access Management (PAM)**: A system that controls and monitors access to critical systems and sensitive data by users with elevated permissions.

54. **Public Key Infrastructure (PKI)**: A set of hardware, software, policies, and standards used to manage public-key encryption systems.

GLOSSARY OF KEY TERMS

55. **Ransomware**: A type of malware that encrypts files on a victim's system and demands a ransom for the decryption key.

56. **Risk Assessment**: The process of identifying, evaluating, and prioritizing risks to an organization's assets.

57. **Risk Management**: The process of identifying, assessing, and mitigating risks to reduce their impact on an organization.

58. **SOC 2 (System and Organization Controls 2)**: A certification standard for service organizations that ensures they securely manage data and protect privacy.

59. **SIEM (Security Information and Event Management)**: A solution that provides real-time monitoring, analysis, and response to security events in an IT environment.

60. **Social Engineering**: A manipulation technique that exploits human behavior to gain access to confidential information or systems.

61. **Spyware**: Malicious software designed to secretly monitor a user's activities and gather sensitive information without their knowledge.

62. **Tokenization**: The process of replacing sensitive data with a non-sensitive equivalent (token) that has no meaningful value outside the system.

63. **Vulnerability**: A weakness in a system that could be exploited by an attacker to gain unauthorized access or cause damage.

GLOSSARY OF KEY TERMS

64. **Vulnerability Management**: The process of identifying, assessing, prioritizing, and mitigating vulnerabilities in a system.

65. **VPN (Virtual Private Network)**: A technology that encrypts a user's Internet connection, providing secure access to private networks over the Internet.

66. **Whitelisting**: A security measure that allows only approved or trusted programs to run on a network or system.

67. **Zero-Day Vulnerability**: A previously unknown vulnerability in software that has not yet been patched or addressed by the vendor.

Wishing You the Best in Your Cybersecurity Journey

As you come to the end of this book, I want to take a moment to congratulate you on your dedication and hard work. The path to mastering cybersecurity is not always easy, but every step you take brings you closer to becoming a skilled professional capable of making a real difference in this ever-evolving field. Whether you're preparing for your Security+ exam, advancing your career, or simply deepening your understanding of cybersecurity, know that you're not alone in this journey.

The world of cybersecurity is vast and dynamic, with new challenges and opportunities emerging every day. The knowledge you've gained throughout this book will serve as the foundation for tackling those challenges. But remember, learning doesn't stop here. The best cybersecurity professionals are lifelong learners who stay curious, adapt to new technologies, and remain vigilant in the face of new threats.

As you prepare for the exam and beyond, stay confident in your abilities. You've put in the effort, and that commitment will pay off. Keep challenging yourself, ask questions, seek out opportunities to grow, and, most importantly, stay passionate about making the digital world a safer place.

WISHING YOU THE BEST IN YOUR CYBERSECURITY JOURNEY

I truly believe in your potential to succeed, and I'm excited for the great things you'll accomplish in the future. Keep pushing forward and never stop striving to improve yourself. The world of cybersecurity is waiting for you, and there's no limit to what you can achieve.

Good luck and remember—your journey is just beginning. Stay determined, stay focused, and above all, stay curious!

Best of luck in all your endeavors,
Kodi A. Cochran

Index

A

Acceptable use policy (AUP), 420
Access control policy, 421
Active learning techniques, 431
Acunetix, 93
Advanced persistent threats
    (APTs), 29, 30, 112, 199, 239,
    332, 345, 350, 404
Adware, 70
AI, *see* Artificial intelligence (AI)
AIS, *see* Automated indicator
    sharing (AIS)
Alert fatigue, 206, 207
Alerting systems, 243, 244
Angler phishing, 65
Anomali, 45
Anomaly-based detection, 239–241
Anomaly detection, 198
Anomaly detection systems,
    344, 345
Application logs, 181, 233
Application scans, 130
APTs, *see* Advanced persistent
    threats (APTs)
Artificial intelligence (AI), 15, 30,
    118, 265, 352, 353, 425
Asset criticality, 99

Attacker motivation, 100
Attack surface, 25, 26
Attack vectors, 62, 86–89
AUP, *see* Acceptable use
    policy (AUP)
Automated indicator sharing
    (AIS), 356
Availability, 18

B

BC, *see* Business continuity (BC)
BCP, *see* Business continuity
    planning (BCP)
BEC, *see* Business email
    compromise (BEC)
Behavioral analysis, 384
Behavioral analytics, 114, 115, 177,
    214, 291
Behavioral IOCs, 332, 333
BIA, *see* Business impact
    analysis (BIA)
Botnets, 71
Breach notification, 401
Broken authentication
    mechanisms, 130
Brute-force attack, 79, 80

INDEX

Buffer overflow, 74
Burp Suite, 93, 130, 132
Business continuity (BC), 143, 317
Business continuity planning (BCP), 421, 422
Business email compromise (BEC), 66
Business impact analysis (BIA), 318

C

California Consumer Privacy Act (CCPA), 186, 359
CCPA, see California Consumer Privacy Act (CCPA)
Center for Internet Security (CIS), 37, 101
Centralized log management, 220
CERT resilience management model (CERT-RMM), 303
CERT-RMM, see CERT resilience management model (CERT-RMM)
CERTs, see Computer emergency response teams (CERTs)
Chain of custody, 395
CIA triad, 17–19
CIS, see Center for Internet Security (CIS)
Civil liberties, 402
Clone phishing, 65
Cloud activity logs, 182
Cloud computing, 15
Cloud security, 31, 32

CMS, see Content management system (CMS)
COBIT, see Control objectives for information and related technologies (COBIT)
Command injection, 77
Commercial threat intelligence services, 53
Common vulnerabilities and exposures (CVEs), 96, 97, 129
Common vulnerability scoring system (CVSS), 98, 124, 127, 138, 139
Communication plans, 388
Compensating controls, 102
Compliance, 10, 11, 154, 159, 160, 409, 429
CompTIA, see Computing Technology Industry Association (CompTIA)
CompTIA CySA+ exam
  confidence, 443, 444
  creating study plan
    adapt and refine your plan, 432
    assess your starting point, 430
    consistent study schedule, 431
    practice exams, reinforce learning, 431
    set clear and achievable goals, 430

456

INDEX

day before exam
   high-yield concepts, 442
   mental readiness, 443
   quick-recall tools, 442
domains, 430
entry-level certifications, 427
formats, 427
hands-on practice
   critical skills, 435
   home lab setting up, 435
   open-source threat intelligence and incident response, 436
   simulation and cloud-based labs, 435
practice exams and review mistakes
   identifying weak areas and adjust your study plan, 437
   improve exam stamina and time management, 438
   and reinforce key concepts, 439
   understanding exam format, 437
preparation concepts, 428–430
study materials
   hands-on labs and simulations, 433
   official study guides and books, 432
   online forums, study groups and discussion boards, 434
   practice questions and mock exams, 433
   video tutorials and online courses, 433
theoretical knowledge, 427
time management
   elimination process, 440
   leave time, 441
   PBQs, 441
   prioritization, 440
   setting realistic pace, 440
CompTIA IT Fundamentals (ITF+) certification, 3
CompTIA Security+ certification, 3
Computer emergency response teams (CERTs), 54, 355
Computing Technology Industry Association (CompTIA)
   certifications, 3
   CySA+ (*see* Cybersecurity Analyst (CySA+) certification)
   defined, 3
   performance-based assessments, 3
Confidentiality, 17, 18, 402
Configuration management, 101
Conflicts of interest, 403
Containment
   business operations, 281, 282
   communication, 282–284
   defined, 279
   types, 279–281

457

INDEX

Content management system (CMS), 146
Contextualizing risk, 99
Continuity plans, 318
Continuous improvement, 141, 162, 225–227, 320, 362, 363, 398, 399, 404, 405
   importance, 324
   metrics, 326
   training and awareness, 325
Continuous monitoring, 237–239
Continuous vulnerability management
   defined, 163
   reasons, 163, 164
   strategies, 164–166
Control objectives for information and related technologies (COBIT), 37, 411
Correlation analysis, 199, 200
Credential-based attacks
   authentication, 78
   best practices, 85
   defined, 78
   goals, 79
   impact, 84
   types, 79–83
Credential stuffing, 80
Crisis management plan, 392
Critical assets, 99
Critical thinking, 14, 16
Cross-site request forgery (CSRF), 93

Cross-site scripting (XSS), 75, 92, 130, 132
CrowdStrike Falcon, 41
CSRF, *see* Cross-site request forgery (CSRF)
CVEs, *see* Common vulnerabilities and exposures (CVEs)
CVSS, *see* Common vulnerability scoring system (CVSS)
Cybercriminals, 31, 41, 57, 74, 86, 96
Cyber kill chain, 60
Cybersecurity
   best practices, 2, 32–36, 187
   centralizing log collection, 185
   concepts, 1
   context, 177
   culture, 424
   data collection, 178, 179
   data integrity, 184, 185
   data sources
      concepts, 179
      types, 179–184
   emerging trends, 30–32
   frameworks, 2, 32–36
   goals, 178
   parsing, 194
   professionals, 366
   regulatory requirements, 185, 186
   risk management, 412–414
   tools, 39
   visualization tools, 200–202

INDEX

Cybersecurity Analyst (CySA+)
  certification, 3
  benefits, 6
  career changers, 8
  CS0-003 version, 4
  domain
    incident response and
      management, 5
    reporting and
      communication, 6
    security operations, 4
    vulnerability management, 5
  exam format and structure, 13
  IT professionals, 7
  mindset
    adapting to change, 15
    critical thinking, 14
    team collaboration, 15, 16
  overview, 12
  purpose, 12
  responsibilities, 9–11
  security analysts, 7
  students and early-career
    professionals, 8
  technical teams and
    management, 11
  time limit, 13
Cybersecurity
  analytics, 196–200
Cybersecurity landscape, 25
Cybersecurity policies
  defined, 419
  examples, 420
  types, 420–423

Cyber threats, 8, 15, 49, 111, 177, 199, 404, 407, 412

D

Dark web monitoring, 53
Database scans, 131
Data breaches, 305, 375
Data-driven hunting, 385
Data enrichment
  benefits, 211
  defined, 209
  security incidents, 209
  techniques, 209–211
  threat detection accuracy,
    212, 213
Data exfiltration, 387
Data loss prevention (DLP), 22
Data normalization
  challenges
    handling large volumes,
      194, 195
    resolving inconsistency,
      195, 196
    streamlined processes, 196
  and parsing, 187, 191–194
  steps, 190, 191
    data fields, 188, 189
    duplicate/irrelevant entries
      elimination, 190
    time zones, 189
Data parsing
  cybersecurity, 194
  in-depth analysis, 191

459

INDEX

Data parsing (*cont.*)
  log analysis tools, 191, 192
  Python, 192, 193
Data protection, 401
Data protection and privacy policy, 420
DDoS, *see* Distributed denial-of-service (DDoS)
Defense-in-depth strategy
  advantages, 23
  components
    application security, 21
    data security, 22
    endpoint security, 21
    IAM, 22
    monitoring and logging, 23
    network security, 20, 21
    physical security, 20
  defined, 19
  implementation, 24, 25
Denial of service (DoS), 76, 105, 215, 305, 374
Development, Security, and Operations (DevSecOps), 166–168
DevSecOps, *see* Development, Security, and Operations (DevSecOps)
DGAs, *see* Domain generation algorithms (DGAs)
Diamond model
  components, 61
  intrusion analysis, 37
Digital forensics teams, 310

Disaster recovery (DR), 317, 422, 423
Disaster recovery plans (DRPs), 318
Distributed denial-of-service (DDoS), 71, 105, 357, 374
DLP, *see* Data loss prevention (DLP)
DNS analysis, 211
Domain generation algorithms (DGAs), 211
DoS, *see* Denial of service (DoS)
DR, *see* Disaster recovery (DR)
DREAD, 106–108
DRPs, *see* Disaster recovery plans (DRPs)

E

EDR, *see* Endpoint detection and response (EDR)
Elastic Security, 252
Elastic SIEM, 219
Elastic Stack (ELK Stack), 219
Email phishing, 28, 63
Endpoint detection and response (EDR), 21, 40–42, 116, 117, 182, 253, 273, 311, 336, 380, 381, 385
Eradication, 284, 288
Escalation protocols, 388
Event correlation, 221
  benefits, 206–208
  defined, 202
  effectiveness, 202

INDEX

identifying lateral
  movement, 204
importance, 204
multistage attacks, 203
rules, 205, 206
sources, 202
use cases, 202
Exploitability, 99
Exploits
  attackers, 123
  best practices, 77, 78
  defined, 73
  types, 73–77
  vulnerabilities, 73
External communication, 389, 390

F

False negatives, 216
False positive rate, 224
False positives, 216, 244, 245
Fast flux, 211
Federal Information Security
  Modernization Act
  (FISMA), 417
Federal Trade Commission
  (FTC), 401
File-based IOCs, 329, 330
Fileless malware, 88, 89
Firewalls, 20, 72, 102, 336
FISMA, *see* Federal Information
  Security Modernization
  Act (FISMA)
Forensic analysis

activities, 393
chain of custody, 395
creating incident report,
  396, 397
defined, 393
post-incident analysis and
  reporting, 395, 396
tools, 394
FTC, *see* Federal Trade
  Commission (FTC)
Forensic tools, 311

G

GDPR, *see* General Data Protection
  Regulation (GDPR)
General Data Protection
  Regulation (GDPR), 186,
  305, 359, 399, 416
Geo-IP data, 209, 210
GLBA, *see* Gramm-Leach-
  Bliley Act (GLBA)
Governance, 408
Governance, risk management and
  compliance (GRC)
  audits and assessments,
    418, 419
  concepts, 408, 409
  continuous improvement and
    adaptation, 424, 425
  cybersecurity, 412–414
  cybersecurity policies, 419–423
  defined, 407
  frameworks, 410, 411

461

INDEX

Governance, risk management and compliance (GRC) (*cont.*)
    future trends, 425
    importance, 409
    life cycle, 415
    regulatory standards and frameworks, 416–418
    senior leadership, 412
    testing and drills, 423, 424
    treatment and mitigation, 414
Gramm-Leach-Bliley Act (GLBA), 155
GRC, *see* Governance, risk management and compliance (GRC)

H

Hacktivists, 57
Hashing algorithms, 18
Health Information Technology for Economic and Clinical Health Act (HITECH), 156
Health Insurance Portability and Accountability Act (HIPAA), 126, 155, 156, 186, 306, 400, 417
HIPAA, *see* Health Insurance Portability and Accountability Act (HIPAA)
HITECH, *see* Health Information Technology for Economic and Clinical Health Act (HITECH)

Host-based scanners, 94–96
Host-based scans, 130
Hypothesis-driven hunting, 112, 113

I, J

IAM, *see* Identity and access management (IAM)
IBM QRadar, 218, 252
Identity and access management (IAM), 22
IDS, *see* Intrusion detection systems (IDS)
Incident communication plans, 283
Incident detection, 243
Incident identification and response, 9
Incident reports, 388, 396, 397
Incident response (IR)
    automation, 312
    communication and reporting, 292, 293
    containment (*see* Containment)
    continuous improvement and feedback loop, 398, 399
    decisions, 348, 349
    defined, 245, 268, 365
    documentation, 277, 278
    effective communication, 387
    eliminating threats, 284, 285
    ethical considerations, 401

INDEX

external communication, 389, 390
forensics, 393–398
forensics teams, 287–290
goals, 268, 269
identification, 274
initial assessment, 276, 277
insights, 212
internal communication, 388, 389
legal and compliance considerations, 305–307, 399–403
life cycle, 270, 271
management, 5, 429
maturity (*see* Maturity models)
metrics, 405
new threats/gaps, 321
objectives, 246
open-source threat intelligence, 436
patch management and security updates, 285, 286
phases, 246, 247
playbooks, 298–300
policy, 297, 298, 421
policy updates, 322, 323
post-incident activities, 294, 295
post-recovery, 291, 292
preparedness, 269, 270
public relations and crisis management, 391–393
reporting and accountability, 403
roles and responsibilities, 272, 307
security culture, 323, 324
security measures, 321, 322
speeding up detection and remediation, 347, 348
testing, 304, 305
third-party partners, 309, 310
threat landscape, 404, 405
tools, 310, 311
tools and resources, 273, 274
training and awareness, 323
transparency and responsibility, 403
updating policies and procedures, 320
Incident response planning (IRP), 24, 295, 296
Incident response team (IRT), 248, 271, 272, 307–309
Indicators of attack (IOAs), 113, 114
Indicators of compromise (IOCs), 38, 51, 113, 275, 276, 313, 383
advantages, 338, 339
collecting and analyzing, 334, 335
power, 333
reasons, 333
security measures, 258
security tools, 336
sharing and updating, 337, 338

463

INDEX

Indicators of compromise (IOCs) (*cont.*)
    types, 329–333
    usage, 334
Information security management system (ISMS), 35, 158, 411, 418
Information sharing agreements (ISAs), 360
Information sharing and analysis centers (ISACs), 54, 55, 262, 355
Information sharing environment (ISE), 356
Insecure session management, 93
Insider threats, 29, 58, 112, 282, 376, 377
Integrity, 18
Internal communication, 388, 389
Internal *vs.* external threat intelligence, 51
International Organization for Standardization (ISO), 158, 159
Internet of Things (IoT), 15, 31
Intrusion detection systems (IDS), 9, 20, 30, 34, 231, 336, 379
Intrusion prevention systems (IPS), 9, 20, 231, 336, 379
IOAs, *see* Indicators of attack (IOAs)
IOCs, *see* Indicators of compromise (IOCs)

IoT, *see* Internet of Things (IoT)
IPS, *see* Intrusion prevention systems (IPS)
IR, *see* Incident response (IR)
IRP, *see* Incident response planning (IRP)
IRT, *see* Incident response team (IRT)
ISACs, *see* Information sharing and analysis centers (ISACs)
ISAs, *see* Information sharing agreements (ISAs)
ISE, *see* Information sharing environment (ISE)
ISMS, *see* Information security management system (ISMS)
ISO, *see* International Organization for Standardization (ISO)
ISO/IEC 27001, 2, 35, 158, 411, 418
ISO/IEC 27002, 159, 411, 418
ITF+ certification, *see* CompTIA IT Fundamentals (ITF+) certification

K

Keyloggers, 71
Keylogging, 81, 82
Key performance indicators (KPIs), 200, 223–227
Kibana, 201
KPIs, *see* Key performance indicators (KPIs)

464

INDEX

L

LogRhythm, 40, 118, 252
Logs, 180, 181, 225
    benefits, 236
    challenges, 236, 237
    collection and aggregation, 234, 235
    correlation, 235
    defined, 233
    types, 233, 234
Logstash, 191, 196
Long-term containment, 279, 280

M

Machine learning (ML), 118, 177, 198, 265, 352, 353, 425
    applications, 214
    categories, 215
    challenges, 216, 217
    defined, 213
    security systems, 213
Malicious traffic, 183
Malware, 27, 371, 372
    best practices, 71, 72
    defined, 67
    goals, 67
    methods, 67
    types, 68–71
Managed security service providers (MSSPs), 309
Man-in-the-middle (MITM)
    credential interception, 83
    exploits, 76

Maturity models
    defined, 300
    frameworks, 302–304
    levels, 300–303
MCQs, *see* Multiple-choice questions (MCQs)
Mean time to detect (MTTD), 223, 326
Mean time to respond (MTTR), 224, 326
Media communication, 391
Metasploit, 132
MFA, *see* Multi-factor authentication (MFA)
Microsoft Sentinel, 219
MITRE ATT&CK framework, 36, 37, 59
ML, *see* Machine learning (ML)
Monitoring security systems, 9
MSSPs, *see* Managed security service providers (MSSPs)
MTTD, *see* Mean time to detect (MTTD)
MTTR, *see* Mean time to respond (MTTR)
Multi-factor authentication (MFA), 22, 66, 72, 80
Multiple-choice questions (MCQs), 13

N

National Institute of Standards and Technology (NIST), 33, 124, 157, 158, 270, 417

National vulnerability database (NVD), 97
Nation-states, 58
NDAs, see Non-disclosure agreements (NDAs)
NDR, see Network detection and response (NDR)
Nessus, 43, 91, 95, 131
NetFlow, 382
Network-based IOCs, 330, 331
Network+ certification, 3
Network detection and response (NDR), 254
Network device logs, 180
Network discovery tool, 91
Network logs, 234
Network management, 3
Network scanners, 90–92
Network scans, 130
Network segmentation, 281
Network traffic analysis, 381, 382
Nexpose, 132
NIST, see National Institute of Standards and Technology (NIST)
NIST Cybersecurity Framework (CSF), 2, 33, 34, 157, 302, 410, 411
NIST SP 800-53, 157, 418
Nmap, 91
Non-compliance, 11, 154, 416
Non-disclosure agreements (NDAs), 360
Non-technical stakeholders, 16, 172
NVD, see National vulnerability database (NVD)

O

Open-source intelligence (OSINT), 52
OpenVAS, 43, 91, 131
Operational intelligence, 50
Operational threat intelligence, 259
OSINT, see Open-source intelligence (OSINT)
OWASP ZAP (Zed Attack Proxy), 93

P

Paid intelligence feeds, 53
PAM, see Privileged access management (PAM)
Password spraying, 82, 83
Patch compliance rate, 170
Patching schedule, 101
Patch management, 101
　challenges, 151–153
　defined, 147
　process
　　deployment, 149, 150
　　discovery, 148
　　testing, 149
　　validation, 150, 151
　role, 147

Payment Card Industry Data Security Standard (PCI DSS), 126, 157, 306, 400, 417
PBQs, *see* Performance-based questions (PBQs)
PCI DSS, *see* Payment Card Industry Data Security Standard (PCI DSS)
Performance-based questions (PBQs), 13, 434, 437, 440, 441
PHI, *see* Protected health information (PHI)
Phishing, 28, 372
  attacks, 81
  best practices, 66, 67
  campaigns, 62
  defined, 62
  forms, 63–66
Policy development, 10
Post-incident activities, 294, 295
Post-incident review, 395, 396
Postmortem analysis, 404
Predictive models, 214
Preparedness, 269, 270
Pretexting, 28
Privacy rights, 402
Privileged access management (PAM), 22
Privilege escalation, 74, 75
Protected health information (PHI), 155, 400, 417

Q

QRadar, 40, 118
Qualitative risk assessment, 413
Qualys, 43, 95, 132
Quantitative risk assessment, 413

R

Ransomware, 27, 69, 305, 350, 351, 371
RBAC, *see* Role-based access control (RBAC)
RBVM, *see* Risk-based vulnerability management (RBVM)
Recovery, 289
  critical systems and prioritize restoration, 315
  metrics, 315, 316
  objectives, 314, 315
  testing and updating plans, 319, 320
  validation, 316, 317
Recovery point objective (RPO), 315, 423
Recovery time objective (RTO), 316, 422
Remediation
  compensating controls, 102
  configuration, 101
  incident prevention, 102, 103
  patch management, 101
  test patches, controlled environment, 101

INDEX

Residual risk, 171
Risk assessment
    factors, 97
    organizational goals and
        regulatory
        requirements, 100
    scoring and
        prioritization, 98–100
    vulnerability, 137, 138
    vulnerability management, 97
Risk-based vulnerability
    management (RBVM)
    business continuity, 143
    critical vulnerabilities, 143
    defined, 142
    resource constraint, 142
    steps, 143–145
    threat intelligence, 145, 146
Risk identification, 26
Risk management, 409
Risk matrices, 139
Risk matrix, 98
Role-based access control (RBAC), 22
Rootkits, 70
RPO, *see* Recovery point
    objective (RPO)
RTO, *see* Recovery time
    objective (RTO)

S

Sarbanes-Oxley Act (SOX), 154
SAST, *see* Static application security
    testing (SAST)
SCA, *see* Software composition
    analysis (SCA)
SCCM, *see* System Center
    Configuration
    Manager (SCCM)
SDLC, *see* Software development
    life cycle (SDLC)
Security information and event
    management (SIEM), 2, 9,
    23, 34, 39, 40, 117–119, 177,
    178, 200, 231, 263, 273, 291,
    311, 336, 347, 369, 377, 378,
    386, 399
    advanced monitoring
        tools, 252–255
    challenges, 256, 257
    data sources, 217
    defined, 249
    features, 220, 221, 250
    functions, 250, 252
    goals, 217
    implementation, 221–223
    integration, 183, 184
    monitoring tools, 256
    objectives, 249
    organizations, 250
    platforms, 217–220
    and security tools, 257
    tools, 252
    usage, 249
Security investments, 227
Security logs, 234
Security operations, 4, 368, 428
    activities and processes, 366

components, 367–369
defined, 365, 366
elements, 231
goals, 367
monitoring and detection
  importance, 382
  tools and
    technologies, 377–382
threat intelligence, 344
types of incidents, 371–377
  (*See also* Security
    operations centers (SOCs)
Security operations
  centers (SOCs), 231, 263
  components, 370
  defined, 368
  mission, 369
Security orchestration, automation
  and response (SOAR), 178,
  254, 255, 312
Security policies, 345
SentinelOne, 42
Server logs, 180
Shared responsibility model, 31
Short-term containment, 279
SIEM, *see* Security information and
  event management (SIEM)
Signature-based detection, 240,
  241, 344
Situational awareness, 207, 208
Smishing, 64
SOAR, *see* Security orchestration,
  automation and
  response (SOAR)

Social engineering, 28, 373
SOCs, *see* Security operations
  centers (SOCs)
Software composition analysis
  (SCA), 167
Software development life cycle
  (SDLC), 21, 166
SolarWinds attack, 86
SolarWinds supply chain
  attack, 351
SOX, *see* Sarbanes-Oxley Act (SOX)
Spear phishing, 28, 63
Splunk, 40, 118, 218, 252
Spyware, 27, 69, 70, 371
SQL injection, 75, 92, 130–132
Stakeholders, 141, 320
Static application security testing
  (SAST), 167
Statistical models, 198
Strategic intelligence, 50
Strategic threat intelligence, 259, 260
STIX, *see* Structured threat
  information
  expression (STIX)
STRIDE, 104, 105
Structured threat information
  expression (STIX), 337
Supervised learning, 215
Supply chain attacks, 86, 87,
  260, 350
System Center Configuration
  Manager (SCCM), 149
System logs, 233
System restoration, 289, 290

INDEX

T

Tactical intelligence, 51
Tactical threat intelligence, 258
Tactics, techniques, and procedures (TTPs), 36, 38, 48, 51, 112, 259, 384
TAXII, *see* Trusted automated exchange of intelligence information (TAXII)
Technical stakeholders, 172
Telemetry data, 181
Threat actors, 57, 58
Threat feeds, 262
Threat hunting, 241, 242
    defined, 112
    forms, 383
    goal, 112
    methodologies, 112-115, 384, 385
    operationalization, 347
    role, 346
    security technologies, 404
    tools, 115-119, 385-387
    uncovering, 346
Threat intelligence, 344
    AI and ML, 352, 353
    analysis, 48, 49
    applications, 353, 354
    automation, 263
    benefits, 356, 357
    best practices, 360-362
    challenges, 264
    collaboration and information sharing, 354-356
    comprehensive approach, 260
    continuous improvement and adaptation, 362, 363
    defined, 49
    detection and prevention, 344, 345
    emerging threats, 349
    feeds, 183
    frameworks, 37, 38, 58-61
    future trends, 265
    hunting (*see* Threat hunting)
    incident response, 347-349
    integration, 210, 261, 312, 313
    legal and compliance issues, 357
    liability, 360
    life cycle
        analysis, 56
        collection, 55
        dissemination, 56
        feedback, 56
        planning, 55
    privacy concerns, 358
    proactive, 362
    proactive approach, 49
    RBVM, 145, 146
    regulatory compliance, 358, 359
    security operations, 344
    sharing and legal considerations, 354
    sources, 52-55
    types, 50, 51, 258-260 (*See also* Threat intelligence platforms (TIPs)

Threat intelligence platforms
(TIPs), 43–45, 262, 263, 347
cybersecurity operations, 339
defined, 339
features and benefits, 340, 341
functions, 339, 340
large enterprises, 343
reasons, 340
small-to-mid-sized
organizations, 343
solutions, 342
Threat modeling
defined, 103
methodologies, 103–108
steps
assess vulnerabilities, 110
attack scenarios, 109
identifying assets, 108
mitigations, 110, 111
Threats
analysis and evaluation, 62
APTs, 29, 30
defined, 27
insider, 29
malware, 27
phishing and social
engineering, 28
Time to detect (TTD), 169
Time to remediate (TTR), 169
TIPs, *see* Threat intelligence
platforms (TIPs)
Tracking CVEs, 96
Trend analysis, 197, 198
Tripwire, 95

Trojans/Trojan horse, 69, 371
Trusted automated exchange of
intelligence information
(TAXII), 338
TTD, *see* Time to detect (TTD)
TTPs, *see* Tactics, techniques, and
procedures (TTPs)
TTR, *see* Time to remediate (TTR)

U

UBA, *see* User behavior
analytics (UBA)
Unsupervised learning, 215
User behavior analytics (UBA), 376

V

Virtual private networks (VPNs), 21
Viruses, 27, 68, 371
Vishing (voice phishing), 28, 65
Volatility, 386
VPNs, *see* Virtual private
networks (VPNs)
Vulnerability management, 5,
10, 47, 428
auditing, 160–162
complexity, 123
components
assessment, 127
discovery, 127
prioritization, 127
remediation, 128
reporting, 128

Vulnerability management (*cont.*)
    concept, 125
    configuration systems, 124
    continuous (*see* Continuous vulnerability management)
    defined, 89, 90
    frameworks, 153
    importance, 124–126
    life cycle
        asset discovery, 135, 136
        concept, 134
        identification, 136, 137
        prioritization, 138, 139
        remediation and mitigation, 140, 141
        reporting and review, 141, 142
        risk assessment, 137, 138
    limitations, 133, 134
    metrics, 169–171
    potential risks, 124
    RBVM (*see* Risk-based vulnerability management (RBVM))
    regulatory requirements, 154–159
    reporting, 171–174
    risk assessment, 97
    scanning tools and techniques, 90–96, 129, 131, 132
    types, 129–131
Vulnerability scanners, 42, 43

W

WAF, *see* Web Application Firewall (WAF)
Web Application Firewall (WAF), 94
Web application scanners, 92–94
Web-based threats, 132
Whaling, 64
Windows Server Update Services (WSUS), 149
Wireshark, 382, 387
Worms, 27, 68, 371
WSUS, *see* Windows Server Update Services (WSUS)

X

XSS, *see* Cross-site scripting (XSS)

Y

YARA, *see* Yet Another Recursive Acronym (YARA)
Yet Another Recursive Acronym (YARA), 386

Z

Zeek, 382
Zero-day exploits, 73, 74, 345, 351
Zero-day vulnerability, 87, 88, 133

GPSR Compliance

The European Union's (EU) General Product Safety Regulation (GPSR) is a set of rules that requires consumer products to be safe and our obligations to ensure this.

If you have any concerns about our products, you can contact us on

ProductSafety@springernature.com

In case Publisher is established outside the EU, the EU authorized representative is:

Springer Nature Customer Service Center GmbH
Europaplatz 3
69115 Heidelberg, Germany

www.ingramcontent.com/pod-product-compliance
Lightning Source LLC
LaVergne TN
LVHW010332260326
834688LV00036B/678